The
Blacksmith's
Daughter

THE STRANGE STORY OF ANN STAIGHT

As one who, walking in the twilight gloom,
Hears round about him voices as it darkens,
And seeing not the forms from which they come,
Pauses from time to time, and turns and hearkens;
So walking here in twilight, O my friends!
I hear your voices, softened by the distance,
And pause, and turn to listen, as each sends
His words of friendship, comfort and assistance.

Longfellow
Entry in Josie Staight's album

Opposite: Ann Staight

The Blacksmith's Daughter

THE STRANGE STORY OF ANN STAIGHT

Susan Oldacre

ALAN SUTTON
1985

For Peg

Alan Sutton Publishing Limited
Brunswick Road · Gloucester

Copyright © Susan Oldacre 1985

First published 1985

British Library Cataloguing in Publication Data

Oldacre, Susan
    The blacksmith's daughter : the strange story
    of Ann Staight.
    1. Staight, Ann   2. Great Britain—Biography
    I. Title
    941.081'092'4   CT788.S69/

    ISBN 0-86299-234-6

Cover picture: detail from Waiting *by John Everett Millais.*
Birmingham Museum and Art Gallery.

Printed and bound in Great Britain

Contents

Shrove Tuesday. February 21st 1882.

Called Mary at 7. 9 filled up jug of water for a good wash.
drew some water after 9.30. washed glasses. Annie came down &
J.P. appeared at 6. When we had breakfast I dusted bar &
parlour. Annie did our rooms. 9 Nan. we cleared away breakfast
things. She did down & usual work. Mrs B. altering her dress.
Mary doing some washing for herself. I went into the Park for
us just before 11. I went on with my errand
work. We had rather late dinner. Mary made some pancakes
after dinner which were not finished. I took Philip a
pancake. He seemed very pleased with it. Saw Amy & Herbert
by lake. Annie lay down till the afternoon for a little while.
I did some writing. Mr & Williams called, but Annie did
not see him. Mr Lilly and Mr B. a rabbit yesterday, & he & I had good
today. Two young gents on the billiard room after dinner.
J.P. B. got up to tea. Mr Lilly came to see him in the evening &
brought oranges, cresses & lettuce. I went to Miss C's before 6,
& back at 6.35. Annie finished her Marseillaise case for her.
Cousin Sarah quilted it with red satin. I finished errand
work on neighbours case. J.P. Philip & J. His this evening
& others.

'A goodly dwelling, and a rich'

When I first came across Ann Staight's diaries I knew nothing at all about her. Her family and the village she lived in were little more than names to me. It was natural, having discovered her, that I should be interested in her. Without deliberately searching for parallels or coincidences, there were several obvious ones. We were both the same age (when she stopped writing and when I started). We were both single. We had the same origins, the same rural background – villages in north Gloucestershire – where we also shared farming and milling connections. We were both unashamedly bookish, with indeterminate literary leanings.

Having read the diaries, and supplemented the information in them from various sources, it seemed to me that here was a story worth telling, or re-telling in Ann's words and mine. Ann Staight was a blacksmith's daughter. This did not sound too auspicious at first (it conjured up a poor sort of life and an immobile one – I had the notion that village folk did not travel) but I hope to show that despite certain limitations and hardships Ann's life was, up until its final episode, quiet and contented and comfortable, for she enjoyed a large, united family circle, a long and loving friendship, an unusually pleasant environment. Her life spans the mid- to late-Victorian era (she lived from 1855 to 1892) and her story is very much of its time both in its outcome and in its preoccupations. With greater opportunities in education and employment, with improved women's rights, with rapid advances in medicine, both physical and psychological, Ann Staight's story could not be repeated today. It *is* a Victorian tale.

Ann is not a 'family chàracter' now; there is no family folklore about her and no one living who knew her, and this makes her as much a character in a book (she is known only through her diaries) as a real personage. At this distance of a hundred years the barriers between fact and fiction blur so that it seems natural for me to say that she has, I think, no close counterpart in Victorian fiction. The governess, the seamstress and the servant girl are well-known to us from that fiction. Equally familiar is the social life of the well-to-do girl in the upper echelons of society, eager for marriage to make her

7

life more interesting. Less well documented is the situation of a girl like Ann Staight who is not in the lowest income group and not obliged to work.

The diaries cover barely ten years of Ann Staight's life, less than one-third of it, so this book is less a biography than a view of a girl, her family and her village, seen at the distance of a hundred years. The result reveals my preoccupations as well as Ann's, highlighting some of the differences between her times and mine (in such matters as medicine, attitudes to death, clothes, words, poetic taste), and placed, I hope, in a literary and a regional context. The setting, Ann's 'unusually pleasant environment', was another reason, another incentive, for telling the story. My roots lie in Gloucestershire as Ann's did. I had gone away, to school, to university, to work, I had been educated and employed as she had not. But the ties with the land persist in me, reality and fantasy inextricably mixed as imagination works on memory. I may not live there again but that I will, in that Cotswold country, is a dream I nurture and which nurtures me. Ann's diaries were a link with, a part of, a long ancestral link with the land, and they offered a way of writing about that land.

At the outset, however, Ann's village was as much a mystery as the girl who lived there. I had visited Dumbleton perhaps once as a child though it is barely ten miles from my own Gloucestershire village. Unlike Eric Delderfield, who has written of the area 'the finger-posts have many quaint names on them, including Dumbleton and Wormington, which always seem to me to have come straight out of Hans Anderson's fairy-tales',[1] I was not charmed by the name, which seemed too close to other unappealing words – *dumb, dumpy, dumpling*, even *tumbledown*. It was the village where the grandfather I had never known was buried, alongside his in-laws, those equally unknown Staights. For a child, graves offer no welcome, and I am certain this state of ignorance would have remained unchanged, had not the diaries brought me again to this physically-near but psychologically-remote place, Dumbleton . . .

* * * *

Dumbleton lies in the Vale of Evesham, so close to a county boundary that its precise location has often caused confusion: its postal address is 'Evesham, Worcs' (now that cumbersomely-named

8

county Hereford and Worcester), but it lies just inside the north Gloucestershire border. This is a neglected bit of the county. Many people in Gloucestershire, even in north Gloucestershire, have not heard the name; books about the county rarely include it. The county boundary follows for a while the main Evesham–Cheltenham road, and the village is located just west of it. Because it is away from this fast, frantic road, busy with lorry traffic transporting the Vale's fruit and vegetables, and not on the way to anywhere except itself, Dumbleton has escaped attention. It is a small place (less than three hundred residents in 1984), tucked under its own hill, between the Cotswold escarpment and another outlier, the much larger and more famous Bredon Hill, celebrated by the poet A.E. Housman and more recently by the local writers John Moore and Fred Archer. On the side of Bredon Hill, and almost directly opposite Dumbleton across the valley (the signposts almost face each other across the main road) is the tiny hamlet of Grafton, about which John Drinkwater wrote a poem, not widely known like Housman's, which begins

> God laughed when he made Grafton
> That's under Bredon Hill . . .[2]

There is nothing obviously *funny* about Grafton, and the divine laughter surely reflects God's sheer delight and satisfaction at the creation of this pleasant place.

Taking, not the Grafton turning, but the one to Dumbleton from the Evesham–Cheltenham road, one passes close to two adjacent village farms, The Bank and Cullabine. The difference, the discrepancy, between these two names – the one so dull and prosaic, the second so much more colourful – is explained by the fact that Cullabine Farm was named after the family who lived there in the 18th century. These two farms would be important for the Staights later on – both are lived in by Staights today – but not in the 1880s, when they were secluded by their own orchards. Now our interests lie at the opposite end of the village street, where church, Hall and Villa are to be found. Along the cottage-lined village street – little changed over the years, except for the addition of a few new houses, and still without street lighting today – one passes Dumbleton's oldest house, the Old Rectory (some of its timbers are said to have come from old ships in Tewkesbury dock nine miles away). Almost opposite, but set way back from the road, so that it looks like a distant doll's house, is The Villa, the home of three, possibly four,

9

successive generations of Staight blacksmiths. It is reached by turning down the side lane named, not unnaturally, Blacksmith's Lane.

At the end of the village street, before it turns left into the road named Nutmeadow (pronounced Nutmedder by some of the locals) is the village shop, Dumbleton Stores, which was formerly the butcher's shop. Across the road from the shop, near the entrance to the churchyard, is a fountain, an oddly-shaped monument to a former 'lord of the manor', Edward Holland, who built in 1830 the Victorian mansion glimpsed through the trees behind the church. Dumbleton Hall today is no longer a private residence but a convalescent and holiday home for Post Office employees. Snuggling beneath Dumbleton Hill, part of which is actually called 'Hall's Hill', the guests of the Post Office look down over grazing sheep and peaceful parkland to the mellow Cotswold stone of the church, one of three in the deanery (of Winchcombe) to be dedicated to St Peter.

The interior of the church is plain, almost austere. Most of the windows are filled with plain glass and the white walls are relieved only by plaques commemorating members of its two great families, the Cocks family of old Dumbleton Hall, the Hollands from the new hall. One memorial of 1765 tells how Sir Robert Cocks 'after sustaining with Christian fortitude and resignation the most affecting loss of an Amiable wife and three children in the course of a few days from a Cruel Distemper' died shortly after them. His youngest daughter survived her parents, but only briefly, dying in 1767 'untainted with the Follies and Dissipation of the age in which she lived . . .'. This pattern of calamity, of a 'Cruel Distemper' striking a family, of the daughter surviving the parents only to die a different death soon afterwards, would be repeated in Dumbleton over a century later.

The most splendid memorial in the church, near the altar, is a monument to Sir Charles Percy, who married into the Cocks family. A follower of Essex, Elizabeth I's favourite, Percy's adventures included expeditions to France and Ireland, a spell – as prisoner, not custodian – in the Tower of London, and in 1603 *he* was the envoy who took the news of Elizabeth's death to her successor James I in Scotland. After such dramas, life in Dumbleton must have been, to say the least, tame, and Percy asked a London friend to keep him posted of news and happenings there. A notice by his tomb tells visitors that 'he wished not to be taken for Justice Silence or Justice Shallow, two characters in Shakespeare's *Merry Wives of Windsor*.' And also in the second part of *Henry IV*. Although the experts will

10

have it otherwise,[3] I like to fancy that Shallow's house in Gloucester-shire is in Dumbleton, even if Shallow is not to be Sir Charles Percy. (After all, it is likely Shakespeare knew it: Dumbleton is within a day's walk of Stratford-upon-Avon.) Shallow's servant Davy consults his master, 'Sir, shall we sow the headland with wheat? . . . Here is now the smith's note for shoeing and plough-irons. Now, sir, a new link to the bucket must needs be had . . .' and later, Shallow shows Falstaff his orchards: 'You shall see my orchard where, in an arbour, we will eat a last year's pippin of my own graffing . . .' Falstaff is impressed: 'Fore God, you have a goodly dwelling, and a rich.'[4] *Corn, horseshoes, apples.* Such matters are precisely the concerns of those Staights about to be encountered in the churchyard beyond the north door.

Above the north door, on the outside of the church, is its most original feature: a curious carving of a strange figure whose identity has been variously interpreted. He may be an ancient fertility symbol, a Green Man 'with the ears of an ass and three pieces of foliage springing from his mouth' (Arthur Mee). Or the Devil with his evil branches. In the early days of the 20th century, villagers called him 'the cat o' nine tails', who acted, presumably, as a threat or warning to sinners. This fits (the ears are far more like a cat's than an ass's, and there are exactly *nine* tails) but the little figure is much older than the corrective instrument of that name. Whoever he is, he is more comic than demonic, his impish face surveying the north side of the churchyard, watching the graves in what was customarily regarded as the devil's (his?) domain, the shadowy north aspect discouraging people from wishing to be buried there, though in fact this does not seem to have been the case at Dumbleton (the oldest graves, including the Jacobean table tombs, are evenly distributed around the church), perhaps because the north side was the side most immediately accessible from the village.

Almost the first graves one sees on entering the churchyard, or on leaving the church by the north door, are a group, arranged irregularly in three rows, spanning two hundred years from 1763 to 1964, and all commemorating members of the Staight family, not far in fact from the Villa in which many of them had lived. (There are more Staight graves on the south side of the church, but they are all twentieth-century ones.) In the middle row of the group, its headstone facing east towards the Hill, is one of the oldest, and certainly the most remarkable of the group, an eighteenth century headstone, which rates a mention in *The Buildings of England* as one of 'three well-preserved examples of a local type of excellent

11

CHURCH NORTH DOOR DUMBLETON 6

Dumbleton church: left, the north door with the cat o' nine tails; above, view from Joe's house of the church and the Holland fountain. The oldest Staight family tombstone (detail below) is near the large north transept window

low-relief headstones . . .'.[5] At the top of the stone is a coat of arms, containing three torches and three upturned horseshoes, supported on one side by a winged mythological figure and on the other by a neatly bridled and saddled horse. This splendid design has to mean a blacksmith or generations of blacksmiths are buried here, and it does, but sadly the coat of arms is an invented one, its 'sham armorial bearings' only the artistic licence of the local mason, Samuel Hobday.[6]

The stone is crumbling now, but most of the words below the coat of arms are legible. The space is divided into two panels. On the lefthand side, Robert Staight, who died in 1792 at the age of 57, has an epitaph reminiscent of Alexander Pope:

> *Untaught to flatter let this Tablet shew*
> *Assembled Virtues that distinguish few.*
> *Though manly, gentle, just, but not severe*
> *Courteous to all in thoughts, in words sincere,*
> *A Friend to pity, as a foe to pride,*
> *None worthier liv'd, none more regretted died.*

There had been Staites at Dumbleton in the 17th century, but Robert was the first of the line of blacksmiths at Dumbleton who concern us now. His forebears were blacksmiths at the nearby villages of Toddington and Gretton. The Staights seem to have been centred at Gretton. There were a lot of them. In the Index of Baptisms* for 1664–1757 at Winchcombe Church (Gretton did not then have its own church) there are as many Staights – spelt in various ways – as there are Smiths. The surname is a local one and Staite is listed under Gloucestershire in one book on surnames, under a *topographical list of peculiarly local surnames*.[7] Robert Staight and his first wife, Mary Pitman, lived first at Gretton, where they had five children, before moving to Dumbleton, where they had more. Mary's surname, Pitman, was used as a family name for her children both before and after her death.

The rest of the space on the coat of arms gravestone commemorates three of Robert's sons, all called Thomas. Thomas Staight had died before his father, in 1789, aged 28. He has the familiar lines 'Reader prepare to follow me.' The soft Cotswold stone has crum-

---

* Amongst these Baptism records are two oddities: a charmingly named illegitimate child, Meadow, daughter of Mary Ashley of Stow, *spuria* (the church's way of indicating illegitimacy at that time) in 1711; and in 1747

Sept 8. Cunosoa Almsbury. This child was exposed and preserved by dogs which defended it from the swine.

bled away so that the medium as well as the message endorses the fragility of earthly things:

> *Reader prepare to follow me*
> *For as I am so shalt thou be*
> *Thy body too must come to Dust,*
> *. . . prepare to die thou must.*
> *. . . . ain Death is sure;*
> *. . . . . and Christ the cure.*

At the top of the righthand panel is the epitaph of another Thomas Pitman Staight, Robert's son by his second wife Sarah Crump, who died at the age of two years and three months:

> *An infant's Fate may make a parent sad*
> *An infant's Fate should make a . . . glad*
> *Rapt out of life ere Cares and Woes begin*
> *I knew no Sorrow for I knew no Sin*
> *Death has no Sting for him who dies so young,*
> *Reader repent since thou hast liv'd so long.*

The next Thomas Pitman Staight – the only one to reach middle age (he died aged 49 in 1833) is mentioned with his wife at the foot of what Ann Staight calls 'our stone'.*

The splendid gravestone, the 'blacksmith coat of arms', and Robert Staight's gentlemanly epitaph prepare us for the unusual status of Charles, Robert's grandson and Ann Staight's father. The eldest son of the third, epitaph-less Thomas, Charles's grave is nearby:

> In loving memory of
> Charles Pitman Staight who died 8 January 1892 Aged 73 years
> Also Ann his wife who died 11 January 1892 aged 73 years
>
> Also two of their children
> Edward Drinkwater died 2 April 1864 aged 2 years
> *Ann died 29 June 1892 aged 36 years*†
>
> Also Henry, brother of the above Charles Pitman Staight
> who died 25 March 1859 aged 32 years
>
> I am the resurrection and the life

No decoration – nothing to indicate that Charles was a blacksmith

---

* 'Mr Gardiner from Evesham . . . cleaned and painted our stone.' (June 10, 1884)

† My italics.

too – no noble epitaph, just those familiar words (St John 11.25) from the beginning of the funeral service. All very ordinary, utterly unmemorable. Except that someone lingering here might just wonder how it was that the man and his wife died within three days of each other in January 1892, and might wonder too why their daughter Ann died so soon after them.

* * * *

Robert Staight probably inhabited the Villa (its deeds reveal nothing of its earliest ownership) and it is possible he built it. Charles's father, the epitaph-less Thomas, certainly lived there, and either he or Charles extended it. Thomas's ownership is confirmed by a note attached to the Sale papers of the Dumbleton Estate in 1822:

> The Manor is co-extensive with the Parish, the whole of which belongs to Earl Sommers except one farm belonging to Jesus College, Oxford, Rectory and Glebe Land and one small House, Garden, and Orchard belonging to the said T.P. Staight.[8]

The original Dumbleton Hall had been allowed to deteriorate with the decline of the Cocks family during the 18th century. Samuel Rudder's new *History of Glos.* (1779) speaks baldly of this decline: 'No gentleman's family is resident in Dumbleton, and part of the mansion house, the seat of the late Sir R. Cocks, has lately been taken down.' With Edward Holland's acquisition of the Estate in 1822, a new Hall was built, and a gentleman's family was resident in Dumbleton once more. Holland gets a brief mention in Cobbett's *Rural Rides* (1830). William Cobbett, who rode quite close to Dumbleton, staying on nearby Bredon Hill, mentions that 'Holland, one of Baring's partners, or clerks, has recently bought an estate of Lord Somers, called Dumbleton, for, it is said, about *eighty thousand pounds.*'[9]

Edward Holland lived with his large family in the Hall he built till his death in 1875. One of his guests was his cousin, the novelist Elizabeth Gaskell, for whom the squire and his village were synonymous ('Does Dumbleton really think of asking Julia?' *Letters*, 8 May 1862). Mrs Gaskell was 'about halfway' through writing her *Life of Charlotte Brontë* (1857) when she stayed at Dumbleton in 1856, and her eldest daughter Marianne would stay here on numerous occasions before becoming engaged to Thurstan, Edward's eldest son, whom Ann Staight mentions in her diaries. On one such visit, Mrs

Gaskell hoped that her daughter would return home 'brilliantly well from the care-free life, and good air of Dumbleton' and a couple of days later she urged Marianne 'Do get strong in the quiet and good air of Dumbleton'.[10]

The village, undisturbed and undisturbing, is ideal for convalescence. There is more spectacular Cotswold country, there are prettier villages – nearby Stanton is one – and more dramatic juxtapositions of village and landscape, but Dumbleton would be hard to match for its air of tranquillity, an established and continuing tranquillity. The countryside is homely, its slopes and coppices unlikely to tax or tire the convalescent walker. Some, from harsher terrains, call it 'soft country' here. Even the nearest town, six miles away, does not evoke the usual images of township, but rather of markets and market gardens. The proportion of people to land feels just about right. Mrs Gaskell's confidence in Dumbleton's restorative powers seems to have been widely shared, certainly by the Staights, and finds endorsement today in the role of Dumbleton Hall, the same house (though now enlarged) where Mrs Gaskell and Marianne stayed.

Edward Holland's death in 1875 was a great loss – as agriculturist and MP he was well known, and 'his private virtues and public labours' had been widely recognised. An obituary described him as 'a type of the highest ideal of an English country gentleman'.[11] Because there were so many children to be supported (Mrs Gaskell mentions 12, The *Evesham Journal* obituary cites 10), Thurstan did not inherit the Estate, which was put up for sale once again. The publicity material was predictably lavish in tone: 'The Dumbleton Hall Estate forms part of the fertile and far-famed Vale of Evesham . . . the society in the neighbourhood is everything which can be desired, Dumbleton Hall being in immediate contiguity to several first class residential estates.'* The Estate was sold, this time not for eighty thousand pounds but for £180,000, to the Trustees of two young gentlemen called Eyres. Six years later, the youthful landowner, Henry William Eyres, would die in Naples at the age of 24, in April 1881. (The East window in Dumbleton church commemorates him. Ann Staight noted its installation in her diary in October 1887 'Mrs Eyres had new window (painted) put in over Communion Table in our church'.) After the presence of a strong man and public figure at the Hall, there was now instead a widow in her early twenties and,

---

* These would include, all within a 5-mile radius, Wormington Grange, Toddington Manor, Stanway House, Sudeley Castle, all mansions of architectural and social importance.

The Villa: front view of house, and view showing the back of the house and the adjoining smithy

from August 1881, her baby daughter, Caroline Mary Sybil Eyres, whose birthday celebrations would form a highlight in the village calendar.

The Estate which the Eyres' Trustees purchased in 1875 still comprised with a small exception the whole of the village of Dumbleton. Most of this small exception was the property of Charles Pitman Staight, who had taken over the Villa at his father's death. The Villa was thus something of an anomaly in this feudal village where virtually every property belonged to the Estate, to the lord of the manor. The Villa is certainly unlike any other house in Dumbleton, and fits no category: not farmhouse, not rectory, not mill, not cottage. A villa has been defined as 'a country mansion or residence occupied by a person of some position and wealth . . . usually of some size and architectural elegance and standing in its own grounds'.[12] The Villa stood in its own grounds, certainly, but was less grand than the definition suggests. From the village street the front of the Villa is visible today: it looks deceptively small from this side, a Jane Austen house in soft pink brick, the sort of house to have been lived in by genteel maiden ladies rather than by a blacksmith's family. From this side one has little notion either of the outbuildings behind the house or of the activities once pursued there.

The front door opened on to a hall. To the right, a parlour, a small room seldom used except by Sarah Staight, Charles's elder daughter, for her sewing; to the left, a much larger 'front room' where the whole family could gather to eat or to sing around the piano. Behind this room was the kitchen, with pantries and larders leading off it. Outside the garden door at the side there was a paved area, 'the court' with a pump; later a vine would grow on the sheltered wall. There were two staircases in the house, one leading from a back room beyond the kitchen into a back bedroom. There were five bedrooms, and also a long narrow windowless room called the 'long closet'. Charles Staight and his wife had adjacent rooms at the front of the house. The two blacksmith brothers shared a room, the two sisters shared another, and there was a spare bedroom. No bath room. Baths were taken in a tin tub. Ann mentions scrubbing the WC well but does not say where it was.

At the back of the house was a brewhouse, with a fireplace, where the family often ate, and where Ann did the washing. Despite its name beer does not appear to have been made here. Cider, which is much simpler to make, was tunned not in the brewhouse but in the woodhouse! The smithy itself was next door. Ann Staight never refers to forge or smithy in her diaries, only to the 'shop', and there are references to the 'shoplids' which I take to be a two-part door of the stable variety. There were numerous outhouses including a penthouse (a word whose meaning has changed dramatically over a hundred years so that today we envisage a luxury rooftop apartment rather than an outhouse with a sloping roof at the side of the house), places for poultry and pigs, and for the storage of wood and coal. Near to the 'shop' was a detached cottage, facing across the fields to the neighbouring village of Wormington. After vacating the Villa for her eldest son, Charles Staight's mother lived here with her two younger sons and a maid. By 1880 the cottage was occupied by the widow of the former Dumbleton Estate agent and her maid.

The garden was as spacious as the house, containing the flower garden which was the domain of Sarah Staight, a herb garden, and areas for the cultivation of fruit and vegetables. Tom Staight kept bees here. Adjoining the garden was a large orchard, containing not only the ubiquitous apple and pear trees, but other fruit-trees too – medlars, plums, apricots. In springtime there was the blossom to enjoy, dainty flowers in white and pastel pink, and in late summer the fruits, green and purple, red and russet, to be gathered in. The privacy of the family was ensured by the orchard, which separated it from the butcher's shop and from the village street itself, and which made the location of the Villa an ideal one, secluded but not isolated. The orchard, which was large enough for Ann to get lost in at night on at least two occasions, provided a second route to the village. The family could either take the garden path to the lane which runs at right angles to join the village street, or they could walk across the orchard. This latter course was the direct route to the butcher's shop, and this short cut was in regular use, not just because the family were great meat-eaters, but because Charles's third son, Joe, was the village butcher.

* * * *

THE VILLAGE BLACKSMITH

Under a spreading chestnut-tree
The village smithy stands;
The smith, a mighty man is he,
With large and sinewy hands;
And the muscles of his brawny arms
Are strong as iron bands.

His hair is crisp, and black, and long;
His face is like the tan;
His brow is wet with honest sweat,
He earns whate'er he can,
And looks the whole world in the face,
For he owes not any man.

Week in, week out, from morn till night,
You can hear his bellows blow;
You can hear him swing his heavy sledge,
With measured beat and slow,
Like a sexton ringing the village bell,
When the evening sun is low.

And children coming home from school
Look in the open door;
They love to see the flaming forge,
And hear the bellows roar,
And catch the burning sparks that fly
Like chaff from a threshing-floor.

He goes on Sunday to the church,
And sits among his boys;
He hears the parson pray and preach,
He hears his daughter's voice
Singing in the village choir,
And it makes his heart rejoice.

It sounds to him like her mother's voice
Singing in Paradise!
He needs must think of her once more,
How in the grave she lies;
And with his hard, rough hand he wipes
A tear out of his eyes.

Toiling, – rejoicing, – sorrowing,
Onward through life he goes;
Each morning sees some task begin,
Each evening sees it close;
Something attempted, something done,
Has earned a night's repose.

Thanks, thanks to thee, my worthy friend,
For the lesson thou hast taught!
Thus at the flaming forge of life
Our fortunes must be wrought;
Thus on its sounding anvil shaped
Each burning deed and thought.[13]

Henry Longfellow (1807–1882)

Charles Staight's smithy at the Villa, unlike Longfellow's, was tucked away from the street, out of sight, his bellows and anvil a fascination for his near-neighbour the Rector rather than for the school children. Here, while his sons grew up, Charles had worked the business with an apprentice and a servant. He had married in 1845 a local farmer's daughter, Ann Peart, in Cheltenham Parish Church. They had seven children, five sons and two daughters, only one – the last – dying in infancy. By 1880, when the diaries begin, Charles was sixty years old (so was his wife Ann) and a Master Blacksmith, running the business with two of his sons, Thomas and John, but in fact working only when their absences or illnesses required. Life expectancy was shorter then than it is now, and fewer men attained the biblical three-score-years-and-ten. Charles had put his affairs in order, making his Will in February 1880. His widow was to remain at the Villa, the property to be held in trust for all his children 'in equal shares as tenants in common'. There was no differentiation between sons and daughters in its terms – he was very fond of his daughters – or between those sons in the business and those outside it.

Life had treated Charles well – better than Longfellow's black-smith, who has lost his wife and is reduced to tears when reminded of her by the sight of their daughter singing in the church choir. Longfellow has got the church bit exactly right

He goes on Sunday to the church
And sits among his boys

for church, to Charles Staight, is as central in his life as the forge. Not only had his work and his family prospered, and he had his health and strength, but he was regarded as a pillar of church and village, earning the nickname of 'Mayor Staight'. A skill of his remembered by reputation in the village today (nobody living can go back this far, of course, but parents' comments are recalled) was his ability to soothe ruffled passions at parish meetings.

The village blacksmith of the 19th century possessed an authority which seems curious to us today, and one not looked for in his modern counterpart, the garage owner. Certainly the forge fulfilled a function not required of the garage, that of providing a meeting place and news centre. A horse will need around ten sets of shoes a year, depending on the amount of roadwork it does. So Charles would see his customers on a regular basis every five weeks or so. This continuity of contact is significant. In a village like Dumbleton *without a public house* this social side became even more desirable. The absence of a public house does not only mean the villagers cannot

Charles Pitman Staight, Master Blacksmith and 'Mayor of Dumbleton'; his
wife Ann and his daughter Sarah

buy a drink; it also keeps outsiders out. The village becomes self-contained, not open to the outside world. Dumbleton was already isolated by its location. The smithy at least brought people in from beyond the village confines, and from neighbouring villages: Wormington, Stanton, Childswickham. It even operated in some ways like a hostelry. Charles would take the more well-to-do customers into his front room for tea or cider while their horses were shod; the others chatted in the shop or the kitchen. His curious status as a private householder, a man of property in a village of tenant farmers and tied cottagers, further enhanced his position. Everyone else was at the mercy of the family at the Hall; Charles was not. He was, like the house he lived in, an anomaly. A kind of social junction, he was clearly respected by gentry and cottagers alike, hence the 'mayoral' status. This resulted in a very comfortable state of affairs. The danger is that as head of a large and well-placed family in a small village he is a central figure, almost larger than life. What happens to a large family when it loses the man at its head?

Before the mid-19th century it was customary for a man to name his first son after himself, and his second son after his father. This is what Charles Pitman Staight did. His four sons are Charles Pitman, Thomas, Joseph Harry and John (the fifth, Edward Drinkwater, named after a friend, died in infancy). Charles' eldest son went to Swindon, probably to be apprenticed as an engineer, but ended up as a publican, and at the age of 35 was landlord of the Red Lion at Moredon, near Swindon. Although he visited Dumbleton regularly, his sister Ann, the diarist, never went to Moredon. This is odd considering the amount she does travel, but she is clearly not as close to Charley as to her other brothers. He had married Fanny Grinnall from Sedgeberrow, a village close to Dumbleton, and the only time Ann mentions Fanny in the diaries is when 'Charley's wife' has a new infant (she had seven). Away from Dumbleton, Charles and his family are not part of this story.

The other son who has broken away from the family and the village, though he was to return shortly, is the third son, Joseph Harry. In 1880 he was in London learning the butcher's trade. Although Joe returns to Dumbleton, as village butcher, he has acquired an independence which other members of his family lack. Once Joe was installed in the butcher's shop, Charles would spend much of his time with his third son: Joe seems to be the favourite son, and after him undisputed head of the family. He was a big man, a monumental man. Even as a child he was so freakishly big – in middle age he was reputed to weigh 22 stone – that he was invited to join a circus. The Rector's son[14] boasted of his size to his Bretforton cousins, but he chose the wrong people to boast to – their local butcher was 28 stone! Longfellow's village blacksmith is, physically, an exact description of Joe:

> . . . *a mighty man is he*
> *With large and sinewy hands;*
> *And the muscles of his brawny arms*
> *Are strong as iron bands.*
>
> *His hair is crisp, and black, and long;*
> *His face is like the tan. . .*
>
> *And looks the whole world in the face,*
> *For he owes not any man.*

The remaining two sons, Thomas (32) and John (22) work in the family business. They are the quiet ones, overshadowed by the jolly Joe. They live at home and show no inclination to leave it. Tom is mild, unassertive; John, as the youngest child, is a little spoilt. Their work was not confined to shoeing horses. Often their work took them out of the shop – to horses too lame to come to them, or to farms to make iron implements or repair machinery (erecting iron fencing, fixing tanks, mending steam-engines). The versatility of the blacksmith is revealed in a note of Ann's 'Tom mended lid off sugar-tin, Father's candlestick, top of kettle lid and my patten ring today' or 'T. Teal called to ask our people to look at church door lock'. Tom is more the farrier, John more of an engineer. Besides these activities, they are also farmers, managing the family property, variously known as Charity or Manor Farm at nearby Wormington, and like both their brothers, Tom and John will end their careers as full-time farmers. For their recreation, both boys enjoy music: Tom sings in the church choir, and John plays the piano.

There are three women at the Villa: Charles's wife Ann, and their two daughters, Sarah and Ann. Charles's wife is a shadowy figure in the diaries, seen mainly in kitchen or sick-room, presiding at births and deaths. Sarah, her eldest daughter, a much more forceful character than her mother, has taken over. It is Sarah, at 28, who runs the Villa – the house and its occupants – with a firm hand, competent in all domestic and medical matters and in such different activities as arranging the church flowers and killing poultry.

And so to the diarist herself, Ann Staight. The name is short, plain, terse. The hero of Mrs Henry Wood's *East Lynne*[15] approved the name Ann because it was 'simple and unpretending'. Ann Staight is like her name, simple and straightforward, and these qualities will be reflected in her diaries, though just occasionally we will have a glimpse of a different, more mysterious person. Ann Staight would without doubt have considered herself the least important member of the family group. She was the second youngest child, and younger than Sarah by five years. Despite being very much in Sarah's shadow she was devoted to her, and they worked well together. It is evident that the members of the family to whom Ann is closest are its strongest characters – her father, Joe and Sarah. Ann is proud, not jealous, of Sarah's superior skills – in sewing, in cooking, in housekeeping – and the diaries will not tell us much about sibling rivalry.

In a house with, at that time, no servant, Ann does the work of a servant, the cleaning, washing, scrubbing. She assisted with the cooking, acting as kitchenmaid rather than cook. Neither sister had outside employment, and indeed both were fully occupied at home, vital workers in the family business. It was a good partnership, and a good friendship too. In the book that was partly written at Dumbleton Hall, Mrs Gaskell quotes a letter from Charlotte Brontë to a friend:

> You . . . know full as well as I do, the value of sisters' affection to each other; there is nothing like it in this world, I believe, when they are nearly equal in age, and similar in education, tastes, and sentiments.[16]

Ann and Sarah, as we shall see, did not share identical interests, but they certainly shared the sisterly affection which Charlotte Brontë herself enjoyed. Together for most of the time, they needed to get on, but their separations supply a register of their affection: when apart, they correspond with each other frequently.

There was only one cloudy area regarding the sisters' attachment, and it was one with which Charlotte Brontë was not confronted. Sarah had an admirer in the village, the miller Leslie Legge. Sarah's attitude – to Leslie and to marriage – is never precisely defined. Marriage to him would offer positive benefits, of course, but it would mean giving up a comfortable home in a pleasant village, power and influence over the five adults there for a more modest, a more solitary existence elsewhere. Sarah is the only one of Charles' four unmarried children currently confronted with this dilemma. It is remarkable that here are three adults, who appear to have no marriage plans and no romantic attachments either. We are so preoccupied with such matters today that such a state seems impossible. Yet they clearly enjoyed a happy family life. There is music and laughter. (One small instance: 'After tea I cut two plates full of cheese (strong) to put in oven. We all had some for supper and did *laugh* over it well.') No sense of deprivation drives them outside the family unit: rather, people from outside come inside it. The companionable symmetry of two boys, two girls, at home made outside society less than essential. The boys will not start looking for wives until they are on their own at the Villa, the family life having abruptly ended. Ann, coming late into a large family, is preoccupied by it. For her recreation, apart from the family, she delights in friendship, flowers, music, books. And she keeps a diary . . .

The family was literate but not literary. They could all read – this is clear from the diaries. They wrote much less. Charles Staight occasionally writes, and not only for himself – 'Old William Hampton came before breakfast to ask Father to do a little writing for him' – but there is no mention of his wife writing. None of the men are letter-writers: they are doers, men of action. When away from home, Ann receives letters only from her sister. We know that Sarah kept a diary when she was a girl (mainly a record of her poultry-keeping) for it was read decades later to the dying John by his daughter-in-law, and what may have begun as an imitative childhood habit with Ann developed into a major adult activity, into her main form of recreation. It is not clear what diaries, if any, Ann had kept before the 1880 notebook. Certainly the first entries there are tentative and sketchy. As her friendship with Annie Biscoe of Enfield develops, the entries lengthen and she writes *for* Annie: they certainly exchanged diaries regularly in the early 1880s. Her enjoyment of writing and her fondness for Annie combine to make the diary-writing a great source of pleasure. There was limited scope for other writing in her life, apart from letters to family and friends (she was the family's main correspondent, and even when staying with her grandmother or uncle she writes letters *for* them), and more mundanely, writing the bills for her father after each quarter day. Ann talks much about doing her 'writing up', often missing family gatherings to go upstairs to do it. It is as if the writing-up becomes more important than the events being recorded. She clearly enjoyed writing; to record her doings, however humdrum, was a passion. Did other blacksmiths' daughters write so avidly?

The extent of Ann's formal education is unclear. There had long been a charity-school at Dumbleton, initiated by one of the Cocks ladies of the Hall, 'for teaching all the poor children to read, knit and spin.' The earliest log-book of the present village school begins in

27

1888, and there are no earlier school records available, either in the village or in the County Record Office. Sarah and Ann were of course of school age before the Education Act of 1870 but they certainly went to a school of some sort, perhaps a Dame's school. (Ann shows Annie Biscoe a book about *School* on one occasion, and Sarah lists a Lesson Book amongst her books.) Although Ann had only, presumably, a modest village school education, she read anything that came to hand – the *Evesham Journal* at home, the *Family Herald*, *Argosy* and *Supplements* at Enfield – and we know she read Dickens and George Eliot as she mentions some of their books in her diaries. The result is that she writes easily and legibly, and rarely repeats herself. Her spelling is surprisingly accurate, though she did hesitate over 'gossipped' as her rendering of it shows, and piano practice is invariably spelt with an 's'. When Joe drives the ragman to Broadway – 'Joe took Sis to Broadway, also the che-ffioneer', Ann's version does not tally with the French original of chiffonier or cheffonier. Only in one area, however, does her spelling waver, and that is in the area of surnames. It was a time when names were spelled phonetically and variously: the name Staight itself is found in other forms (of which Staite is the most common) though it will be spelt in its final form throughout this book. Wedgwoods are sometimes spelt with an 'e' in the middle, Mr Reeve is sometimes Mr Reeves. As for punctuation Ann much prefers the comma to the full stop. She writes in an abbreviated style, as though time and paper were scarce (they probably were). She is painstakingly accurate, changing 'grey dress' to 'slate dress' or 'best dress' to 'drab' if she finds she has made a mistake. She avoids repetition and likes alliteration: twice she speaks of 'cleaning candle-sticks and corners' – an unlikely combination of ideas but not of sounds. There was no gas in Dumbleton (there isn't any today either) and she was writing only by oil-lamp or candlelight. It is remarkable that the result is so neat and clear.

We may assume that her diaries were not read by the family, not even by Sarah, yet their contents are not confidential. Was this natural reticence or a deliberate censorship? There is never any criticism of anyone, no personal remarks, feelings are never revealed, or secrets told, and these are the things on which great diaries thrive. The only indication of emotion is in the handwriting itself, which may change from being neat and regular to large and wild and blotchy in times of stress.

Leaving aside the notebook, the early diaries contain entries which are long and leisurely (eight diaries for two years) and Part Two of this book deliberately reflects this spaciousness. Then the character of the entries changes in marked fashion for the last two diaries, for reasons which will be examined later. The entries become short ones, and Ann no longer wrote every day. She never intended telling a story, but in the final diaries (Part Three) her sense that she has no story of her own to tell becomes stronger. And then, suddenly, they stop, just when the *drama* of her life is beginning; and the rest of the story has to be unearthed, uncovered elsewhere.

PART ONE
The Notebook

The Notebook

I
Enfield

The small notebook which Ann Staight purchased in Enfield in the summer of 1880 may have been her first diary. On its front cover, inside the circular device which forms part of its cover design, she wrote:

> Annie Staight
> Dumbleton
> June 15th / 80
> Memorandum.

Inside the front and back covers of the notebook Ann listed her purchases and expenses for June and July 1880. The first item, appropriately for a diarist, is an inkstand. It and the 'little pocket book' listed later each cost one shilling. Her expenditure for the two months totalled £2 6s. 1d., of which by far the biggest item is the single train fare from Evesham to Paddington at 9s. 6d. Amongst such girlish items as 'pink and blue ribbons 10d.' and 'gloves 3s. 1d.' is a purse for her father 1s. 6d., two bottles of polish for her boots 6d., 2d. for church, and 'Book (Oliver Twist) 6d.'.

The notebook contains entries for June and July 1880 at the front and for the period December 1880–March 1881 at the back, entries which encapsulate in miniature Ann's two worlds at this time – at Dumbleton and Enfield. The pocket book opens, without preamble, with her travelling from one to the other: 'Returned with Miss Biscoe to Enfield Tuesday June 15th/80. Sarah came with us in pony and trap to Evesham . . . we reached Enfield about 9.'

It is appropriate that Annie Biscoe figures right from the beginning of the diaries, indeed from the very first line. The friendship between the two Annies* is central to the diaries and may have been

---

* To avoid confusion between the two Annies, and as Annie Biscoe was actually christened Annie, the diarist is called Ann throughout this book.

the original reason they were written. At this stage the friendship was clearly a new one, hence the 'Miss Biscoe', a formality which is immediately discarded. There is no indication, here or elsewhere, of how or when the two girls first met. Ann's brother Joe was learning the butcher's trade in London and it is possible she had visited him there before. In any event, Ann was going to stay with Annie at the Biscoe home in Enfield, Middlesex, and Joe, with another friend of the family, Mrs McGlinchy, met the two girls at Westbourne Park, the stop before Paddington. Their journey, though not a difficult one, was fourfold: by horse and trap from Dumbleton to Evesham, by train on the Great Western Railway to Paddington, by Metropolitan line to Liverpool Street, and from there a forty-minute train journey took them north to Enfield. Joe escorted the woman as far as Liverpool Street station; Mrs McGlinchy left them at Rectory Road station, which was close to her Stoke Newington home.

While the profession of Annie Biscoe's father is not revealed in the notebook, the fact that he was an active man with his own stables does emerge, as he drives daughter and guest hither and thither on their holiday excursions. For this visit was pure holiday, in sharp contrast to a later one. There were visits three days running to Alexandra Palace in Muswell Hill, named after the Princess of Wales and opened in 1875 as North London's answer to the Crystal Palace. It offered a wide variety of entertainments: Ann mentions a horse show, a circus, picture galleries. The organ was one of the finest in Europe, but Ann had her priorities: 'Had some coffee and cake and listened to the organ'. The girls shopped in Enfield – gifts from Annie included, significantly, a writing case – and they went to church there, 'to St Andrew's church. Canon Gregory from St Paul's preached in aid of the missions to Madagascar'. Visits to friends of the Biscoes included a picnic tea in a hayfield, a novel experience for Ann who never had tea out of doors at home:

> Mr Biscoe had the grey horse and 4-wheel carriage and drove us to Mr Gayfer's in the afternoon. We had tea in the hayfield, took up the things with horse and trap, the boy took up a faggot, we made a fire, boiled the kettle, had strawberries and cream etc. for tea. Afterwards we all went for a long walk over the farms to see the lambs (240) . . .

But the main interest of this time was brother Joe's courtship. Only fifteen months separated Joe and Ann – a smaller gap than between any of the other children – and they had been baptised together. Ann would naturally be curious about the woman he planned to marry. To heighten the interest, Joe's fiancée, Miss

Louisa Rose, was four years his senior. But she was hardly the experienced woman of the metropolis ensnaring the country boy. She was not a city girl at all but the second daughter of a Surrey cattle dealer from the picturesque parish of Wotton, near Dorking. Her mother's family, the Dibbles, had run the Wotton Hatch Inn* for over three hundred years and for a time Louisa Rose lived at the inn, acting as barmaid for her Dibble aunt and her husband John Legge. When this uncle returned to his native South London, Louisa visited him there. Quiet and retiring, she was the perfect foil for Joe's extrovert nature. She was, furthermore, small and slender beside his massive frame. Meetings cannot have been frequent, with Joe in North London and Miss Rose in Balham, but the day after Ann arrived at Enfield

> Joe and Miss Rose came down for an hour or two, we had a little music. They left directly after supper, Annie and I went to the station with them.

Music, something the three women had in common (all three played the piano, and Annie Biscoe and Louisa Rose sang solos) would ease the shy early stages of acquaintanceship.

Ann left Enfield on 29 June 1880.

> Annie and I went out shopping. I bought a tiny purse for Father, salad spoon and fork for Mother, and *little pocket-book for self*. We had early tea, Mr and Mrs Biscoe went for a short drive after, and on their return I said good-bye. Annie came with me to the station, and stayed till train started.

It was a short train ride down the line to Rectory Road, where Ann stayed with Mrs McGlinchy for a few days. Mrs McGlinchy had been a Staite before her marriage, and came from the Tewkesbury area, but as she is never called by a more familiar name it would appear there was no direct family relationship between her and the Staights. But she certainly knew Joe well and accompanied Ann to visit him at his Swiss Cottage lodgings. There Ann finished letters to 'Sarah, Annie B. and Miss Rose and posted them in Fairfax Road', the three names denoting neatly her various stages of intimacy with the recipients: sister, friend and prospective sister-in-law, the three key women in her life.

---

* A notice in the hotel explains the name: Wotton means the farm by the wood, and a hatch is a gate generally leading to a common. The inn was formerly called the Evelyn Arms after the Evelyn family who lived at Wotton House and lie in Wotton church, and of whom the most famous member is the 17th-century diarist John Evelyn.

An excursion to Hampton Court was foiled by rain and when Ann returned to Evesham on July 3rd it was raining there too:

> When I reached Evesham it was very wet. John was there, but had to wait to send a box by Birmingham train. Mr Wedgwood [the Rector of Dumbleton] had wagonette and pair there, and brought me home with Mrs and Miss Wedgwood.

*　　*　　*　　*

II

Dumbleton

Five months later, on December 7th 1880, Ann began writing again, from the other end of the notebook, and she would write on till forced to a halt – in March 1881 – by the homecoming entry quoted above. In the intervening period, Joe had married, in September 1880, his Miss Rose, not in her remote and romantic parish church at Wotton, but at St Mary's Church in the Balham High Road which was near the home of her uncle, John Agar Legge, one of the witnesses at the ceremony.[17] After the wedding the bridal couple travelled to Dumbleton, where Joe succeeded Alf Dudfield as village butcher at the house-and-shop just across the orchard from the Villa. Louisa Rose, who had celebrated her thirty-first birthday three days after her wedding, had not been working at the time of her marriage. In *Our Village*, published earlier in the century, Mary Russell Mitford had this to say of the name Louisa:

> *There are some names which seem to belong to particular classes of character, to form the mind, and even to influence the destiny: Louisa now – is not your Louisa necessarily a die-away damsel, who reads novels, and holds her head on one side, languishing and given to love?*[18]

As befitted her gracious name and gentle ways, Louisa Rose delighted in possessing pretty things – a tea-set of dainty white bone china decorated appropriately with tiny pink rosebuds: a REGARD ring, engraved 'In memory of dear Mother died July 22nd 1871', today missing all its stones – the ruby, emerald, garnet, amethyst, ruby and diamond – which explain its name; and bracelet charms which included – a tiny emblem of her new life – a mother-of-pearl pig. If this Louisa was a die-away damsel, she had to change fast. Overnight Louisa Rose became Louie the butcher's wife. While the bride

36

received callers in her neat front parlour (Ann noted that on January 10th the Rector's two youngest daughters called 'to pay the wedding-visit'), out at the back Joe did his slaughtering.

There were then no public abattoirs, and behind Joe's house and stables was the outhouse where the slaughtering was done. Without the refinements of cold storage the butcher killed animals as he needed their meat, or when their injuries or misbehaviour necessitated:

Joe killed a beast Wed., had it from Mr Smith's [of the Bank Farm], it knocked down their little gate and jumped the big one

and

Tom up to Joe's to help him, got a beast from Mr Smith's he had to kill, broke its leg

and Joe's own stock were not exempt: 'Joe obliged to kill calf, been bad all along'.

The proximity of the two families worked to the advantage of both. The Villa Staights collected their meat, milk, butter and cream from Joe's, and they supplied him with poultry. They used his horses and traps, but on the other hand they helped with his slaughtering, haymaking, fruitpicking, cider-making. The slaughtering was an opportunity for the men to get together: 'After tea, John went up to Joe's for an hour helping kill a pig' or 'Father and Tom up at Joe's till after 9 (he was killing a sheep)' and they helped Joe with his own animals 'Joe down soon after eleven, fetched Tom and they stayed up with a cow till 2 a.m.' If Joe was indisposed, one of the brothers delivered the meat for him. When Joe took Louie out for the day to visit relations, in the evening the brothers would go up 'to light the fire and wait for them coming'. In this commune-like arrangement, the Staights shared their assets and achieved a state of near self-sufficiency. This living in peaceful and productive harmony in a garden setting appears – is – ideal, idyllic. But there *is* a darker side of the picture even in this peaceful place. 'The world's sharpness like a clasping knife' is *there* too, and here is an early example of it, the far-from-pretty proximity of the slaughterhouse to the bride's dainty parlour.

So the winter of 1880 was one of adjustment for Louie. Not only was the abattoir at the back door, but she also had to contend with the initially daunting proximity of in-laws. Every Sunday she would meet the whole family at church *en masse*, and she and Joe would

Seller

2 – 1 Hhd Cask, 1 – ½ Ditto,
18 Gal Do. 2 Taps & Keeper   £ 1 .. 10 .. 6

Shop

2 Blocks, salting Tub, weighing Machine,
Sett of Weights, 2 Saws, 2 Cleavers,
Spring Balance, 4 Knives & Steel, Hanging
Lamp, Meat Basket, Wood Rail & Crooks,
Steel yards   £ 4 .. 10 .. 0

Slaughterhouse,

Cratch, Tub, Pole Axe, 4 Gambrels,
Crooks, & Sundries.   £ 0 .. 18 .. 0

Harness Room

Sett of Harness & Trap, Bridle & Saddle,
3 Collars, Roller, Halters, Bits, & Sundries   £ 0 .. 1 .. 0

Yard

Pig Trough, Water Tub, Chaff Box,
3 Pails, Clothes line, 2 Ladders, Door –
Scraper, Ringing Machine, 2 Hay Forks
& Hay Knife, Brass Kettle & Sidian, ~~1 Do~~
~~Hurdles~~ Mattock, Hoe, Shovel, & Sundries   £ 1 .. 15 .. 0

Left, part of the inventory of the butcher's shop and house, 1880; above, Louisa Rose; right and below, two views of the butcher's house and shop (the larger one shows Joe and family c.1890)

spend Sunday evenings at the Villa, where there would be music and singing. Her father-in-law called in every morning for meat and milk – and to talk to Joe – and there would be frequent visits from her sisters-in-law, the formidable Sarah and the quieter Ann. By the time Ann resumes writing in the notebook, the shy bride has become the working wife, happy with her husband and her home and rarely seeking society or entertainment beyond the family circle.

The second part of the notebook starts abruptly, and the lack of any explanatory or introductory note suggests that Ann had written elsewhere in the interim, and that lack of loose paper compelled a return to the pocket book. Paper can be a problem: elsewhere in the diaries she has to borrow paper from Louie, and an important document will be written on butcher's stationery!

The first entries place the reader firmly in a *country* context, opening with a meet of the local hunt. This would have been the North Cotswold Hunt, though nowadays two other hunts, the Cotswold and the Cotswold Vale Farmers, cover nearby territory.

Dec 7th 1880. Hunting here, met at Wormington [the next village], the boys went on the Hill, had good sport, killed two foxes by the Hall, horsemen and dogs all went down the village and back. Old gentleman came to have a shoe fastened, waited in the front room for the boys to come, had a glass of ale and biscuits. I went to the shop and up to Joe's, did not stay long, they were very busy, Joe killing pigs, and Louie busy with the butter . . .

Wed Dec 8th. Joe went to Tewkesbury Fair, John drove him to Beckford [station] to meet 9 train, he bought fat heifer and two sheep . . .

Friday 10th. It was a lovely day, almost like Spring. Sarah was gardening in the afternoon . . . (Two men and a woman with baby about the village this week, causing some consternation, being seen at queer hours).

Sunday 12th. Sarah stayed to cook, all the rest went to church, Mother and I a little later. Mr Wedgewood not very well, Mr Stewart did duty for him both services . . . (Saw Joe's large photo and small ones that arrived Sat. from London, very bad ones all of them.)

This is the first reference to the failing health of the Rector, the Rev. Robert Wedgwood. A grandson of the potter Josiah (and son of Josiah's eldest son John), Robert had been at Dumbleton since before Ann's birth, and not only was he the only Rector she had known, but a near neighbour, and, too, a prominent figure in a very limited village community, a Justice of the Peace and Chairman of the Board of Guardians of the Winchcombe Union which was responsible for the poor and infirm of the area around Winchcombe, including Dumbleton. Presented to the living by his cousin Edward Holland of

40

Dumbleton Hall, Robert built a new Rectory at his own expense in 1853 (Squire Holland contributed the bricks from the village brick-yard) which he then presented to the church – a gesture which more than hints at the Wedgwood family wealth. The Rectory,* a large, ugly redbrick house in the severe early Victorian style, stood at the top of Nutmeadow (the road built by Holland as a grand tree-lined approach to his Hall) and was thus well-placed for the Rector's three areas of obligation, church, Hall and village. Robert Wedgwood was now 75 and would henceforth share his duties with various local clergymen including his second cousin, the Rev. Frederic Holland (Edward's second son) who was Vicar of Evesham. Occasionally Robert's older bachelor brother Allen, a retired clergyman, would help out. He was always near at hand, for he lived with Robert, his wife and four daughters at the Rectory. Robert was an old father (his four daughters were all in their twenties) but there was an explanation for this as I learned from the son of a subsequent Dumbleton Rector. Robert had first married a woman twenty-five years older than himself. After her death, he married again, this time a woman twenty-five years younger, by whom he had the four daughters.

Robert's decline, Ann's developing friendship with Annie Biscoe, and the severe winter of 1880–1881 dominate this second half of the notebook, as Ann gets into her writing stride after the sketchy early Enfield entries. The year 1881 opened with her working on the Squire's bill – there would not be a Squire much longer – and the Rector reviewing the events in the parish of the past year:

> Mr W preached his *annual* sermon in the afternoon, 14 christenings, 2 weddings, 15 deaths . . .
>
> (January 2, 1881)

Births neatly balance deaths in this survey of 'hatches, matches and dispatches'. One hundred years later the Rector of Dumbleton was still lamenting the lack of weddings in the village. Two marriages a year is a good year.

In the severe January weather, the blacksmiths were particularly busy 'roughing' the horses, using long-headed nails to prevent them slipping on the icy roads:

> The boys did not go to Wormington till after tea, were obliged to go roughing . . .

* The house deteriorated and was demolished early in the 20th century. A new house was built on the site and a small modern rectory was built in the centre of the village.

Thursday 13th. Father and the boys very busy roughing all day. It came on to snow fast about 11, Sarah got in all the clothes and had the stove on in brewhouse to burn up slack [coal-dust] and dry the clothes. Joe slipped up going to Beckford, made him very stiff and sore, he slipped up in Evesham Monday too, says it is smooth tips on his boots so the boys tell him he must be roughed . . . There was a parish meeting at the school to decide about a fresh rate, Mr W[edgwood] promised to get information Sat. at Winchcomb. . . .

Tuesday 18th. Tom and John busy arranging stove in kitchen, answers capitally. I cleaned up the coal house . . . A very rough cold wind.

Wednesday 19th. The wind not quite so rough this morn, but it has been a deep snow, and drifted tremendously, some sheep in the Short Ground had to be dug out and driven up this orchard, couldn't get along the field. Boys very busy clearing snow away . . . did not work in the shop at all. . . .

In these conditions, what Professor Mingay has called 'a ferocious blizzard' causing severe sheep losses,[19] travelling was difficult, almost impossible. A visitor at Mr Wedgwood's ran into trouble: 'The train he left Evesham by got blocked up, they had to stay in it all night, and couldn't get far next day.' The sharp frosts continued – Sarah made apple jelly with the apples 'touched with frost' – until the end of the month:

January 27th. Rapid thaw today, we were later getting up. Grange coachman came before we had breakfast, so we had to wait till after 9

and on the 29th

Sis and I busy all day cleaning, every place very wet, still thawing, not much snow left . . .

The delayed breakfast remained a problem! '1st Feb. Breakfast ready at 7.30, had to wait till nearly 9, boys over at the Rectory boiler . . .'

Like Christmas Day in the middle of winter, so St Valentine's Day relieved the February gloom. In an age of sentimentality, it was a perfect opportunity for lavish expressions of sentiment, and these were not confined to exchanges with the opposite sex. Friendship was celebrated just as much as romantic love. Ann and Annie, who corresponded regularly, exchanged Valentines. They were also exchanging diaries regularly ('I received Diary', 'Received D–, only one string on one end loosely, not sealed at all') and from now on the frequently-used word is always abbreviated to 'D–'.

Two days after Valentine's Day Ann received a second one, its source less obvious.

I had a Valentine come with Taunton postmark, they were all anxious to open it, thought it was a letter from Mr Cook, the address looked like his writing. Had my large new album down and put in photos out of old one this afternoon. (John had Valentine but I did not know till last night, from AB [Annie Biscoe] and I think Tom had one too, but did not see his.)

The 'large new album', to which Ann refers, possibly a 25th birthday present from her parents the previous October, is a large, lavish, leatherbound book complete with lock and key. In the front a loose sheet gives her instructions to the album-maker:

A.S. In about ½ inch Old English letters
not the date, as at first ordered.

Her wishes had been duly executed, and the initials A.S. gleam out from the cover in gold Gothic script. Inside, the very first photograph is one of Sarah, who has precedence over Ann's parents (side by side on the second page) and Joe and Louie, who follow soon after. Beside Sarah's portrait is a tinted one of an attractive fair-haired boy, John in his teens. On the *final* page of the album is a photograph of Tom, calm and broad-browed, beside one, the very last in the book, of Ann herself. These two photographs are late ones whereas the ones of Sarah and John are youthful ones. This careful placing illustrates special affinities within the family, both the importance of Sarah to Ann, and the way the brothers and sisters 'paired off'. Sarah and John were always close, particularly in later life. As first daughter and youngest son/last child they enjoyed privileged positions in the family structure, Tom and Ann, as second son and second daughter, are less well-placed, their status reflected, perhaps unconsciously, by their position in the album. Among the many unidentified photographs in the album one only is well-labelled – a photograph of Queen Victoria's daughter Princess Louise and her husband the Marquis of Lorne, who were married in 1871.

Ann's autograph albums and birthday books and scrap books (in the notebook she mentions clearing out her desk and taking downstairs 'a lot of odds and ends for scrapbook, bits of poetry etc. out of newspapers') did not survive their peregrinations as the photograph albums did, but would contain the same sort of sentiments – the value of friendship, the importance of noble deeds – which abound in the albums of Ann's nieces (some introduce the sections of this book). One such entry, written in *three* of her nieces' albums around the turn of the century, is called *Good Advice*, and its exhortations to *do* and not to *dream* were certainly fulfilled by Ann:

Left, the only identified photograph in Ann Staight's album: Princess Louise, fourth daughter of Queen Victoria, and her husband the Marquis of Lorne; right, unidentified couple, possibly Sarah and Arthur Young

Good Advice

Be good sweet maid
Let those who will be clever.
Do noble deeds
Not dream them all day long,
And so make life, death,
And that vast for ever,
One grand, sweet song.

This is, in fact, the *third* verse of a poem by Charles Kingsley. By the end of the century it was misquoted and mispunctuated, as a glance at the original reveals:

A Farewell: To C.E.G.[20]
(Feb. 1, 1856)

My fairest child, I have no song to give you;
No lark could pipe in skies so dull and gray;
Yet, if you will, one quiet hint I'll leave you,
For every day.

I'll tell you how to sing a clearer carol
Than lark who hails the dawn or breezy down;
To earn yourself a purer poet's laurel
Than Shakespeare's crown.

Be good, sweet maid, and let who can be clever;
Do lovely things, not dream them, all day long;
And so make Life, and Death, and that For Ever
One grand sweet song.

The album version has acquired a new title and a new form. The *Good Advice* verse is tailor-made, in both length and content, for the Victorian girl's album. The 'noble deeds' which have replaced Kingsley's original 'lovely things' were a notion particularly dear to the Victorians, as another album entry (in Josie Staight's album) testifies:

Whene'er a noble deed is wrought,
Whene'er is spoken a noble thought,
Our hearts, in glad surprise,
To higher levels rise.

That is Longfellow again, very much the spokesman of his age.[21] 'Work' is thus imbued with sanctity. Doing things, working, even something as lowly and menial as Ann's 'I cleaned all spittoons and six or seven pairs of boots', 'I scrubbed out WC well,' is noble, is being good. Work, housework, occupies a large amount of Ann's time. What is surprising is that she *writes* so much about it. We might think that doing the work would be bad enough, without describing it in detail in a diary afterwards. Ann clearly views her work in a different light. Carlyle wrote 'Man is sent hither not to question, but to work: "the end of man," it was long ago written, "is an Action, not a Thought"',[22] and while Ann may have known nothing of Carlyle, her diary embodies his creed. She writes down her work, not her thoughts. With her desire for neatness and order she would derive some satisfaction from housework anyway, but by ritualising it and writing about it, she derives more. Washing, for example. In a large household, and one with three men employed at particularly dirty work, without (at this stage) either servants or washing machines, the washing operation alone was a colossal task, and not confined to a single day, as a glance at Ann's diary makes clear.

> January 1881
> Monday. We commenced washing, finished coloured clothes and hung out, put whites all in soak, and washing and put scald on fine things for first boil, left off before 7 pm . . .
>
> Tuesday. Was up at 7, went straight to washing and kept on till 10 at night. Mother left off at 8. Finished washing and wrung out everything ready to hang out . . . snowed in afternoon and again in the night.
>
> Wednesday. Sharp frost, fine day, hung out everything and tidied up brewhouse . . .

The chore often makes inroads into her evening leisure. If she starts late she may be at it till bed-time ('Then set to at my washing, and didn't finish it till 11 o'clock') but she can still feel playful at the end of the operation:

> Mother came in [from washing in brewhouse] about 9, but I was not in till 9.30, finished washing and wrung out most of it . . . Had a little game with the boys while they were washing, and finally sprinkled soapsuds freely to get rid of them . . .

The division of labour between the Staight women is clearcut: it is always Ann and her mother who wash. Sarah, as the eldest daughter, enjoys the choice of household tasks: she may starch, she sometimes irons, but she never washes. While Ann spends much of her time at the washtub, Sarah's superior skills are employed elsewhere. Her sewing skills are revealed early in the notebook. While Ann works on a *morning* petticoat or Tom's *second-best* coat, Sarah works on something more elaborate: 'Sis made Aunt Moseley a pretty cap of ecru lace and cerise satin.' When Ann re-covers dress buttons with new silk, it is 'with Sarah's instruction and assistance'. Ann assists Sarah with the cooking – she makes a vast quantity of apple puddings and milk puddings – and occasionally tries her hand at bread-making: 'Baking today, I made one loaf myself, had some difficulty in getting it *any shape*, but looked alright baked'. There is a definite programme of work: she talks of doing her 'regular Saturday work' or her 'upstairs work'. The domestic routine imposes an order and a structure on her life, and it is one that she does not resist or resent.

*   *   *   *

Ann's desire for order and her need for rites and rituals was met, of course, in another area, by the church itself. In the notebook she devotes a good deal of space and significance to the Rector's demise. By the beginning of February 1881 Mr Wedgwood was still able to be in church, but usually one of the other clergymen 'did duty' for him.

> Sunday Feb 13th 1881. Mother went to church with us, commenced snowing as we started, and turned out a cold, miserable day. Mr Stewart did service, all but sermon, Mr W preached that, and told us he should not be able to do both services any more, nor go about the village as of old, but he hoped to help in the church, and see his sick people in their homes, he was suffering from one or two complaints . . .

For someone with only a week to live, Mr Wedgwood's reference to 'one or two complaints' demonstrated remarkable understatement. The very next Sunday he was dead:

> Sunday Feb 20th. Was not up till 8.30, all the others were up, the bell passed out at 8 o'clock, we did not hear it at first, but imagined it to be some child dead. About 10, Tom and John had been to Joe's, came back to say Mr Wedgwood died very suddenly about 1 o'clock this morning (he told us in his sermon last Sunday his heart was affected). Miss Hettie [Robert Wedgwood's daughter Henrietta] was fetched home this evening from Prescott where she was visiting. Only Tom and John went to church in the morn., and Joe. I went in the afternoon with them. Louie was not there, very few people, no singing all day. Mr Steward did duty and asked for prayers of the congrega-tion for the bereaved family . . . It was a miserably wet cold day. We had no one here in the evening and came to bed about 10.

The next two days are taken up with the washing marathon. Then:

Above, Dumbleton Rectory; below left, the Rev. Robert Wedgwood with his four daughters: from left, Annie (in riding habit), Eliza (crocheting?), Henrietta and Eleanor; below right, the Rev. Allen Wedgwood, older brother of Robert

Wednesday 23rd.

Father's birthday. Father had a letter, pretty card and nice mittens from Annie. We had large Xmas pudding today, and roast beef. Miss Wedgwood sent Father a note to say the funeral would be at 3 Friday afternoon, they were not asking anyone, feeling sure everyone that could would go and follow their late friend and minister to his last resting-place. Sis gathered a basket of snowdrops and some heath [heather], and took across to the Rectory this afternoon. Miss Eliza [Robert Wedgwood's youngest daughter] sent a note back in the basket thanking her and would be glad of some more Friday morn . . .

Louie had called five days earlier to see the snowdrops, which bloomed every February in the Villa garden in great profusion, and still do.

The funeral, for which Ann's father bought a new black hat, was attended by more than four hundred people, and Ann's account is even more detailed than that of the local paper, the *Evesham Journal*. Their accounts are very similar, the only discrepancy being that the *Journal* cites six bellringers bearing the coffin; Ann says eight.

Friday, 25 February 1881.

Busy putting things straight and clothes ready for funeral. After we had finished dinner, Annie Dudfield called, stayed an hour, had been to Mrs Dunn's. Mr Fawdry called about the same time and had some dinner, then went on to the Rectory. All the Guardians of the Poor of Winchcomb District came to follow, many clergymen and most of the Dumbleton people assembled in the Rectory gardens, to follow after the relatives.

The grave (near to the church gate leading to the Rectory) was lined with yew, and bunches of snowdrops placed round the edge of the top, looked very pretty. The school children (such a number) stood, a row on each side [of] the path, many of them had a little bunch of snowdrops. Mrs Walker, Mother and Mrs Dunn waited in the church, I stayed with them, Sarah and John did not go, Tom and Joe followed [the coffin], and Father stayed in the churchyard to keep order.

The bell did not toll once all the day. 8 of the ringers carried the body under-handed, the coffin covered with splendid wreaths and crosses. Mr Randall (steward of the estate) brought Mrs Wedgwood, Mr Stirling [brought] Miss Wedgwood. Messrs. Ricardo and the other Miss Wedgwoods were to have walked together but, I think, the three Miss Wedgwoods walked together, each of the ladies carried a wreath or cross. The church was full. Mr Fred. Holland and Mr Stewart were the officiating clergymen. After the body was laid in the grave a muffled peal was rung by the carriers. Mr Thurstan Holland [Squire Holland's eldest son] and Mr and Mrs Hutton came to the funeral.

Uncle William, Mr Reeve, Mr Fawdry and Mr Rushton (the artist) came here to tea. Mr Reeve and Uncle stayed till after 8, they took Annie Dudfield home. Tom went up to Mrs Walker's for her (A.D. had asked Mr Reeve if he would take her). The cuffs were shown to Mr Reeve, and Sarah asked Mr

Reeve if he should like to know the lady who sent them, and promised to invite him over when she comes. A.D. put in her little spoke, and Sis cramped her *proper*. A.D. and Mr Reeve put their names in my book. We had a beautiful sunshiny day.

There is an abrupt switch here, from the almost professional reporting of a public event to the minutiae of domestic life. 'The lady' is Annie Biscoe and the cuffs demonstrated her needlework skills. Ann is clearly impressed by the way her sister, known for her sharp tongue, deflates Annie Dudfield, the daughter of Dumbleton's former butcher, and a contender for the attentions of Mr Reeve.

The Sunday following a funeral was almost as important as the funeral itself, with full attendance by the bereaved family, and in this case, further commemoration of Robert Wedgwood.

Sunday. After 8 when I appeared, not much snow, had been a frost, came on a rapid thaw, made it miserably dirty. Mother went to church with the rest of us, Sis did not go all day (her face swollen). Mr Stewart did duty, Mr Halsey Ricardo brought in Mrs Wedgwood, Miss Wedgwood played the organ, Mrs Edward Halsey stayed with her. The other Miss Wedgwoods were at church with Mrs Wm Halsey, Mr H. Ricardo, and a Mr Allen. Mr Stewart preached a beautiful sermon, taking for his text II Cor IV 18th verse 'While we look not at the things which are seen etc.' [but at the things which are not seen: for the things which are seen are temporal; but the things which are not seen *are* eternal.] He spoke of our late Rector, but in such a way as not to try the feelings of his family, urged all to go to Sacrament next Sunday morn. and told us he hoped in the afternoon of next Sunday to read to us a sermon written by Mr W a few days before his death, which he had himself intended to preach to us the morning he was called away.

In the afternoon Mr Fred. Holland did duty. Mr Halsey Ricardo played the organ. Mr Fred. gave out the wrong hymn for the second, Thomas Teale came out and corrected him. The sermon was very touching. The church was full, but there were not many dry eyes. Mr Fred* took for his text Genesis V.24 'And Enoch walked with God [:and he *was* not; for God took him.]' He spoke of the years Mr Wedgwood had lived and worked among us, of the friendship existing between him and the late Mr Holland, who gave him the living nearly 50 years ago, but the Rector [i.e. the former Rector Samuel Garrard], then an old man, lived on for 20 years, at his death Mr W came here, and proved a friend to all. After the sermon the 8th hymn was sung 'Abide with me'. Mother and I went in with Louie, but did not stay, she came down with us to see the little pigs, went back directly to see about their tea, it

---

* Six months later, the Rev F.W. Holland, or Mr Fred. as Ann calls him, was himself dead, at the early age of 43. He died alone on a mountain, having dropped behind his brother Thurstan and the rest of the party on a Swiss climbing holiday. As former Vicar of Evesham, there was naturally great consternation at the news, and at the request of the editor of the *Evesham Journal* Thurstan wrote a full and moving account of his younger brother's tragic end (Sept 10, 1881).

snowed a little . . . Joe and Louie came down at 8, had supper and stayed till 10 *but we did not sing.* [my italics]

As on the day of the funeral, Ann moves naturally between spiritual and temporal matters, between (to re-iterate St Paul) the things which are seen and those which are not, between

> *Heav'n's morning breaks, and earth's vain shadows flee*
> *In life, in death, O Lord, abide with me*

and the newly-born piglets.

The very next day, Mr Reeve, clearly the object of some interest both to Ann and Annie Dudfield on the day of the funeral, appeared unexpectedly with a friend, causing a flurry of excitement:

> We put away dinner, and I was dusting front room, had not lit that fire, and the stove fire was out, [when] Tom brings in young Mr Reeves and a friend. Mother and I laid cloth and dinner in front room, and brought them in. Mother made a fire *while I tidied myself* [my italics]. Alf Dudfield called before they had finished, to pay his bill, he had some dinner, but did not stay very long. Mr R's friend played several pieces to us by ear, he left at 2.30 to walk to Evesham to do some business, and was then going home to Chelt[enham]. Mr Reeves stayed till nearly 4.

Mr Reeve's visit appears to be purely social: it was not combined (as visits to the Staights often were) with having horses shod or bills settled.

The little notebook was now almost full, the short entries for early March about to collide with the earlier ones written from the other end of the notebook.

> Sunday March 6th. Not up till after 8, found the hen dead that has been ailing so long, also 7 live chicks in the nest in manger, and afterwards 3 more dead, had slipped out of nest and couldn't get back; and another was dead in shell. Did not go to church morn. Went in the afternoon, Mr Stewart read to us the sermon written by Mr Wedgwood a few days before he died.

Here the space ran out, and so we do not learn any more about the posthumous sermon of Robert Wedgwood. In an age where the squire could appoint more or less anyone to the living in his gift, Edward Holland's appointment of a relative, and one from a wealthy family at that, appears most inauspicious. But Robert Wedgwood had been an ideal appointment, a man something like Mr Irwine in *Adam Bede*,[23] a story of Midlands country life which (though it is set a century earlier) bears many resemblances to this slow-changing

Gloucestershire parish. (Its author, George Eliot, had died just before Robert, in December 1880.)

Robert Wedgwood's tombstone in the churchyard at Dumbleton bears the words

In loving Remembrance of Rev. Robert Wedgwood MA who died Feb 20 1881 aged 75. When I awake up after thy likeness I shall be satisfied with it. Psalm XVII, 16.

a text (taken from the Book of Common Prayer) which makes better sense if given in full: 'But as for me, I will behold thy presence in righteousness: and when I awake up . . .'. Later on a plaque was erected in the nave of the church, (its text adapted from that of Frederic Holland's sermon 'He walked with God and he was not; for God took him'), commending 'one whose genial kindness, wide sympathies and sterling worth endeared him to all his neighbours.' The Staights were literally amongst Robert Wedgwood's closest neighbours, and it is singularly appropriate that Ann's account of his last sermon is halted by that earlier diary entry which had recorded an instance of his neighbourliness – the lift home with him from Evesham station. Not all Rectors were esteemed and commemorated by their parishioners in this way – Robert's successor was not – and the space apportioned to Robert Wedgwood's obsequies in Ann's little notebook is another commemoration. Eleven years later her portentous encounter with another minister-magistrate would go unrecorded.

PART TWO
The Early Diaries

The Rising Sun, Enfield

The Early Diaries

Enfield 1882

'By Enfield lanes and Winchmore's verdant hill'
(Charles Lamb)

After the notebook there is a gap of about one year. Ann clearly wrote a diary during this time but it has not survived. There follow, after this break, ten consecutive diaries, not in notebooks but in home-made coverless diaries, all using the same cream paper, folded in half, with thread sewn and tied through the centrefold. The diaries vary in thickness, and the number of sheets used in each varies considerably, so that the period covered by a single diary might be a couple of months only or, as in the final diary, as much as five years. The ten diaries cover nearly ten years, from February 1882 to December 1891.

During the undocumented year, Dumbleton lost its youthful squire (Henry William Eyres, only 24, died at Naples in April 1881) and acquired a new Rector. A *third* uncommon happening was the 1881 Census. For the Staights, the major event of the year, the biggest upset, was the loss of Louie's first baby (named Louisa after her) on the day of her birth in August. In October, just before her twenty-sixth birthday, Ann went again to Enfield for a visit which was to last eight months. It is not known how long a visit was envisaged when she set out, but it will become clear it was longer than her parents liked. Drastically altered circumstances at Enfield explain Ann's prolonged visit, for this was no holiday.

The notebook had made no reference to the nature of Annie Biscoe's home, which was – *a public house.* Annie Biscoe's father Ebenezer, besides owning livery stables, was landlord of the Rising Sun, an old and well-known inn in Enfield's Church Street. Ebenezer had been an exceptionally active man, described (later) in the *Enfield Gazette*[24] as 'a keen man to hounds, a zealous host when feasts were held in his upstairs room, and a livery stables proprietor.' (That upstairs room welcomed, at different times, such disparate bodies as the Enfield Baptists, the Oddfellows' Lodge, and the Cricket Club.) But now all that was changed. Ebenezer was seriously ill, with an undiagnosed lung condition. His days as horseman and huntsman were over, and the livery stables had been sold to Mr Welch. The Rising Sun, however, still had to be managed. With her father unable to work it is likely that Annie Biscoe looked to her friend as an ideal person to help the family through the crisis. Although Ann was a friend, a guest, she was a worker, and she worked as hard, probably harder, than any employee. After her singularly domestic life in the small village she could now sample a kind of independence, as well as the added novelties of town and inn.

In 1881 Enfield's population was climbing rapidly from 19,000 (Dumbleton's for the same year was 139). Charles Lamb, who had lived in Enfield ('a dreary village') for eight years from 1827–1835 came to hate it: 'Enfield, where we are, is seated most indifferently upon the borders of Middlesex, Essex and Herts., partaking of the quiet dullness of the first, and the total want of interest pervading the two latter counties.' For him, comparing it to London, it was very much a country backwater, 'a little teazing image of a town about one, country folks that do not look like country folks, shops two yards square' and so on.[25] As one of the 'country folks' herself, Ann's reaction to Enfield, many years later, was rather different. She was used to visiting towns – usually Evesham, Tewkesbury and Cheltenham, occasionally Gloucester or Worcester – but not to living in one. After the limitations of Dumbleton's shopping facilities (only Joe's butcher's shop and Mrs Walker's post-office and general-stores) she enjoyed Enfield's rich diversity. For her it was not a village, let alone a dreary village. The Biscoes lived near the centre of the town. Church Street was and is the High Street of Enfield, and it also linked Enfield's two railway stations, the Great Northern at Windmill Hill and the Eastern Railway at Enfield Town, both thriving concerns despite their gloomy and forbidding station buildings. Church Street was thus a main thoroughfare, wherein there was much to be seen (or missed!):

March 8. Sanger's Circus went by, but I was only in time to see the last van . . .

The Rising Sun was close to, but not part of, what was (and still is) the prettiest, most picturesque part of Enfield, Gentleman's Row. Its cottages and quaintnesses include Clarendon Cottage, where Charles Lamb and his sister Mary lived, and Lamb had found the Rising Sun a useful landmark for directing friends to his lodgings: 'Pass the church, pass the 'Rising Sun', turn sharp round the corner, and we are the 6th or 7th house on the Chase.'[26] There was no mistaking the pub by the time the Biscoes lived there: apart from the inn sign itself and the welcoming lamp above the door, the brewers advertised their ales in large letters on boarding above the ground floor windows and again in larger letters at roof level. Beyond the inn was a small group of cottages, then the tall gates and drive of the imposing Chase Side House; opposite the inn, on the north side of Church Street a high wall enclosed another sizeable house and garden called Little Park. The inn was thus located at the quiet, unlit, residential end of the busy thoroughfare, enjoying the best of both worlds. Now the inn and the large private properties are all gone. The Eastern Electricity showrooms occupy the site of the inn and Chase Side House has been replaced by the Enfield Central Library.

* * * *

For the unsophisticated country girl the initiation into being a barmaid would have been slow and difficult. Not only had Dumbleton no public house; even if there had been one, it is unlikely that the shy and abstemious girl would ever have gone inside it. Like Louie at the Wotton Hatch, Ann makes an unlikely barmaid. But by the time the diaries re-open, she has been at Enfield for four months, and the initiation is over. She is comfortable in her role as barmaid. She likes keeping things clean and tidy, she is used to *serving*, and in addition, there is much pleasure to be had in chatting to the regular customers, 'our particulars' as she calls special friends.

Life at Enfield appears easier than at Dumbleton. There are more people here to do the work – Mrs Biscoe, Annie, Ann, as well as Mary the maid and Sam the potman, and the work itself is less arduous. Ann has more leisure here than at home, and this is reflected in the diary, where the entries are long and neatly written (with often a whole page devoted to one day). There is more time too for music – she has piano lessons at Enfield and daily practices – and for sewing, crewel work and crochet. At Dumbleton the women are there to serve the men and life is geared around the business. Breakfast, for example, is not eaten till the boys get back from shoeing a horse or repairing the Rectory boiler. Here too there is a business to run, but the women can run it themselves. In fact, it is the *women* who are dominant here: Mr Biscoe is an invalid upstairs, his son Henry is an infrequent visitor from Kent, and Sam is a servant.

Ann, like Annie, belonged to that section of society which did not require its daughters to take outside employment. It could afford to keep them at home, though not in idleness. This experience at Enfield is the nearest Ann will get to outside employment and the furthest she will get from her family. The signs are that she thrived on the experience.

The diary, which indicates by its very opening that there *were* earlier ones, starts appropriately for a Victorian diary, on the subject of health, and with Ann in what will become a familiar, ministering, role:

> Thursday, February 16th 1882. Continued.
> After we came up to bed, Annie was very ill for an hour or two, but would not let me fetch anything to relieve her. Gyp barked tremendously for an hour; at ¼ past 1, I put on some of my clothes, and armed with the whip, went down, thought perhaps the door was left undone but it was not. Showed Gyp the whip, and came back. Kept our gas in a little all night, thinking Annie might feel ill again.

Mr Biscoe's hunting whip, no longer needed in the hunting field, had been appropriated for home use. Next day

> I brought Annie some breakfast up, but she *would* get up . . . Mr B got up before tea-time, but terribly low-spirited. The Dr came this afternoon and Annie (after much persuasion from me) spoke to him about herself. He sent her some medicine, and told her she must not worry.

With her father so ill Annie was hardly able to heed such advice. The doctor himself was worried by Mr Biscoe's illness, later described as 'an affection' of the chest. At this stage, however, Ann was writing that he was 'still very low' (February 19th and 20th) as if she expected him to stop feeling so low and thus to recover. Her concern with other people's health (not with her own, which is excellent) extended beyond the Biscoes' private quarters to the customers in the bar – Mr G. Ellis had a bad foot, Mr Williams looked ill, Philip 'not feeling just right' – and even to strangers:

> Some poor man in bar this morning with two dreadful black eyes, and face all swollen up, said three men fell on him near Covent Garden about 6 last night, and would have taken his carpetbag and box from him had not two gentlemen appeared on the scene to help him.

A landlord was, of course, a well-known figure in the community. Mr Biscoe had been born in Enfield and had spent most of his life there; he was well-liked. When no one came to see him Ann commented on the fact: 'No one to see Mr B this evening. I sat with him two or three times for a little while.' Visitors came often or sent all manner of foods to tempt his appetite: 'Mr Tilly sent a rabbit yesterday, and two pigeons today.' Other appetisers included a slice of salmon, some skate, an eel, a sole, cresses and lettuces, besides the more traditional invalid's gifts of oranges and grapes. There are flowers too, including regular parcels from Sarah at Dumbleton. Unlike his Dickens' namesake, the generous nature of this Ebenezer[27] showed itself even in illness, for he asked for 'some spirits and tobacco' to be sent to Ann's father as a birthday gift.

By early March the doctor's portentous pronouncements intensified:

> The Dr pronounced him worse, and *very feeble* . . .
> The Dr came, said he saw a great change in Mr B . . .

Ann went to Youngs the butchers for steak, 'but Mr B couldn't touch it when it was cooked.' He has ceased to figure as a person, only as an invalid having bad or less bad nights. He never came downstairs, where the smoky atmosphere of the bars – very few men were non-smokers at this time – would have been a deterrent. The tenor of Ann's daily bulletins changed. Instead of 'still very low', it was now 'Mr B not any better' or 'Mr B much weaker' or 'Mr B very very bad night'. They convey a clear message, that there could only be one outcome. That outcome seemed imminent on Sunday March 5th

> Mr B had very very bad night, Annie went to the Doctor's at 11 . . . Dr Jones came before we had finished dinner, told Annie she had better telegraph for HB, that he thought Mr B was sinking fast . . .

It would have been better if he had sunk fast. It would take Ebenezer Biscoe, who was only fifty-seven, another month, painfully, to die.

The two girls could not go out very much in these circumstances, except to shop or to church. There were no more visits to Alexandra Palace. But they were not left alone. In a public house, the people came to them, and two girls in their twenties were an added attraction for the (almost exclusively male) customers:

> Monday March 13th. G. Ellis and W. Marshall over this morning, stayed nearly an hour, offered to take us two girls to Epping Forest one day . . .

CHJ came in early in evening, did not stay long, had been to a funeral. Gave me a lovely camellia he had in his coat, two nice buds and a tiny one too . . .

TT called early, did not stay, came in later with all the others of Fire Brigade, in their uniforms, their helmets looked very nice, 9 of them, they were out with engine.

At the beginning of the diaries Ann enjoyed dressing up to go out; she enjoyed clothes and colour –

Commenced dressing to go out, put on blue dress, and hat, and pink necktie for first time. Annie wore her white hat, and light jacket. I wore her watch and silver chain today

but by the middle of March it was no longer appropriate to be dressing so brightly:

Sunday March 12th. I put on black clothes again, and put away coloured in portmanteau.

There were sunny spring days, Ann noted rather wistfully, but she stayed at her post:

Sunday March 19th. Another lovely day, but we did not go out . . . we settled up in sitting room to have quiet afternoon, but people kept calling all the time . . . Annie very angry with me, for saying something unkind

and

Another lovely day. Mr B much weaker. After dinner I washed up in bar, Annie lay on sofa . . . In the evening Annie stayed with her father an hour or more, when she came down looked dreadfully ill, nearly fainted, I got her some brandy and water, but it was ½ hour or more before she could get over it.

A diversion at this time was the wedding of Annie's cousin Sarah Young. Sarah, who was three years older than Annie, lived in London, but the two girls had spent much time together and were friends as well as cousins. While they did not attend the wedding of Sarah and Arthur Young (weddings were mainly private affairs and not social occasions), the Enfield girls were busy making gifts for the newly-weds, handkerchief and nightdress cases, a brush-and-comb bag, a pincushion, table mats, and a smoking cap. Ann persevered at the routine sewing, but the more intricate operations were referred to Annie or her mother. 'I kept at cushion all evening when not in

60

bar, and did all but berries . . . finished edge of cushion, made lining and partly stuffed it with Dumbleton bran that eggs came in . . .'.

*   *   *   *

Just as the death of the Dumbleton Rector had occupied a large amount of diary space in the little pocket notebook, so the dying of Ebenezer Biscoe dominates these (three) Enfield diaries. It is not that Ann is obsessed with death. There is just a lot of it about.

> Saturday April 1st 1882. . . . Annie went in town. While she was away, Mr B rang the bell, Mrs B went up to him, found he was in dreadful pain, sent for the doctor, Annie came home, and went up too, the Dr said he *might* rally. Mrs B lay down in sitting-room for a little while and Annie stayed with Mr B after dinner. I washed up and attended to bar . . . Annie telegraphed for Henry at 6, he arrived here at 12 in time for Mr B to see and speak to him.

It was the third time in a month that Henry had been summoned from Chatham. Annie fetched the nurse, and all arranged themselves for the night. Ann is quite specific about where everyone is. Annie and her mother moved between sitting- and bed-room, the nurse settled on the parlour sofa, Henry went to bed, and Ann herself went off to bed at about one o'clock when 'Mr B was easier and dozing'. It was a short night.

> Sunday April 2 1882
> Before 3, Annie came up and woke me, told me Mr B died in his sleep about 2.15. I dressed and came down in parlour. Mrs B., Annie, Mrs T [Mrs Taylor the nurse] and myself had some tea, then Annie went upstairs with Mrs T to do what was necessary. I stayed with Mrs B. They finished and had tidied the room by 5 . . .

After breakfast at six Annie wrote letters, including one for the undertaker, and Sam delivered them. 'We did not call Henry, he had his breakfast in bed, and stayed till ten.' Henry was in bed when the undertaker called, and later he 'upset Annie before tea by something he said; till then she had been wonderfully calm.' Henry was not, it has to be said, much help, though he did accompany Annie to the cemetery 'to choose the spot where Mr B should lie.' Visitors at tea-time did not know of the death till they saw the blinds drawn.

Next day Mr Coote the undertaker and his men arrived with the coffin and carried it upstairs, through the billiard room and on up to the private quarters, 'Annie and Sam were with them, they put Mr B in the coffin and left him in sitting-room . . . I sent Miss C a note saying I could not have any [piano] lessons this week.'

Tuesday April 4th 1882
We had a very bad night, Annie could get no sleep at all, so we got up, came down at 6, then went up to see Mr B and into his bedroom . . . I had a very long letter from Sis enclosed in canister of flowers (she had not then received our sad news). Annie and I put a few in his hand and placed every one of the others on his breast, a lovely hyacinth first . . .

When Mrs B and Mrs Y [Mrs Young, her sister] came downstairs Annie went into the sitting-room with them, to see the dear one in his coffin. It seemed almost too much for Mrs B. After she felt a little better, she decided to go out for a little while, so Annie ordered the phaeton from Mr Welch's, and we (Mrs B, Mrs Y, myself and Gyp) started at 11, had a beautiful drive, the man took us up Baker St. round Forty Hill, Clay Hill and home Chase Side way, were back at 12.30 . . .

Not only was a drive one of Mrs Biscoe's pleasures; it would also be a reminder of happier times when her husband, and not Mr Welch, owned the livery stables. While they enjoyed the drive, Annie registered the death. The death certificate[28] gives the cause of death as 'Phthisis 18 years', that barely pronounceable medical term for consumption or tuberculosis, and states that Annie Biscoe, daughter, was present at the death. The Rising Sun is not mentioned, the address of the licensed victualler given as 'Church Street, Enfield'. He, and it, were clearly well-known.

Ann was concerned for her friend, who was unable to sleep at this time. In the afternoon she tried to rest 'Annie was lying down in little bedroom, but could not get any sleep then or nights'. Just when she had settled down to look at patterns for mourning clothes, the undertaker arrived: 'Mr Coote came to fasten lid on coffin, and she went up to stay with him.' The women were almost entirely occupied with organizing their mourning. Annie went with her sister-in-law Kate into London to Rylands, Wood Street, to buy new outfits. Mrs Hobbs in Enfield began to make up a dress for Annie in black cord. Kate trimmed hats for Annie and Ann with satin and lace, then began work on the black veils. The women sat over their sewing till after midnight. None of the garments they made or re-made – polonaises, dolmans, ulsters – are worn today.

The Rising Sun, which had stayed open on the day of Mr Biscoe's death, remained firmly closed on the day of his funeral.

Good Friday, April 7th 1882. We closed the house all day (and Sam nailed notices to the doors) because of the Funeral.

Annie dressed carefully, putting on the jet jewellery she had been given by Mr Tilly a few days earlier, 'lovely jet bracelets, earrings and necklace with pendant'. Her Uncle Young arrived with more, and Mrs Biscoe presented Ann with a pretty brooch and some bracelets. Jet was the only form of jewellery permissible for mourners, and the Victorian women (most of whom would be mourning for somebody for a considerable part of their lives) certainly made the most of the concession. None of the women attended the funeral, for Mr Biscoe had requested the most simple funeral possible. The cortège was therefore a very small one, only eight men in two broughams. Everyone else waited at Lavender Hill where the cemetery's graves had replaced the former lavender fields. The women waited at home.

> We had dinner in billiard room. Mrs Garrard [next door neighbour] sent in a nice wreath of flowers, and Mr Myers [JP] a lovely cross. About 2.30 Coote and his men arrived . . . at 3 they all started for the cemetery. (Mrs Young forgot some of the jewellery and a nice cross of artificial everlasting flowers that Arthur had sent, so Kate went to fetch them, and got back just after the mournful procession had left; Sam took the cross and followed after.) They were not very long away, we had tea in billiard room, Mr and Mrs Garnham called and had some but did not stay long as their carriage was waiting. Nearly all Mr B's old neighbours went to see him laid in his last resting place, Sam said the church was full. (The Misses Biscoe sent a pretty bouquet to go on their Uncle's grave.) After tea Mrs B, Mrs Y, Kate, Annie and I went for a little walk round reservoir, we left Mr Gayfer, Mr Young and Mr Logsdon with Henry, the others had gone, they left after the Will had been read. . . .

The next morning flowers arrived from Dumbleton: 'By first post came some flowers from Sis (boxes very much crushed, short note enclosed)' which the girls took to the grave on Easter Sunday.

> Easter Sunday, April 19th 1882
> We had our breakfast before 9, Annie got up soon after, did the bar, and made a nice wreath with Sis' flowers (she had enclosed wire and moss for it) . . . Soon after 2, Annie and I started for the cemetery, taking the wreath and a few loose flowers in box, we placed it on the head of grave, and left all the others on, did not stay many minutes, we both got very tired before reaching home, it was so dusty and warm. Mrs B very lowspirited while we were away, went to lie down after our return, and Annie lay on sofa.

Enfield is full of hills, as its street-names indicate: Clay Hill, Forty Hill, Lavender Hill, Windmill Hill, and many more – and an uphill walk from Church Street to the cemetery one and a half miles away *is* a tiring one. Taking the flowers to the grave was the nearest to church that Ann managed that Easter Day. It was the only Easter in the diaries that she did not get to church. (The following year, in

Dumbleton, as if to make up for the omission, she would go three times on Easter Sunday). She served in the bar instead, releasing the mourners (Annie went to church, and Mrs Garrard from next door came in to sit with Mrs Biscoe).

A few days later, on Friday April 14th, one of the regulars brought Annie a copy of the local Tottenham paper 'with account of Mr B's funeral'. This was the *Tottenham and Edmonton Weekly Herald,*[29] published that same day. On page seven, under the *Enfield* news and before the report of the Enfield Petty Sessions, is the heading *The late Mr Ebenezer Biscoe*. It begins

> *Another representative of that good old style of country yeomen whose ranks are gradually being thinned has gone to his rest. During the last quarter of a century or more no man has perhaps been more familiar in local, social, and sporting circles than that of the late Mr Ebenezer Biscoe, and it is no mere stereotyped mode of speech to say that his death will be deplored not only by a very large section of the residents of Enfield, but also by a host of friends for miles round, to whom the deceased gentleman had endeared himself by his uniformly genial, honourable and manly conduct . . .*

The obituary enlarged upon the circles in which Mr Biscoe had moved, and his activities in the First Volunteer Corps, the troop of Yeomanry Cavalry, the Lodge of Forestry and the Masonic Fraternity – and then turned, by contrast, to the illness which had put a stop to all of them. He had died from 'an affection of the chest' which had baffled the skill of physicians, caused his relatives much anxiety and himself six months of acute pain. The deathbed scene itself offered the obituary writer an irresistible opportunity to use a great number of highly emotive words and images dear to Victorians – the hand-holding, the devoted wife, the constant vigil, the beloved husband, besides the rich potential of death itself:

> *. . . terminated fatally on the early morning of Sunday 2 April, not, as has been reported, during the absence of his attendants, but peacefully grasping the hand of his devoted wife, who, as usual, was keeping a constant though weary vigil, seated at the bedside of her beloved husband.*
> *The funeral obsequies took place on Good Friday, and in strict accordance with the expressed wish of the deceased, all superfluous ceremonial appendages were dispensed with, and a rigid simplicity in every aspect observed . . . The cortege consisted of a car, of plain design, with glass panelled sides, and two ordinary broughams. In the latter were Henry Biscoe, only son, his two brothers James and Thomas, and two cousins Mr Thomas Biscoe of Tottenham, and Mr Stephen Biscoe, and Messrs. H. Young (of London), W. Logsdon, and J. Gayfer. At the Chase Cemetery a large and select concourse of friends of the deceased assembled. . . . Coffin was a plain oak with black furniture, covered with floral tributes, including a superb cross from James Meyer, Esq., JP, a large and handsome wreath from Mr Garnham (a very old friend, of*

Gower St., London) and several tastefully made wreaths etc. from the nieces and female relatives of the deceased. The burial service was read by Rev. E. H. Egles and funeral arrangements entrusted to Messrs. Coote and Sayer.

Two things strike the reader of Ann's recent diary entries: surprise that there should have been even a rumour that Mr Biscoe died alone, and the absence of any reference to Annie. Although Ann was not exactly an impartial reporter, it is unlikely that Mr Biscoe died alone (if he had been alone, the time of his death could not have been specified so precisely in her diary, and furthermore the death certificate[28] states that Annie was present at the death). All the credit for his nursing went to Mrs Biscoe, and it was the nieces, not the daughter, who were singled out for their tastefully made wreaths. Annie's central role is reduced in the obituary to a bit part, to a mere 'female relative of the deceased .

Not everyone saw the paper, however, for next day 'Two strange gentlemen came in and asked for Mr B, and seemed very much shocked when I told them the sad news.'

*   *   *   *

Seventeen years earlier, Mrs Gaskell had expressed her confidence in the therapeutic effects of 'the good air of Dumbleton'. The Staights, apprised of the news by the regular correspondence between Ann and Sarah, were now thinking along the same lines. With the flowers from Dumbleton came an invitation to Annie to go there to rest and recuperate. She accepted gratefully, arranging to go down there some two weeks after the funeral. Before leaving Enfield, a boyfriend of hers (only ever referred to as HW by Ann) came to stay on an overnight visit. Ann tactfully stayed in the bar while they played cards and chess in the parlour. This seems to be the nearest thing to a special attachment. Both girls enjoyed the attentions of the customers, the little gifts, the flirting and teasing ('JJ tried to tease me all he could' – Ann the country girl must have been an obvious target for teasing), but their friendship with each other was more important than any other. Because of this, Ann felt it keenly when Annie left for Dumbleton. The parting was made harder by the disappearance of Annie's dog Gypsy the night before she left, just after a visit from Mr Gayfer to whom Mrs Biscoe had presented her late husband's hunting whip. Sam and Mary, then Annie, searched the town, but without success. Annie would have to leave, not knowing what had happened to her dog.

Friday, April 21st 1882

Annie down first before 8, I followed; she commenced putting up spirits, Sam helped carry pots, I did bar. After Annie finished spirit work she did our room and finished packing, had my portmanteau and her own hat box. She put in lots of things for Sis' millinery chest and hearth-rug work and some bottles of spirits for Father. Still no tidings of Gyp. I attended to bar all morning. We had dinner at 11.30. Just before 12 Mr Sewell came in with Gyp, an old man (a stranger) had brought her into the town to try and find the owner, Mr Sewell knew the dog so brought the man in with her (We supposed Gyp followed Mr Gayfer a little way, then was afraid to come home. The stranger took her in, and kept her all night.) Annie was so delighted, and looked quite a different girl . . .

Gypsy's return was well-timed. Minutes after she returned, at noon, Annie set off for Paddington, escorted by Sam.

We had a long afternoon. I tidied bar, read a bit, then did my writing up. Mr Long brought some flowers this morning at 10.30, it was too late for Annie to go then to cemetery, so Mary went before 5 this evening. Mrs B cut two nice bits of westeria for her to take too. She put them all in the trough, brought the others home and burnt, except one Marchal Niel which was not faded and which was needed for one corner. I changed my dress after tea, filled water-can for upstairs, put out tea, c-soda, tobacco, matches etc. We had early supper soon after 7. It had seemed such a long afternoon . . .

The rare repetition of the 'long afternoon' is more telling than any emotional outpouring.

A postcard next day confirmed Annie's safe arrival at Dumbleton, and her first letter 'addressed to Mrs B but written to us both' arrived a few days later. In it she reported that Will Rose, the third of Louie's five brothers, had arrived there before her, looking very ill. Ann did most of her writing of letters and diary, and her reading, while Mrs Biscoe rested in the afternoons. The diary-writing continued unabated. Even tooth-ache did not prevent it. Rather, it shortened the night, thus increasing the time for 'writing up':

Awoke before it was light with bad faceache, bore it till 6, then got up, took a dose of Car[bonate] of Iron, dressed and came downstairs, took some of Annie's medicine in kitchen, then settled myself in parlour, and did writing up, then lay on sofa till Mary came . . .

Ann, as we will see again and again, had a childlike faith in the efficacy of all medicines.

When she was not reading the local papers, she would be devouring the *Family Herald*, which Mary bought every week. This sounds a thoroughly respectable, wholesome publication. In fact it

66

was one of the first mass publications, a penny weekly which was read almost exclusively by servants, shopgirls and the wives of unskilled labourers.[30] While intended, as its name suggests, for whole families, it primarily served to offer escapism to housebound women. It contained letters and advice columns besides plenty of stories, a high proportion of which were romantic. It is interesting how it is always the servants, Mary or Sam, who buy the paper, but Ann devours it each week with undisguised relish:

> Mary took the mangling, and brought F. Herald, which I read (Wed. 26 April)
>
> I read F. Herald in bar, the others talked away in parlour (Wed. 18 May)
>
> Sam fetched F. Herald, I had a good read (Wed. 24 May)

The *Family Herald* is not mentioned at all until after Mr Biscoe's death. It would have been inappropriate to buy and enjoy romantic pulp while someone was dying in the house. When she was not reading the *Family Herald*, Ann was reading *Hard Times*, one of the less popular novels by the immensely popular Charles Dickens. There appear to be some ironies here – that Ann was reading escapist literature at a time in her life when she was most out in the world, not closeted by family life in a remote village (where the magazine was not available); and that she was reading *Hard Times* at a time when her own times seem to be at their lightest.

*   *   *   *

The end of April brought particularly inclement weather:

> Saturday April 29th. Very wet morning. In afternoon wind rose very high, and continued very rough all night, did considerable damage . . .

There was wildness within the inn also:

> After 10 [pm], a woman with baby called, asked me if I knew what she could get a cab for to Botany Bay [on the road to Potters Bar, probably named because for a long time it had been remote, possibly inaccessible, in Enfield Chase]. Sam went to Welch's to see, she had left her baby in perambulator outside. Sam's pal followed him out, went against peram – and turned it over (baby being underneath). The poor woman rushed out, and seemed wild for a time, thinking the youngster was killed, but it only got a bruise on the cheek . . .

and the next day's entry continues the theme of wildness, though it also illustrates Ann's fondness for food and for flowers.

Sunday April 30th 1882 (The strange minister preached) . . . Left Mrs B in bed, she did not feel inclined to go out, and seemed anxious for me to go to church. With Mary's help I donned my new costume, she let me out Billiard Room door. I sat in pew below Mr Logsdon's, hurried out of church, home a little past 12.30. Changed my dress, then we commenced dinner. Had nice chop each, tomato sauce, potato; 2nd course rhubarb pie and custard. Before we finished DR came in, only stayed a few minutes as he could hear dinner was not over . . . Later on came Mr Thomson (we had a sharp storm then), he stayed talking some time, I couldn't understand him much but said 'Yes' and 'No' as well as I could. He gave me lovely Marchel Niel . . .

Ann's responses must have been adequate, for on Mr Thomson's next visit he presented her with a jonquil. He would hardly have expected his gift of the perfect Maréchal Neil tea rose to be given away. It found its way, as usual, to the cemetery, taking pride of place in the centre of the cross-shaped container. While Mary saw to the flowers, Mrs Biscoe and Ann set out for the reservoir and to Winchmore Hill across the fields. On their walk they saw several branches torn off the trees in the gales and 'one large elm tree in a lane blown right up and the iron railing with it . . .' After their return, although it was Sunday, they found not all the customers were well-behaved.

A dirty old soldier and his wife in (forbidding-looking pair). Sam was home early, this old man kept on jawing loudly, Sam tried to stop him several times, but couldn't & as he became very saucy Sam put him out and sent the woman after him.

Ann had recorded the marriage of Prince Leopold, Duke of Albany, Queen Victoria's fourth son, on Thursday 27 April, and another royal event was mentioned at the beginning of May, when the Queen officially opened Epping Forest:

Saturday May 6th 1882. . . . Beautiful day. Lots of people gone to see the Queen open Epping Forest to the public today. Very quiet afternoon, very few customers in evening.

A public event of a very different sort was recorded the next day.

Sunday May 7th 1882
Dressed and went to church in new clothes . . . Home at 12.30, changed dress, had roast veal for dinner, DR in just as we had done, stayed a little

while, afterwards Mr Thomas, he told me two dreadful murders committed in Ireland on Sat. (Lord Cavendish and Mr Burke stabbed before they had been there 6 hours.) At 2.30 we closed, put on our things, and taking Gyp, started for Bush Hill . . .

In fact Mr Thomas's date was not quite accurate: 'The Phoenix Park Murders' of the Irish Secretary and his under-secretary occurred on May 4th, two days after Charles Parnell, the Irish 'home ruler' had been released from prison.

But news from Dumbleton mattered more. There had been a letter from Annie early in May, grumbling at the lack of news from Enfield and feeling sorry for herself: she was 'very poorly and Will Rose much worse.' Her mother and Ann both wrote by return, urging her to stay another fortnight, and get properly well. They were alarmed to hear a few days later that she was 'far from well, no sound sleep yet'. Mrs Biscoe asked Ann to ask Sarah 'to have advice for Annie and get her some composing medicine'. When 'Philip', the local pharmacist at Enfield (presumably Ann puts his name in inverted commas because it was the name of the chemist's shop) saw Ann alone in the bar, he showed her a letter from Annie telling him how ill she felt and asking if he could send her anything; 'he said he had not done so as he wanted to see me first, but he would send powders tomorrow, and advise her to see a doctor.' Ann wrote circuitously to Sarah via her Moseley relations (a ruse to avoid alarming Annie) saying how anxious Mrs Biscoe was about Annie and that she wished her to return home if she did not improve.

Sarah duly took Annie to a local doctor in Tewkesbury, Dr Devereux, who told her she needed 'completely setting up' and prescribed medicine and pills. She was told to see him again a week later, and this time she went with John, whose hip 'had not been right since Christmas when F. Smith's hunter ran away with him.' Because Annie felt far from well and found walking tired her, she had taken to riding, (which one would have thought was more arduous). There were no horses at the Villa but Joe had two, so she rode whichever was available, having borrowed a saddle and made herself a habit. She kept Ann apprised of the home news: she and Sarah had visited the Morrises at Dumbleton Mill, and had been escorted home by Leslie Legge and Cormell Morris. 'Will Rose no better, still there; W. Legge [Leslie's brother Willy] called with his brother yesterday, was going back to London in afternoon, Annie not much taken with him. Uncle Joe to be married Whit Sunday, Grandma much better, Mrs Dunn much the same.' Uncle Joe's

69

wedding was another Joe-Louie union, for Ann's youngest uncle Joseph Peart, a publican, married Louisa Webb, an innkeeper's daughter. It is likely that the Biscoes and Staights had originally met through a 'pub' connection. Although there was no public house at Dumbleton, there are various links: Joseph Peart at Kemerton, Charles Staight Junior at Swindon, Louie's Dibble relations at Wotton, were all innkeepers; and Annie Biscoe's brother Henry was a brewer's clerk who had friends at Gloucester.

Annie had asked if she could be spared for another week, and was urged to stay ten days or longer. This was generous on her mother's part, and on Ann's. Mrs Biscoe had lost her husband, and was missing her daughter. Almost every day there are references to her grief: 'Mrs B fetched down Mr B's top boots to rub and hang up in kitchen, seemed very low-spirited after . . .' The same entry continues on the subject of food, and whatever Ann's spirits, they could be relied upon to be lifted by her interest in food and her healthy appetite: 'Mrs Young arrived about 4, brought haddock (which we had for tea) tripe (for supper) and bit of 'bluey' cheese (Gorgon Zola) and 2 large red herrings.' There is quite as much about food as about flowers in her diaries, the one subject so ladylike and proper, the other almost comical. But for Mrs Biscoe there was not this relief. One afternoon she came down to tea, her dress unchanged, a terrible lapse. 'Felt so ill and faint had some brandy in her tea, and seemed better after . . . Mrs B reading, and seemed herself, so I had ½ hr's practice, but when I came down, found her crying terribly.' Another time Ann found her in the parlour, very upset, so she put her washing aside and attended to the bar. In the afternoon she had to stay there 'I was very sleepy, but had several customers in, read Argosy . . . Mary brought F. Herald, I read most of it.' The unlikely partnership of the grieving mother and her daughter's friend worked extremely well, and they spent their leisure time together, too. On Sunday May 14th, the two women went by train to Finsbury Park.

Hundreds of people there, beautiful park, a few of the lovely rhododendrons just coming out, a nice lake there, some swans and ducks on and some (the first I've seen this year) tiny young ducks. The wind seemed quite cold by the water. We stayed till 5 o'clock, came to Wood Green by Main Line train, waited there ¼ of an hour for Enfield train, home before 6. Mrs B very low and crying after we came in, the house seemed so quiet, but she felt better after tea, we had ham sandwiches . . . Sam home before 10, and gave me a lovely bunch of lilies of the valley.

Ann gave them all away, some in a letter to Annie, some to Philip next day ('I gave him some of the lilies which he begged so hard for last night'), and the rest to a predictable destination half an hour's walk away.

Lady Longford, in her biography of Queen Victoria, has noted how the frank interest in death-bed scenes in Victorian times has been supplanted by sex and the marriage bed in our own 20th century literature.[31] The grave itself was a continuation of the deathbed and the amount of attention paid to it was prodigious. Mr Biscoe in his grave was visited at least once a week, sometimes more often. The grave was decorated with fresh flowers on each visit, lilies of the valley, forget-me-nots from a neighbour's garden, heartsease [small pansy], wallflowers, wistaria from the inn garden, lobelia and begonia plants from one customer, roses and pinks from another, even buttercups.

Everyone looked forward to Annie's return. Customers enquired after her regularly. Only a couple of days after her departure one regular called in for 'biscuit and Burton; talked away some time and left several messages for Annie'. Mr Logsdon, Ann's escort for church, and the town's coach-builder, instructed Ann on May 15 to tell Annie in her next letter 'she needn't be surprised to see him down there after her if she kept postponing her return many more times.' Ann, naturally, was delighted at the prospect of her friend's return, and perhaps she was in need of a break herself: 'Mr Gayfer called before 4, Mrs B was lying down, he couldn't stay long, asked me what was the matter, I didn't look half right he said . . . (Sam said when he was sweeping out, he should be glad to see Miss B. again, he wished she'd never gone.)' Annie's sister-in-law Kate stayed at Enfield for the last two weeks in May, and she, like Mrs Biscoe, turns to Ann if anything is amiss:

Wed May 24th 1882.
I lay down about 12 last night, had a short doze, woke up and couldn't go off again. About 1, Mrs B came to my door, wanted to get some Eno. After she had gone I went to sleep, but about 2 Kate came up. Their light had gone out and Mrs B was not well, so I went down with her. Stayed a little while, then back and put petticoat and ulster on, and down again, lay on sitting-room sofa, and went to sleep. Woke at 5, looked in on the others, both asleep, so I put out their light and went back to bed.

Annie returned on May 26. At 3.15, while the others rested and Ann sat reading (*Argosy* this time, not the *Family Herald*), a telegram arrived for her from John (sent from Evesham at 2.58) to say that

Annie would be at Paddington at 5.25. Kate met her at Bishopsgate and Sam met both at Enfield.

> They all came in together, Annie looking better, and very much sunburnt. She brought ham, bacon, preserved beans, eggs, gooseberries, herbs, cabbage, and lettuce. I helped her unpack and put things away, she was very tired . . . All seemed very pleased to see Annie back. She was seen off by Will Rose and John. W. Rose is no better. We talked away after we got to bed, and kept awake till it was light . . .

The next day Ann read the diary Annie had written at Dumbleton, taking it up in the sitting-room before dinner. A few days later she destroyed it: 'Burnt Annie's D. she wrote at Dumbleton'. The private reading, and the destroying of the secret document suggest highly sensitive material. It is not likely – after major bereavement and in poor health – that Annie's activities at Dumbleton were remotely illicit (and the blacksmith brothers were shy and inexperienced with women), but Ann's life, circumscribed by social convention, her retiring nature and by her confined village life, combined to make her delight in the secrecy of a private document as in the more explicit dramas of the *Family Herald*.

Dumbleton had been a welcome diversion for Annie. Now she had to work through her bereavement, a process temporarily halted for her (though not for her mother) by the Dumbleton holiday. Re-adjustment was slow. On Whit Sunday she was 'very middling and low-spirited' and Ann and Kate left her dressing to go to St Michael's, a newish church (built 1874) on the corner of Chase Side and Gordon Hill, where they were seated only minutes before the service opened with a processional hymn. 'Beautiful anthem, Mr King read prayers, Mr Eagles preached and read lessons. Singing and music very nice, chancel was prettily decorated with scarlet geraniums and fern.'

Annie remained in low spirits all through the week, particularly susceptible to Enfield's noise after Dumbleton's peace:

> Tuesday May 30. Annie and Kate went to Edmonton and Annie had her hair cut quite short (it was so heavy made her head ache terribly and Brand didn't seem to have time to cut it) . . . We had man and two drunken women in parlour. We got rid of them very quietly, but up the town they commenced fighting (the women) and were locked up. We got to bed soon after 11, heard some slight noise after we were in bed, but couldn't find out what it was.

> Wed May 31st. Stanley Garrard drove Annie up to the cemetery and back to speak to the gardener about tidying the grave . . . After dinner she went to lie down in little room. Some men in Billiard Room (there were several there this

morning too) so she moved in sitting room, but couldn't rest, Mr Garrard's pony was kicking away in the street . . .

A visit to Annie's aunt and uncle at the Minories involved the girls in a rare misdemeanour.

Just as we were going to meet 2.40 train, Mr Bell came in, he said he would go to the station with us. As we were going up the town, he asked us if we should like a drive to London, as he intended starting at once. We decided to accompany him, and turned back to the office. The coachman soon appeared, had a nice horse and four-wheel carriage. Annie sat in front and I behind with Mr Bell. He put us down in Whitechapel and we had 2d ride in train to Aldgate. Enjoyed our drive very much, had no rain at all after we left home. Got to the Minories before tea was ready . . .

The Minories, linking Aldgate and the Tower of London, derives its curious name not from any connection with mines but from the Minoresses or Poor Clares whose convent stood nearby. (Today a side street is called St Clare Street and a modern office block St Clare House.) With its modern and commercial buildings it is hard now to picture the street in Victorian times. Although Dickens did not write about the Minories, the area, close to the City and the East End, would have had a distinctly Dickensian atmosphere, the overhead railway creating gloom and shadow beneath it, the nearby river creating mist and fog. A few years after the girls' visit, in the autumn of 1888, the Minories would acquire notoriety in the Jack-the-Ripper case. The street is close to the locations of the multiple Whitechapel murders and is mentioned by name in one of the 'Ripper Letters': 'Beware I shall be at work on the 1st and 2nd inst. in Minories at twelve midnight.'*

But it was not the girls' *destination* which caused concern. Their visit to the Minories was entirely unsensational. The Youngs kept a draper's shop and on this visit, besides seeing the newly-married Sarah and enjoying music and singing, Ann purchased stockings for her mother and sister, scarlet wool for Sarah, grey wool for socks for her brothers, paper collars for herself. She returned home the same night, Mr Young escorting her to her ten o'clock train, while Annie went on to Sarah's new home in Canning Town. Much to Ann's surprise on her return to Enfield, Mrs Biscoe was displeased on learning *how* the girls had travelled to London: 'Mrs B seemed very

* Daniel Farson, in *Jack the Ripper*, (Michael Joseph, 1972) argues persuasively that the Ripper was M. J. Druitt, whose doctor cousin had a surgery in the Minories in 1879, and it is likely that the Ripper operated from here even after his cousin left the district.

upset about us going with Mr Bell. We slept in her room, she had a bad night . . .' When Annie returned home two days later 'Mrs B was cross with Annie about our drive. She slept alone in her own room.' This is the only occasion in the diaries when Mrs Biscoe was displeased with her daughter. Normally they enjoyed a remarkably harmonious relationship, and Mrs Biscoe made no secret of which of her children she most valued. (A few days earlier, with Kate, the four women had discussed, not very diplomatically, 'boys and girls. Mrs B spoke highly of Annie and against HB, Kate did not like it at all, and at last went away.') The day after Annie's return was marked by heavy thunderstorms 'such large hailstones fell this afternoon', but inside the house, the small storm had subsided, for Annie slept with her mother, then all three women slept in Annie's room. This changing around of rooms, almost a musical-beds, is very marked. It is unusual for anyone to sleep alone, even when space allows. At Dumbleton, Ann and Sarah shared a bed, and here at Enfield, Ann and Annie sleep together, with minor variations.

After this temporary hiccup, the days were peaceful, but they were numbered. On June 15th Ann received a letter from her sister, 'said Father and Mother seemed very vexed I did not go home. W. Rose very much worse, his sister and brother had been to see him.' Was Ann feeling guilty about prolonging her stay? There is no word of when she decided to go home, but it was a reluctant departure. The solemn business of illness, death and readjustment had occupied at least seven of her eight months' stay. Things were just getting interesting. She and Annie had made friends with four of the regular customers, Mr Paul, Mr Davenport and two Frenchmen staying temporarily in the town. These four men called at the Rising Sun once, twice, sometimes several times in the course of a day. One day the two Frenchmen arrived with lobsters and cheeses and arranged for the foursome to have a dinner party at the inn the following night. 'They went up in sitting room at 8 and commenced their supper, which occupied two hours, had 10 courses altogether. Sam answered the bell at first for a little while, then Mary, self and Annie served up the different courses. Annie stayed with them a little while and had to drink their health in champagne, each of the four made a short speech in a different language, referring to Mr Leuridan's immediate departure. They had a little music, left punctually at 11, and did not forget Mary and Sam. They all put their names in our birthday books.'

The very next morning the sobering letter from Sarah arrived. The fun was over. It was time to go home. Family obligations had to be met. Ann began to receive farewell gifts from her friends, a silver thimble in a case from Mrs Young, a silk umbrella from Mrs Biscoe, flowers from the men, 'some wild rosebuds' and 'a lovely rose' from the Frenchman who like Ann was about to take his leave of the district.

Monday June 26th 1882 Last morning at Enfield
Before 9, Mr Paul and Mr Duhalde in for a few minutes, they both said goodbye, and Mr Paul gave me a tiny rose. Mrs Garrard came in to wish me goodbye, and I gave her the pincushion. She brought me a few nice flowers and asked me to press them in a book when I got home. Mary helped me down with portmanteau and box (little trunk for my hats Annie gave me). I gave Sam and Mary 1/- each, Sam took the luggage to the Gt. Northern Station. We had some lunch, Mrs B and I started about 11.30 . . . Annie came to the door with me, neither of us very bright at the last . . .

The train journey into the metropolis sounds like something very different, the names of the stations *sounding* consistently rural the closer one gets to Liverpool Street itself: Hackney *Downs*, London *Fields* (the ultimate in pardoxes?), Cambridge *Heath*, Bethnal *Green*. Then Liverpool Street itself, more appropriately named than the others for this part of London with its tiny patches of greenery amongst the grimy black buildings.

The weather, like Ann's mood, was mixed: sunny at Enfield, sunny at Paddington, wet in between the two. She left Paddington at 2.15, waved away by the kindly Mrs Biscoe. Between Reading and Oxford there was a sharp storm, but it was bright at Evesham, unlike that earlier return journey when the Rector drove her home.

Wood [the carrier] was waiting for my luggage and had a note from Sis for me saying Joe was busy haymaking and CM [Cormell Morris] had promised to bring me home. I met him just outside the station. We walked as far as Post Office together, I went in there and scribbled a few lines to Mrs B, walked on nearly to Northwick Arms. CM joined me soon after and took me in sitting room to wait while he had horse put in. It came a good pace home, he called at one house up Sedgeberrow, brought me up to Nutmeadow stile. Sis met me in Joe's ground . . .

*   *   *   *

Dumbleton 1882

'As sure as God's in Gloucestershire'
(Old Glos. saying)

Ann was home in time for another death. Tuesday June 27th 1882, headed *First Morning again at Dumbleton*, was warm and sunny. While her father and brothers were haymaking 'in Joe's ground', (Dudfield's Close and Butcher's Ground totalled eleven acres of pasturage), Ann unpacked and dispensed her gifts. She called to see one invalid, Mrs Dunn in the Villa Cottage ('she seemed very miserable, did not stay long'), but it was Thursday afternoon before she could steel herself to ask after the other. Even then, on her first visit to Louie's, she did not actually see Will, who was now confined to bed. Having come from one deathbed, she was not yet ready for another one, and the imminent death of a young man in his early twenties was harder to accept. 'I stayed nearly an hour, but did not go up to see Will, did not feel up to it. He was no better; after I left he was taken worse, and continued very ill all night.' Will had now been at Dumbleton for two months, and in this time he had endeared himself to all the Staights. Like Louie, his was a quiet and gentle nature, and he had gravitated towards her as his health failed. He had been a Post Office clerk until consumption had rendered him an invalid, as it had Ebenezer Biscoe. Consumptive patients were not then isolated, not, that is, until weakness and breathlessness confined them to bed. Only a month earlier, Will had seen Annie Biscoe off from Evesham station.

Ann went home, after leaving Louie's, to find Leslie Legge sitting in the kitchen. 'I just spoke to him, and came on upstairs, he stayed some time.' His relationship with Sarah was clearly prospering. The brief word, the quick get-away, the observance of the barest civilities – Ann's terse entry denotes the coolness between herself and Leslie, who was back the next afternoon, having walked from Tewkesbury. Ann withdrew to Joe's 'to ask after Will. Louie was sitting with him. I said I'd go up if he would like me to, so I went. Poor fellow looked very ill, but no worse than I expected to see him, his breath very bad, asked about Annie as soon as I had spoken to him and then asked me about Mr B's illness. I stayed about ½ hr.'

How do you tell someone who is dying about someone else's recent death from the same disease? It was a taxing half hour.

Nearly 6 when we had tea, LL stayed, and did not go till 8. John got home about 8 from Worcestershire Agricultural Show at Dudley. Tom went to church and practice. (Prayers every morning now, and Friday evening.) I finished my writing up this evening, had not done any since my return till today. (Poor Will wanted an apple so much, and they can't get one anywhere, he could only speak in a whisper.)

Comfort me with apples, says the Bible.[32] An apple a day keeps the doctor away, says the old rhyme. It is ironical that in this orchard-filled place in the Vale of Evesham, which is famous for its apples, there were no apples for the dying man. Now, with imports, apples are no longer a seasonal commodity and are available all the year round. But this was the very worst time of the year for them: the previous year's crop would have been exhausted by April or May, and the new crop would not yet be ready. (It would be July 19th before the family ate *codlin pudding*, made from young apples which are only edible when cooked.)

Mother went up to see Will in the evening, I had an hour's practise [sic]. Father came home at 10, and told us poor Will had just died. Mother and Dr Fulcher were with him at the last, Louie had gone downstairs for something. Joe had only brought Dr Fulcher a few minutes before.

On hearing this news, Tom went to collect Mrs Teale, and Ann went up to be with Louie while her mother assisted Mrs Teale in the laying-out and final ministrations. 'I saw Will just after I went up, before Mrs Teale touched him; *he looked very happy* [my italics].'

Annie had had difficulty settling down at Enfield after her stay in Dumbleton; Ann too found it hard going. The solution was Work, non-stop activity to blot out time for 'moping'. In any case, the year's second quarter had ended on Midsummer Day (June 24th) and her return coincided with bill-writing for her father: 'After I finished Mr Smith's bill [Bank Farm], I did needlework and sat at it till dusk' and the next day 'I began Mr Smithin's [Cullabine Farm] and Rector's bills, finished them before dusk, and had an hr's *good* practise.' To concentrate her mind she decided to cook the lunch singlehanded, though in fact with assistance from almost everyone: Tom fetched the meat from Joe's (a shoulder of mutton), the maid from Mrs Dunn's peeled the potatoes, Tom and John shelled the peas, her mother made a currant pudding, and Sarah put the rice on to steep.

They all went to church except me, I proposed it, managed cooking very well, but got so hot, burnt meat a little while I was tidying pantry, but I scraped it off.

Her desire for order and tidiness did not, and would not, always stand her in good stead. In addition, she began work on a nightdress case for Annie's birthday in July 'but could not get on well with it.'

Enfield was still in her thoughts when she went to church that first Sunday. Its music was clearly superior to that of the little congregation in the country church:

> I went to church with Father and the boys, very few there, singing sounded so harsh and drawling to me . . . I pressed the flowers Mrs Garrard gave me and put away the withered rosebuds . . . I did some more writing (my D- to Annie).

Will was buried on July 5th." In the diary beside the date is a box enclosing the words W.R. Rose buried . Will's sister Emma and his youngest brother had arrived at Louie's two days earlier, but the two eldest brothers had written to say they were unable to come. Clearly, Louie who was very family-minded, thought this was pretty poor:

> Louie telegraphed again to the eldest to come, but he wired back to Evesham to say it was not possible. Mother went up to see Will for last time, was not long away. I got the boys' clothes out all ready for them to put on, and tidied the places, couldn't settle to anything. Our boys went at 4.30 to be ready to follow. They buried him at 5, the two sisters, brothers, and our three followed . . . Thunderstorms all day, but it was fine while funeral lasted. Have felt less mopish today.

Later on Joe and Louie had a stone put up for Will, who shared a grave with their two infants. The inscription concludes with the words: 'Also William Richard Rose, Uncle of the above children, died June 30th, 1882, aged 25 years.'

No sooner was Will buried and his mourners departed when – the very next day – came news of another young man's death:

> Tuesday July 11th 1882
> Woke very early, lay a long while, heard passage clock strike 5, got up 5.30, lit two fires, John filled furnace . . . Father was back before 10, two letters for me . . . As soon as I could I got away to read Annie's D- alone. Such sad news she sends me today, poor Sarah Young left a widow, her husband only ill a few days and died Sunday evening (9th inst.) about 6, of inflammation of the lungs. Mrs B went up in the afternoon to see how he was, he died before she left. Annie went up yesterday to see her poor cousin, took some flowers, did not stay long, home again at 2, and finished her D- to me, very poorly herself. (Poor Arthur insensible from Sat. night, knew no one.) I wrote a few lines to Sarah, and said I'd send some flowers tomorrow.

Sarah Young had been married slightly less than four months. Next

78

day the other Sarah cut a bunch of white flowers from the Villa garden and packed them into a wooden pencil box for Ann to send the young widow. Already, at the end of the third diary, one of the startling differences between the Victorian age and our own is beginning to show – the high mortality rate, the relentless regularity of death.

*　　*　　*　　*

At this time Sarah Staight was receiving almost daily visits from Leslie Legge of Dumbleton Mill. In a large household it was not always easy for him to see her on her own. His success varied:

> LL came before 7. No one in kitchen, Mother told him to go in, so he did, and stayed by himself for some time, then went out in shop, and back again. He and Sis had kitchen to themselves after for some time while Tom at a church practice, Father at Joe's, and John having a bath upstairs.*

John is not always so obliging, as another entry indicates:

> Sis and LL went in front room just before 9. John had supper, then joined them and practised a little. Tom and parents in kitchen. LL began reading away, he, Sis and John kept at it some time *till at last John left them* [my italics].

Sundays offered time for courtship. Evensong was held in the afternoon, leaving a good stretch of the day free for secular pursuits:

> LL soon appeared [after church], Sis was gone upstairs and did not come down for a long while . . . She came down to shut up poultry, and LL went out after her. I did a little writing while they were all at supper.

> Lovely afternoon and evening. LL and Sis in as the others were finishing, had their supper together. I went downstairs soon after the others went in front room, we had a few hymns over, I played, made sundry mistakes . . .

Leslie was friendly with the two boys as well as interested in their sister. On one occasion he sent them a note proposing a walk on Bredon Hill; on another he accompanied them on a walk in the opposite direction:

> Joe down smoking with Father till nearly tea-time. Boys started for a walk after dinner, Sis lay down all afternoon, she and I went to church in evening, Louie there. We came home through Joe's field, she came to the stile with us,

---

* As there was no bathroom at the Villa, this would mean a tin tub.

Joe milking, Father looking on. I helped Sis get ducks from pool, and came upstairs to do a little writing. Boys not home till 9, had been with LL to Hailes Abbey and to Hailes church, called at Toddington on their way home to see Mr and Mrs Sharp, they were well and as jolly as ever . . .

The ruins of Hailes Abbey (or Hayles, it is spelt both ways) continue to attract both local people and tourists today. The monastic houses of the Cistercians were invariably to be found set apart from society amidst rich farmlands, and Hailes was no exception (the nearest settlement is Winchcombe, three miles away, a pilgrim's way across fields linking the abbey with the little town). Not only did its monks enjoy peace and prosperity but also the inspiration of the hills. The abbey was built at the foot of the Cotswolds, the east window of the Abbey church looking towards them. Nowhere can there be any better setting for the Psalm which begins 'I will lift up mine eyes unto the hills . . .'.[34] Hailes had become an important centre of pilgrimage after 1270 when a phial of the Holy Blood was presented to it, and this is the most likely origin of the old Gloucestershire saying 'As sure as God's in Gloucestershire', meaning He was here at Hailes. But at the Dissolution of the Monasteries the 'Blood of Hayles' was taken to London, examined, and declared to be false. The Abbey was destroyed, all but a group of stone arches.* Hailes church, across the road from the Abbey, it is said to be even older. In July rose trees loaded with blooms hide the graves, transforming the tiny churchyard into a rose garden. Decoration inside is provided by a series of wall-paintings. Over the north wall a scene depicts three ferocious-looking hounds in pursuit of a hare who is crouched under a tree. An appropriate scene for this rural setting, though the brothers may have pondered its spiritual message. On the opposite wall is a more traditional subject, a larger-than-life figure holding a staff in his right hand. He may be the Good Shepherd carrying his lamb or else St Christopher carrying the Christ child, but he is ambiguous too, for whatever he carries has faded in the fullness of time.

Nearby Toddington is visible from Hailes, its church spire rising above the trees. Toddington Manor was built at the same time as Dumbleton Hall but on a much grander scale. I have heard it said locally that the Manor is a copy of the Houses of Parliament. This is wrong (it is more like an Oxbridge college) but there is a germ of a connection here, for the Manor's architect and owner, Charles Hanbury-Tracy, was chairman of the commission appointed to

* Hailes Abbey is open to the public and administered by the National Trust. The ruins are more extensive now than in 1882, having been extended by excavations.

judge the designs for the new Houses of Parliament. He created at Toddington a Gothic fantasy, and its recent role (till 1985) sounds like another fantasy – Avicenna College was a *Moslem* rival to Eton, a public school for Arabs! The Manor's creator is buried in a vast tomb in Toddington church, which stands between the Manor and the picturesque ruins of the original Toddington House. To house the monument the church was completely rebuilt and the new church-cum-mausoleum is large and lofty, more suitable, says David Verey,[35] for London than in this remote country park. The rebuilding was completed in 1879, so the men's sightseeing had combined the very old (Hailes Abbey and church) with the very new (Toddington church). The road home took them past the Toddington fruit farms, reputed to be the largest in the country, and past the two farms, Raymeadow and Cotton's, which separated Dumbleton Mill from the Toddington estate.

After this pleasant summer outing, and the pastoral scene at home – the women strolling home from church, Charles watching Joe at the milking, the two sisters rounding up the ducks from the pond – the night was less peaceful, and Ann's entry shows how uneasy, how threatened, the two girls felt when their father was unwell.

> We had a very bad night, woke up before it was light, heard Mother about. Sis awake too, said she was afraid Father was ill. Mother came out and asked Sis for brandy out of spare room. Sis fetched it, Mother gave Father some and bathed his brow, he felt very ill for a time, but got better and went off to sleep. We couldn't go to sleep for a long while . . .

Next day 'he seemed as well as ever by dinner-time' but in the evening when Ann was practising at the piano 'I had $\frac{1}{2}$ hr's practise, intended having an hour at it, but Sis came in, and said I'd better not, as Father was come home and seemed rather middling, so I stopped . . .'

While Ann worried about her father, Annie at Enfield celebrated her twenty-fifth birthday. The nightdress case was finished in time, with Sarah's help, and next day a letter arrived from Annie.

> Tuesday July 18th 1882
> John met the postman as he took Mr Smithin's horse home, letter for me from Annie . . . (Annie enclosed a funeral card of Arthur Young's for me). I escaped to read my letter alone, then sat down in kitchen to mend an old sheet, Sis making John a waistcoat to wear in shop.

At the same time as Arthur Young's funeral card arrived, Louie was sending out cards for Will, or 'poor Will' as Ann invariably calls him, and one was to Annie. The next day the apples Will had craved in June appeared, in mid-July, for dinner ('We had codlin pudding, very nice'). That day, as Ann sat reading Annie's letters ('burnt all except the last'), Mrs Dunn's maid arrived 'to tell us Mr Allen Wedgwood died about 4.30 this afternoon.'

This was the Rev J.A. Wedgwood, Robert's older brother Allen, who was 85. As oldest son of Josiah's oldest son John, Allen would have been an obvious candidate to enter the family business. But, as we are told in a recent family history,[36] 'the frail, introverted Allen would be a liability in the pottery' and he went instead into the quiet haven of the church. When the living at Maer, one of the Wedgwood seats in Staffordshire, became vacant it was offered to Allen as an easy job for a semi-invalid. There the only notable act he had performed was the marriage ceremony in 1839 of his two first cousins, Emma Wedgwood and Charles Darwin, author of *Origin of Species* (1844). 'More preoccupied with his health than with church rituals, he lived entirely by the clock, becoming agitated if anything interfered with his accustomed daily routines . . . He was amiable, however, and seemed not to mind being the subject of jokes. He was Evangelical but not energetic. As the one cancelled out the other, religious life at Maer was carried out with minimal observance . . .' When their mother was dying, the conscientious Robert went immediately to her bedside; Allen, unable to cope with emotional strain of any kind, stayed at home. He had retired early from his semi-job to live with Robert, first in Wales, then in Gloucestershire, where occasionally he helped Robert with services. As so often happened, and would happen with Ann's brothers, the more delicate members of a family outlived their stronger siblings (it's the creaking gate that hangs the longest) and as we know, Robert died first, in February 1881. Two months later, the Census Returns[37] listed the dependent 84-year-old Allen as head of the household, but the Census Enumerator was unsure how to deal with the curious situation of an inactive clergyman occupying a Rectory: the words 'without cure of souls' have been cancelled out and the word 'clergyman' written above them. Allen moved with Robert's widow and his four nieces from the Rectory to Stanton Court, a beautiful 16th-century house near Stanton church and a much grander home than the Rectory at Dumbleton they had built and vacated. Although he died at Stanton, Allen was buried alongside his brother at Dumbleton on July 24th, a day when Sarah was exasperated by another querulous, cosseted invalid:

Monday July 24th 1882
Service at church at 2.30, Father and Sis went, the Archdeacon came and delivered an address. (Sis gave Mrs Dunn a scolding this morning. She called Sis in to fetch a book downstairs, and then asked her to cover it. Sis asked why the maid couldn't; the girl said she offered to but Mrs Dunn said she wasn't to touch it, and wouldn't even let her fetch it downstairs, so Sis gave her a bit of her mind and left it.) Mr Allen Wedgwood buried here today at 4 o'clock, Father and Joe went, and many of the parishioners, Mrs Wedgwood ill in bed, some of the daughters came, and some cousins. Mother went up to Joe's while funeral was on . . . Sis began papering the wall in Mother's room

and on this occasion Ann is less pre-occupied with the latest funeral than the wallpapering. After devoting so much space to Robert's death and funeral, she had little time – or space – for the weird, weakly Allen, though she did note the following Sunday that Mrs Wedgwood's servants drove over from Stanton to church at Dumbleton in accordance with the convention. And later that year, in November, Miss Annie Wedgwood would bring Charles Staight a present, Allen Wedgwood's dressing-gown.

Just as the Wedgwoods had found their Staight neighbours doubly valuable – both as staunch churchgoers and as providers of poultry and of garden produce – so their successors at the Rectory (from 1881 to 1894), the Rev. and Mrs Francis Willoughby Jones, were also frequent visitors at the Villa. Ann always refers to the Rector as Mr W. Jones (clearly he insisted on the double barrel name). He is often away from the village, visiting or on holiday, and his absences, combined with his short time at Dumbleton, make him a pale replacement for Robert Wedgwood.

Saturday July 22nd. Finished mending my old boots and John took them in shop to level the heels. Sis killed 4 ducks, and commenced picking them, and dressing the feathers (2 for us, 1 for Joe, and 1 for Wm Teale). She did giblets and all for the 3, and did all but giblets for the other one, sent Mrs D's maid with it. Mrs W. Jones called in the morning, Mother went to the door, she wished to see Sarah particularly, Mother told her she was dressing poultry, but she said she wouldn't mind and not hinder her long if she'd go, so Sis went and it was to ask her if she or I would take a class in the Sunday School, she had so few teachers and so many children. Sis said she couldn't upon any consideration, children didn't take to her nor she to them. She (Sis) came out and asked me, I declined, said I shouldn't know what to do with them etc. Mrs WJ said she shouldn't like either of us to go against our wish, perhaps we wouldn't object to go and help at the school treat. Sis said we'd be pleased to. Stayed talking for a little while. (Mr W. Jones came to see Mrs Dunn this afternoon, talked to Father at the shoplids, saw my old boots there, said he didn't know they mended boots.)

The end of July was marked for Ann by successive nights of 'horrible dreams'. Was the cause something in Annie's letter, which arrived on July 25th? 'At 9.30, Pap [her father] brought me Annie's letter, which I read alone at the usual resort.' Today people are more interested in dreams, and analyse their dreams and themselves, sometimes even keeping dream diaries, but Ann does not say what she was dreaming about, only recording the disquiet the dreams provoked.

> Had horrible dreams, woke at 4 (26 July) . . .
>
> Dreaming again very much, woke before 4, had no real sleep after, up at 5.30 (27 July) . . .
>
> Had a very bad night (the worst of all) woke before it was light, couldn't sleep after, tho' I felt *very* tired (28 July) . . .

Against this internal disturbance the days were tranquil summer ones. Joe celebrated his twenty-eighth birthday, the men worked in the garden, and Ann soothed herself with music: 'Had an hour's practice, did not go well . . . tried "Troubadour" and "Blue Bells"', but sometimes she despairs at herself: 'Had an hour's practice, seemed more backward than ever . . . .'.

While we do not learn the nature of the disturbance, the nights are as well-documented as the days. Ann was a light sleeper, and rarely slept late. The nature of the men's work demanded early starts:

> Woke before it was light, heard the boys talking, they couldn't sleep either. Heard them get up about 4 (to go with Joe to try his colt in harness to Stanton)

and 'Woke before 5, heard Tom get up then to go to steam plough.' Sleep is almost as much of a preoccupation as death:

'We had a wretched night, couldn't go to sleep for such a time. About 12 thought I heard some one groan, but Sis said it was John clearing his throat.' An August entry devotes some time to the activities of the previous night besides illustrating the advantages and disadvantages of being a blacksmith's daughter – the hard, dirty work it entailed at the furnace and washtub *and* the news agency value of the blacksmith's shop.

> Monday August 21st 1882
> Last night, Sis and I soon went to sleep, but at 11, some noise woke us, it was the wind shaking the window. Sis fastened nail in, but still it shook, so I put another on other side. Some time before we could sleep again. Boys up before 6, self at 6 but not down till 6.30, stopped to put up hats etc. worn yesterday.

Went down, lit fire, cleared away ashes there and at furnace hole, John filled furnace and chopped big sticks. I lit furnace fire, Sis and I broke a lot of sticks (filled the basket), she emptied gurgeons [the coarser part of meal, sifted from the bran] and took bag away, and I tidied wood-house and brewhouse.

And all this before breakfast!

Nearly 10 when we began washing. John rode with Joe to Beckford to see about breezes [from French braise = cinders; in singular means cinders; in its plural sense, as here, it means small coke, for burning in furnace], we can't have them now till carriage is paid. Fine day but cool wind . . . Mother left off washing at 8, self at 9, we washed all white clothes (except sheets) and put scald on ready to boil. Had supper (giblet pie) and I came on to bed, did a little writing in D till Sis came, she was putting lining on John's old coat sleeve. G. Tandy in shop tonight (home from Squire Woods for a holiday). Said his sister saw Mr Cook in Hyde Park about a month ago, he looked hard at her but didn't speak, had got a young lady with him.

Mr Cook was thought by the family to be the sender of Ann's Valentine the previous year. But by now Ann was much more interested in the men at Enfield, and Annie's regular letters and diaries brought news of them all. When I saw the words 'Lamb's birthday' against Ann's entry for September 17th I assumed, wrongly, that it referred to Charles Lamb, the writer and essayist who had, after all, lived in Enfield for part of his life, but in the course of their correspondence Ann and Annie had coined nicknames for some of their menfriends at Enfield – Lamb, Wolf, Goat. Goat was Mr Paul's nickname, not a very flattering one. For John's twenty-fourth birthday on August 15th, Annie sent him a letter and two songs 'The Lad's Farewell' and 'Old Timber Toes', and there was a letter for Ann, too, saying that the Goat was shortly sailing to America.

*　　*　　*　　*

It was holiday time, what George Eliot calls 'that pause between hay and corn-harvest'.[38] Ann's parents had an outing together on August 3rd, a rare occurrence apart from visits to the ubiquitous Peart relations, when they went shopping in Gloucester. Joe took them to Beckford station for the 9 o'clock train, and collected them there at six. 'Father had treated Mother to new wedding-ring, and steel thimble lined with silver, brought Sis and me a pencil each to write like ink [an early biro?]. Pap bought leather for shop work, Mother a dress for herself, dark grey, 3 new shirts for boys, linen to make Father some best pair thick sheets, and calico . . .'

Ann herself had an outing a few days later.

Monday August 7th 1882 Bank Holiday

. . . Sis put my black flower (I took out of velvet hat) into my white one and I wore it and merino dress to Pershore Show, had Mother's cloak on to ride in. Sis lent me her old blue silk umbrella. Joe brought horse and trap down, we had a bit of dinner, started before 2 (Tom, John, Miss Hughes [a friend of Sarah's who was staying at the Villa] and self). Went through Ashton, Elmley, Comberton, such a lot of turns, put up at Three Tuns . . . Went on the grounds, looked in show tent for a little while, beautiful fruit, vegetables and flowers there, but didn't stay long, it was so warm, and went to look at the Sports. Band of Grenadier Guards there played splendidly and kept at it. Several pieces from Patience, Ehren on Rhine, The Lost Chord, and a 'Sleigh Ride' which took wonderfully. A lot of sports and we watched nearly all, Miss H and I standing in a chair most of the time. One poor bicyclist in one of the races fell and I think was hurt badly, and some part of the Grand Stand gave way, caused quite a confusion for a little while. Donkey racing caused much fun and the boys' race too, the poor fellows jumped hurdle, water other side, all of 'em went bang in it three times . . . Mr Clarke of Hampton came and spoke to us while we were waiting to see fireworks, stayed with us after. The fireworks were very good, especially one 'Welcome to Pershore'. Thousands of people there, but not many we knew. Mr Clarke walked with us to Three Tuns, stayed a little while, then hurried off to catch train. We left before 10, home about 12, I dozed nearly all the way home, was so tired. I left Sis' umbrella in hotel, or else let it slip when we were loading. John turned the wrong way once, and went for Bricklehampton, but not far as we met a woman who told us the right way. Joe was waiting here for horse and trap . . .

This time of year saw the climax of the Dumbleton social calendar, with celebrations hierarchical, horticultural and ecclesiastical. First was the celebratory birthday party of Miss Eyres of Dumbleton Hall. Although this was a *children*'s tea party (and without a guest of honour, for Miss Eyres, at one year old, was not yet able to grace the proceedings with her presence), it gave Ann an opportunity to dress up: 'August 29th. Put out silver ornaments ready to wear to tea-party, tacked frilling in dress . . .' The two sisters set out together for the Rectory where

Mrs Jones's brother came out and told us they were all in coach house at Hall stables, so we went through churchyard. They were just ready to begin, plenty of waiters there . . . The mothers came after tea to watch the games. It kept nice and fine, there were plenty of games and amusements for them, racing chiefly for prizes. At 7 all adjourned to coachhouse again, cake, bread and butter and jam being distributed to the mothers and children. We went home through churchyard, called to see Louie, she was in cellar skimming. Got back before 8, took off my things, put them all in place again, slipped on grey dress . . .

The Flower Show was held a few days later on September 7th. This was always the occasion for a large party at the Villa, the largest party of the year in fact, and the longest, for it lasted all day, lunch, tea, and supper, with intervals for guests to attend the Show itself. It was no mere flower show, but an institution, initiated by Squire Holland, which had lasted nearly half a century. 'Mrs Eyres and Mrs W. Jones both gave prizes for the encouragement of useful work . . . and in other ways *'the classes' and 'the masses' join together on this occasion for mutual improvement and pleasure* [my italics],' commented the *Evesham Journal*[39] approvingly of one Dumbleton Garden Show. Like the Pershore Show but on a smaller scale, there were the flower, fruit and vegetable exhibits to see and enjoy, but also games and competitions, and later on, dancing. A large marquee was erected near the Hall, its supports entwined with flowers. On one side, the farmers' and tradesmen's exhibits were displayed; on the other, the cottagers'. It was very much Sarah's day. 'Sis busy making bouquet and filling the stand with flowers. She sent fern, large geranium and Tom's plant, and John took as well beans, apples and plums.' The *Evesham Journal* reporter was excited by the cabbages, which were 'of prodigious size', and continued 'With regard to the flowers, the Show was about an average one, the most attractive being the table decorations which were in every respect a remarkable display, notably the stand of Mr C. Staight, who took first prize in the tradesman's class.'[40] Sarah, in her father's name, had won first prize for both the 'Best Nosegay' and the 'Best Basket of Cut Flowers'. In Ann's version

We had 1st prizes for bouquet and device, and 3rd for plants and plums, and one for fern. Sis brought a lot home to supper, the Ashton lot, CM, LL, a Mr Minchin (Mr Walker's friend), Miss Sextys, Mr Candy and Cole, we had a little music, singing and games after supper till after 12. (Beautiful day.) Pershore Band.

Staying overnight were aunts and cousins and young friends, and next day the youngsters, who 'had made wicket of 3 sticks, and had old wash stick for bat' improvised a cricket game on the green. Sarah showed the bouquet to Louie, then sent it by Joe to her grandmother at Kemerton. Willy Stanley delivered the prize money a week later: the grand sum of six shillings and tenpence. Of this, Charles Staight gave back one shilling towards the expenses of the next Show. 'Sis gave me 2/6 of the Show money,' reported Ann.

The Show coincided, deliberately, with the time of maximum output and variety in the gardens. At the Villa, the men and women spent their spare time working side by side in the garden. Moments of discord were rare: 'Boys gardening nearly all day. Mrs W. Jones came and paid Sis for chicken. While she was there the boys chopped off the roses in hedge, Sis was very much upset about it.' The apricots had been picked in mid-August and now the apples, pears and plums were picked and packed into pots for Joe to sell in Evesham. Ann does not specify whether he sells them to shops or stall-holders, or apple-women, a term which has become a pejorative one. I remember it used of a local lawyer by my late grandfather, another Gloucestershire man and a nonogenarian. 'He's an old apple-woman', he said, and had to explain that this meant a slow, dithery, ineffectual person, which is hard on the apple-women.

The final event in this threefold celebration was the Harvest Festival:

> We thank Thee then, O Father,
> For all things bright and good,
> The seed-time and the harvest,
> Our life, our health, our food . . .

A week beforehand, the Rector's wife called 'to ask us to do some decorations for thanksgiving, Sis said she would, but I couldn't.' Sarah collected moss from the woods and spent hours in the church, measuring the windows for 'her church-work'. The Festival was held mid-week on Thursday, 21 September.

Sis went to church at 8.30, and to the children's service at 3.30, took little basket of apples . . . I went to church with Tom at 7.30, the church very prettily decorated, Mr Mercier of Kemerton preached a nice sermon, collection towards lighting the church. Lots of people there, Joe sat with us, Mr and Mrs Ludgater and children in his pew.

Joe would soon be seeing Mr Ludgater, the young Rector of Wormington, in less happy circumstances.

*   *   *   *

Meanwhile there had been major developments on another front. Recent letters from Annie had chatted about mutual friends, minor dramas. A stray kitten moved in, uninvited, and caused a mishap: 'Annie, going down cellar stairs Friday, stepped on kitten and fell from top to bottom.' Philip was away for a holiday; the Goat had not yet gone to America; Mrs Biscoe met up with her son Henry at the Minories about an offer for the inn and accepted it; Annie asked about spending Christmas at Dumbleton.

The next letter contained more drastic news and with Ann's low-key reportage it is easy to miss it.

> Tuesday September 12th 1882. . . . Father came down from Joe's about 11 with letters for me from Annie and Mrs McG. She (Mrs McGlinchy) tells me Alf Staite married September 2nd. (Annie tells me of her own engagement. Mrs B very much upset, and Mrs Y[oung] down yesterday afternoon.) I helped with dinner and to clear away. Fire at the Lanes [Lane Farm, east of Cullabine], we heard of at 2, boys went down, took buckets, Father and Sis went too, it kept on all afternoon and evening, barn burnt down and large barley rick (supposed to be set on fire by tramps). I changed dress, wrote to Annie and went to post . . . I went to the fire (Father and Sis had come home before), Evesham fire engine there and a lot of people. I tried to persuade the boys to come home and have some tea, they said 'not yet'. I came back, and did some writing . . . Wood's new horse ran away by the Lanes, threw the occupants out of cart, T. Hopkins's little boy hurt . . .

Competing with the fire drama and the carrier's bolting horse, the other major news item is tucked away inside brackets, as if to reduce, to contain, its impact. Ann of course knew Mr Paul (The Goat) from her Enfield visit, and his imminent departure for America may have precipitated the marriage proposal, but for her friend to become engaged to anyone must have occasioned a terrible sense of loss. Was it a premonition of this that had caused Ann's 'horrible dreams' in July? That night she woke at half past one, 'thought it was nearly morning, lay awake some hours and could get no more sound sleep', and all that week she slept badly and felt unwell. The news had disturbed her quite as much as it had disturbed Annie's mother.

> Had a very bad night, lay awake hours, disturbed Sis too . . . I felt very poorly all day. After dinner, I came upstairs thinking to have a doze but couldn't so went down again . . .

> Sis singed my hair this afternoon, took a lot of trouble over it and I nearly went to sleep . . .

> Father had two doses of last week's medicine left, he wouldn't have it, so I did, and it seemed to do me good . . .

Annie's mother recovered her equanimity before Ann. 'Letter for John from Annie and one for me (she tells me Mrs B now quite recovered from the shock the news gave her. Annie and Mr P[aul] went to London Wednesday and to the Minories . . .'.

Ann was just beginning to accept the new situation when there was cause for worry nearer home. Two days after Harvest Festival, on 23 September,

John took apples to the Mill (C. Grinnall's cider machine [cider press] being down there) and made nice lot of cider. Home with it at tea-time, tunned it afterwards, and he and Tom cleaned court . . . Father at Joe's after he had helped tun, home at 9, said Louie was very poorly, and would like to see Mother. Tom went up with her, they came back 10.30.

That day was Louie's thirty-third birthday, and her second confinement was imminent. It was natural that she should turn to her mother-in-law at such a time. Her own mother had died long before, when she was twenty-one. Sarah and Ann were unstinting with help and friendship but even the omni-competent Sarah had no expertise in this area, and their mother had, after all, borne seven children. Having witnessed the loss of her first baby, Louisa, the previous year, everyone was concerned for Louie now. An added hazard was the lack of a doctor in the village. Joe had to drive to Beckford, Winchcombe or Tewkesbury when one was needed. Two days later 'Father came down from Joe's saying Louie wanted to see Mother (she had just begun washing but left it and went) . . . Louie very poorly, so Joe started to fetch the nurse.'

That evening there was a 'happening' at the School, a conjuring and 'mesmerism' company, a new form of entertainment. Tom and John went, and Mrs Dunn's maid; the others were too preoccupied. Sarah had given the maid 3d for helping her a few days earlier, but the admission fee was clearly more.

She came back about 8, had left Mrs Dunn's key here, said they wouldn't let her in for 3d so Sis sent her off with 3d more. Not out till after 10. Sis went out and met her with the key. The boys came soon after and CM with them, the performance very good they said.

The next evening Sarah called to see Louie, who had still not given birth. The nurse promised 'to send down in the night' if she was worse.

Thursday September 28 1882
Joe's little son born and died today [the words 'born' and 'died' are in larger writing than the rest]

. . . Mrs Fisher came down from Joe's to ask Father to go and help Joe put colt in, he did, and Joe went for the Dr from Winchcomb. Sis back soon after 11, with news that baby boy was born about 10.30, both seemed to be doing well, Dr arrived 5 minutes after . . .

After dinner Joe came down to say they thought the baby would not live. Mr W. Jones out, the boys were going to Wormington, so Sis wrote a note for them to take to Mr Ludgater to ask him to come and baptise the baby. Mother sat with Louie afternoon and evening . . . Father went up to Joe's about 5 and came back to say they thought the baby was dying, and Mr Ludgater hadn't come. Sis went up and persuaded Joe to fetch him. Joe brought Mr Ludgater hardly in time, he had been at home all afternoon but the servant had forgotton to give him the note. He baptized the baby Joseph Harry, and poor little creature died soon after 6.

The urgent baptism before the baby expires is echoed, more melodramatically, in another baptism in Thomas Hardy's *Tess of the D'Urbervilles*, a novel published nine years later, in 1891.[41] Usually of course, baptism was a church ceremony, and the Book of Common Prayer advocates early baptism of children in church, parents urged 'that without like great cause and necessity they procure not their Children to be baptised at home in their houses. But when need shall compel them to do so, then Baptism shall be administered . . .', *need* usually being imminent death. The Private Baptism of Children in Houses is very much geared to children, using often the words 'child' and 'infant', but it anticipates a future time when the child will 'not be ashamed to confess the faith of Christ crucified, and manfully to fight under his banner, against sin, the world and the devil; and to continue Christ's faithful soldier and servant until his life's end.' The incongruity, the pathos, of these big brave words addressed to a tiny baby about to die were not lost on Thomas Hardy, writing of baby Sorrow's improvised baptism by Tess: 'Poor Sorrow's campaign against sin, the world and the devil was doomed to be of limited brilliancy . . . In the blue of the morning that fragile soldier and servant breathed his last.' The campaign of Joseph Harry Staight junior was even less brilliant. He had lived less than eight hours.

In the days following, the women took turns sitting with Louie who was 'as well as could be expected' after a year in which she had lost two children and a favourite brother. Ann was shown the baby by the nurse, 'a pretty little dear'. Today we are reluctant witnesses of death, and this displaying of death and the corresponding desire, even eagerness, to look upon it (closely related to religious belief and the improvement of character) is particularly alien to us. Ann's diary-writing had not stopped, but the writing of the last three entries was much less controlled than usual, with ink blotches penetrating the paper. On October 1st she began a new diary (the fifth) and had recovered her small neat handwriting, as she described a death in the chicken world: 'I went to put chicken in, found one dead under the iron that is put in front of their coop, it had blown down on it.' On the first page of the new diary there is the by-now familiar coffin-shaped heading beside the date.

91

Ann stayed with Louie, while her mother followed with Joe, 'the nurse carrying the poor Babe. Louie very brave, but feeling her loss keenly. The baby looked so pretty in the coffin with flowers all around him . . .'.

* * * *

Annie's next letter enclosed one from her fiancé for Ann.

October 4th 1882. Letter for me from Annie and one enclosed to me from Mr Paul, written Friday 29th Sept. on board ship, from the Irish coast. Two circulars for Father. I read Mr P's letter through and showed Sis, had only time to glance at Annie's first, then finished Mr Smith's bill. Father and I called it over, I wrapped it up, then read Annie's letter. Sis found two more dead chicks, one of the little ones (been middling some time) and one of the best, had jumped up at hole in door to try to get out, and got hung there . . . I read Mr P's letter again, put on dirty dress. I cleared away dust and soot in kitchen, brushed up fireplace, scoured the kitchen all over and dusted well. LL came with bill. Mother in kitchen when he came. Sis went out there to get me a light, and took him in front room. I read Annie's letter again, and last week's. (Annie tells me in hers that Mr P said good-bye to her Wed. afternoon Sept 27th, went on board ship at 7 o'clock Thursday morning. The Lamb told her afterwards that he left London at 12, he sailed for America in 'City of Rome' . . .).

More news of Annie came from another source, and again it was at the smithy that the news was transmitted. During a walking tour from London, Harry Dyer called at Dumbleton, and when Ann's mother went to the shop 'to tell the boys that Joe's sheep were loose, she saw him there and spoke to him. He told her Mrs B and Annie were leaving Enfield, Annie going to live with a cousin, a widow, and Mrs B at Minories.' (Mrs Biscoe was clearly considering living with her sister Mrs Young at the Minories, while Annie teamed up with Mrs Young's widowed daughter Sarah.) Harry Dyer makes no mention of an engagement, clearly not yet made public. Ann did not see Harry herself: 'Went to the shop lids to ask the boys something, but saw they were not alone so shut the door again. Thought afterwards one of the company must be HD.'

Her replies to the engaged couple remained unfinished, for there was an unexpected outing on October 12th.

'Lay till 6.30, dressed, went down lit fire, very misty. John proposed going to Worcester Exhibition, so I got ready, and we rode with Wood to Beckford.' At Ashchurch they changed on to the

Worcester line, and at Worcester headed straight for the Cathedral.

We went to the Cathedral, but service was on, so we did not stay long (Mr Witts was there with a party (his choir, I fancy, he took 12 tickets at Ashchurch). Then we went to the public museum, which was very good, something of all sorts to be seen there, animals, birds, stones etc. ot all descriptions preserved. Afterwards found our way to Exhibition. Lots of people there, but very few we knew. All sorts of machinery there, carpet making going on, boot and glove making, needle making, all the processes. Saw the wool in its raw state, and different machinery at work preparing it for the carpet making. Picture galleries very grand. We stayed in till 6, went little way in town and had some tea, then to the station. Train stopped at all the stations coming home . . . Joe met us at Beckford, Louie looked much better.

This foray into the world of advancing technology mentions the glove industry for which Worcester was famous (Mrs Henry Wood, the famous Victorian novelist and author of *East Lynne*, was the daughter of one of its glove manufacturers) but omits any mention of its equally famous Royal Worcester china. Ann's talk of 'all sorts of machinery there' is a reminder of Dumbleton's relative closeness to the industrial Midlands.

The next evening, by contrast, was an unusually quiet one. Ann's father was with Joe, Tom attended a choir practice, Sarah sat with Louie while John went to fetch back the nurse after her day off, 'so Mother and I had the evening to ourselves'. Ann finished her letters to Annie and Mr Paul. She had written a good deal, to either or both of them, and needed an extra $\frac{1}{2}$d stamp, supplied by her father, for the envelope. Not only was she keeping up the diary-writing but copying out parts of it too: 'Copied out piece of old diary, destroyed old piece afterwards with a lot of blots on.'

A few days later on October 16th Ann wrote '(12 months ago since I went to Enfield)' and there was another anniversary two days later, her twenty-seventh birthday, which warranted a particularly long entry in the diary.

. . . At 9, I changed dress and went to meet postman and bring groceries [from Mrs Walker's shop]. Bessy served me; later on Nellie appeared and invited me in sitting-room, we sat and talked for a bit, then the postman appeared, he was very late. Nellie gave me letters from Annie and A.A. [Alice Anderson, a childhood friend], also two nice books (Martin Chuzzlewit from Annie, and the Mill on the Floss from A.A.). Annie sent me a pretty birthday card, and one from Mrs B too. I came home with my possessions, read letters, then took fowls into Joe's field and fed. (Annie tells me in hers that Lamb said Mr P's ship got in [to USA] on the 5th.) Lovely day. Father said when he came in that Mrs Dunn had got a letter and cheque from Mr Thurstan, wanted it read to her. I went in and read it, stayed a little while, then Sis went and signed cheque . . . I finished off letter to Annie, Sis enclosed short one asking if they would have her a few days next week (trip Monday for the day 5/6 or till Wed. or Thurs. 9/6 from Evesham to Paddington). Sis wrote a few lines to Uncle M[oseley] telling him about excursion, and asking if he'd go, also wrote for Mrs Dunn to Mr T. Holland, I went in and read it to Mrs Dunn, and went to post, and to see Louie, she looked better. I stayed some time, went into churchyard, looked at Mr Anderson's grave, it was rather untidy, home Nutmeadow way. Misses Nettie and Annie Wedgwood had been here while I was away, Miss Nettie going on Monday into a London hospital to learn to be a trained nurse. CM [Cormell Morris] called and had his horse shod, came in and settled, he told our people a poor man was killed at Ashchurch yesterday attempting to cross the line . . .

Mr Thurstan is of course Thurstan Holland, eldest son of the former squire of Dumbleton, Edward Holland, and thus related to Mrs Gaskell. Long before he married her eldest daughter Marianne, Mrs Gaskell had written glowingly of him 'He is so good and intelligent that I am sure you [an American friend of hers] will like him at once . . .', and eager to see him in 1859 after his visit to America, she wrote jokingly 'Could you not find out that Manchester is half way between Dumbleton and London? It is, if you look at geography the right way.' Thurstan remained constant to Marianne during a difficult courtship, 'opposed 1stly because they are cousins (*second*) and 2ndly because she is 18 months older than he – & also because he, though the son of a rich man, has eleven brothers and sisters, and has to make his way in that most tedious of all professions *chancery* law.'[42] The marriage did take place, just after Mrs Gaskell's death, in 1866 and though the Holland obligations in Dumbleton ended with the sale of the Estate, Thurstan's letter and cheque to a former employee's widow in her last years is a typical act of kindness.[43] Similarly, in February 1881, he had taken the trouble to come from London for the funeral of the Rector his father had appointed, his second cousin Robert Wedgwood.

* * * *

Meanwhile, a journey in the opposite direction, from Dumbleton to London, was a major topic for discussion. William Moseley decided to join Sarah and Joe for the imminent rail excursion, and Sarah wrote to Annie 'not to trouble about meeting her at Padd. as Uncle M and Joe would put her right.' On Monday, October 23rd, Ann rose at three thirty to get breakfast for Joe and Sarah:

Nice fine morning but cold wind. Sis down at 4.30, then Joe came (He had sleepless night, and all the others at both houses) . . . I put flowers etc. in carpet bag (we put apples, pears, cabbage, bay-leaves, separate in ham-bag for Mrs McGlinchy last night, also apples, pears, cabbage and piece of cheese for Mrs B), John fastened up the bag and went with Joe up with it to help put horse in. Tom cut some sandwiches and wrapped up, I put small bottle of brandy and water, and helped Sis finish dressing. Tom went up with her, and I soon heard them drive down Nutmeadow at 5.10. Boys came back, and we had our breakfast. (We saw the comet.) . . .

Sarah was away only three days but the sisters kept in touch with each other during this time. Sarah saw most of Ann's 'particulars' at Enfield while she helped Mrs Biscoe and Annie to pack up their possessions. Gypsy the dog had already gone to another home, her future more settled than that of the Biscoes who were to leave The Rising Sun at the end of the month.

John had caught cold the day Sarah went to London and now began a long period of illness, during which he was nursed by his sisters. The weather was harsh: 'We had such a flash of lightning and heavy thunder. Wind rough and cold. Came on to snow about 9, lasted 2 or 3 hours, then rain again . . . I did not go to the poultry till after dinner. Fed all and let out fowls and ducks, got wet through and changed my clothes.' In amongst messy cleaning jobs (she cleaned out the duck house and the pigsty and blackleaded the kitchen fireplace) Ann nursed John, making him gruel, or onion broth, and lending him her books: 'John amused himself reading Martin Chuzzlewit most of the day.' Early in the book he would be amused by a familiar scene, a village forge in nearby Wiltshire. Dickens could exploit, even more than Longfellow, the visual and aural opportunities offered by the smithy:

Then [i.e. early evening] the village forge came out in all its bright importance. The lusty bellows roared Ha, ha! to the clear fire, which roared in turn, and bade the shining sparks dance gaily to the merry clinking of the hammers on the anvil. The gleaming iron, in its emulation, sparkled too, and shed its red-hot gems around profusely. The strong smith and his men dealt such strokes upon their work as made even the melancholy night rejoice, and brought a glow into its dark face as it hovered about the door and windows, peeping curiously in above the shoulders of a dozen loungers. As to this idle company, there they stood, spell-bound by the place, and, casting now and then a glance upon the darkness in their rear, settled their lazy elbows more at ease upon the sill, and leaned a little farther in, no more disposed to tear themselves away than if they had been born to cluster round the blazing hearth like so many crickets.
Out upon the angry wind! how from sighing, it began to bluster round the

merry forge, banging at the wicket, and grumbling in the chimney, as if it bullied the jolly bellows for doing anything to order . . .[44]

While John read on, the sisters thought up appetising meals, and tried different remedies. 'Went up to Joe's to get a little something nice for John's supper (his appetite bad) Joe put some sweetbreads and bit of skirt [of beef] on a plate for me to bring. I put some of them in soak, then cooked them by the book, and John enjoyed his supper much.' At bedtime, John had hot sherry and water and cough pills, but coughed continually through the night, disturbing everyone.

Friday October 27th 1882. We all had bad night, John's cough dreadfully bad, he kept on continually. Tom up a little past 6, and went to Wood's to fetch Kay's Essence of Linseed we sent for yesterday. I took John a dose of the stuff in warm water. It seemed to relieve him almost directly. Sis wrote to Annie and Mrs McG and sent Mrs B a bit of fresh butter in collar box. She went hunting the village for eggs, succeeded in getting 3. John had one for supper, and enjoyed it very much.

To minimise the disturbance, especially for Tom, the sisters moved John into their room and they slept in the spare bedroom. When two days later he was no better Sarah set off for Tewkesbury to ask Dr Devereux to come and see him. He sent medicine and promised to come the next day, when 'he sounded John, said he'd got it very tight on each side of his chest, ordered mustard plaster and linseed meal after, only to have light food, and to stay in bed.' The Tewkesbury doctor prescribes for John a famous Tewkesbury product, used as medicine as well as condiment. As far back as Shakespeare's day the words *Tewkesbury* and *mustard* were synonymous: Falstaff says Poins's wit is 'as thick as Tewkesbury mustard'.[45] The mustard was used externally for chests and rheumatic ailments, and earlier, when Ann's mother had toothache Ann had tried a mustard remedy: 'I rubbed Essence of Mustard on her face, that wouldn't stop it so put ginger-and-pepper plaster on.' John's father consulted the doctor at the same time, grumbling at various symptoms of old age: 'the doctor told him he mustn't worry, or hurry over anything, to wear warm drawers for his sciatica, and told him to keep on with glycerine for ears [for deafness]. John to have senna tea, so Father went up to the shop for some.'

To start with, all three women attend to John in the night. 'Sis went to John at 1, I went at 3 and put out lamp, Mother went to him at 4,' but later Ann bears the brunt of the disturbances: 'I went to John

96

a little before 3, he had a turn of coughing then. I gave him some beef tea, made up the fire, stayed a little while, then back to bed, dozed till nearly 5.30, dressed, went to John and made his fire up.' Joe brought down new milk and cream; Mrs Walker sent grapes from her vine; Sarah cooked him part of a sole specially sent for from Evesham.

Ann was getting behind with her diary – on Sunday, when she caught up, she had written nothing for four days. Her father was getting behind too, and asked her to write to the Broadway blacksmith to ask if he knew of a suitable man to help out in the shop.

> Just as we were going to tea [1 Nov], a blacksmith came (dirty oldish man), said Mr Kemp had sent him, and brought a note from him, saying he had worked for Father before. He had cider and bread and cheese, then Father took him to Midwinter's, who had promised to lodge a smith for us.

Five days later, the man was paid off, having spent most of his time not in the blacksmith's shop at all, but picking fruit with Tom and Mrs Dunn's maid!

While John was ill Leslie Legge had called several times, and one Sunday afternoon he stayed with him most of the afternoon. Both men read. Ann was there too and probably wished Leslie was not.

> At John's request I took my writing into his room. Very rough wind and began to rain at tea-time. LL stayed tea, and after the others had gone to church, came upstairs, talked a bit, and looked at Mill on the Floss . . .

It was a peaceful sickroom scene, the young miller sitting beside the bed, reading about another mill and perhaps comparing Dorlcote Mill with the one he knew, the River Floss and its tributary the Ripple with Avon and Isbourne. He would enjoy the discussion of Tom Tulliver's 'eddication' in the early chapters, especially Mr Riley's comment 'Not that a man can't be an excellent miller and farmer and a shrewd sensible fellow into the bargain without much help from the schoolmaster'.[46] (Whatever formal education Leslie had or hadn't had, he would become increasingly bookish as the years passed.) While he browsed in one of her birthday gifts, and John carried on reading the other, Ann went on writing, the quiet Sunday evening disturbed only by the sound of the church bells: 'Bells began ringing directly service was over, and kept on some time. LL stayed with John till 9, then left, I brought my writing away about 8 . . .' But even after retiring to bed the compulsive writer went on writing: 'Sis and I did John's bed and she put poultice on him. She read and I

97

wrote after we were in our own room till past 11.'

John soon recovered – 'John had a good night, we did not go to him at all' – and he was soon up and going, briefly, into the garden, where on November 7th Ann had spotted a rare sight. 'Frosty morning. CG's cart came, Tom and Joe's boy loaded the fruit, then they went off to make the cider. Joe and his boy helped them tun it in wood-house (I saw a live stoat in the front garden this morning).' John was back at work by mid-November, soon to be immobilised again.

> Friday Dec 1st 1882
> Was dreaming all night, chiefly about Annie and S.A.Y. [Sarah Young] . . .
> John came and told us Wood's grey horse ran away yesterday going into
> Chelt. [Cheltenham] and dashed its brains out against a house . . . Joe
> brought the trap down for the apples (9 pots), Sis busy helping Tom and
> Father to pack them all. John hurt his back this morning (near to the bad hip)
> before breakfast helping lift a big wheel. It got worse, so after dinner he went
> to bed, could hardly get upstairs, Sis rubbed in Essence of Mustard. Joe back
> from Evesham about 7, sold the apples all wonderfully well (Blenheims 11/-
> per pot) and others all dear. The colt had not been out in the dark before but
> very quiet, yet frightened and stopped short coming down Bridge St., nearly
> had Joe out on his back. Tom heard Wood carrier was in bed nearly all day,
> his leg hurt. John's back dreadfully bad tonight, couldn't move himself in bed,
> pain awful for a time. Tom and Sis moved him a little before we went to bed.

Sarah had to dress John for the next few days. When she made a cap for her mother, she used John as 'dummy'! Tom was left to cope in the smithy but had a moment of glory the day before John's accident when he sang a solo 'Gallants of England' at a concert at the school. As for Wood the carrier, he was still 'very much bruised' a week later. It would be Christmas Eve before Mr Jones in church 'returned thanks to Wood the carrier, and his sermon was in reference to it.'

Ann had made another reference to a sermon earlier in the month, on December 10th: 'Tom and I went to church. Mr W. Jones gave us a very nice sermon (the text Proverbs 25th chapter, 25th verse). As cold waters to a thirsty soul, so is good news from a far country.' Did it cross her mind that this text had a local application? It was, after all, a good description of her pleasure in receiving letters from Annie. There *was* good news, too. Mrs Biscoe and Annie would spend Christmas at Dumbleton.

* * * *

Preparations for Christmas were, unlike now, contained within the few days preceding Christmas Day.

Monday Dec 18. Sis went up to Joe's to see the large beast they killed yesterday.

Inspecting animal carcases may not sound too Christmassy, but 'the large beast' would supply Christmas meals for Joe's customers. Free beef for the tenants from the Hall was an expected, and welcome, part of Christmas. On St Thomas's Day (21 December), there were more preparations. The church bells rang early: they *stopped* at 5.30 a.m.! Sarah had been inveigled by Mrs Willoughby Jones into decorating the church for Christmas and after examining the windows for which she would be responsible, she set off into the shrubbery to collect the traditional evergreens, yew, ivy, laurel and holly. The front room, not much used except for Sunday singing round the piano, was prepared: Tom swept out the chimney and the four 'children' carried the carpet outside for a good beating. Ann's mother grated nutmegs, cut peel and stoned plums for her Christmas puddings, though traditionally plum puddings were made earlier than this. Stir Up Sunday[47] at the end of November is so-called because its Collect (the 25th Sunday after Trinity) begins 'Stir up, we beseech thee, O Lord' and also because it was the time, just before Advent, to stir the Christmas puddings.

Ann rode with Tom and John to Evesham in Joe's trap to greet the Biscoes. 'Mrs B and Annie came safely, former looking very sadly, but Annie better. We took the luggage to Railway Hotel, then went into the town shopping. Annie went with Tom to buy his overcoat. Tom called in at Mr Morris' to try to get calves' feet for Joe, but they had none.' It was nearly dark when they reached home at half past five.

It was Mrs Biscoe's first Christmas without her husband, and a sad one for her, but she and Annie helped Sarah with her 'church work' and she was generous with gifts: 'Mrs B gave me a sweet pretty gold watch and chain, and to Sis she gave a lovely bracelet, and Annie gave us a dear little bracelet each from Mrs Young.' Annie also gave Ann a photograph of 'her dear old home'. Numerous Christmas cards were dispatched, many to Enfield. Christmas Eve fell on a Sunday that year, and after church 'poor Mrs Biscoe very low and sad, so when we came out we went through shady walk, and down road, she soon felt better.' Ann and Annie made pikelets for tea, and there was a musical evening with Joe and Louie, Leslie and Cormell. 'We had a nice lot of music. Annie sang some of her Sacred Songs. CM and LL went before 10, the others soon after. Mrs B and us three girls sat talking till nearly 12, after the rest were in bed. Heard the bells ring out midnight peal.'

'Xmas Day, Dec 25th, 1882 . . . Father and boys busy making toast-and-ale, and Mother and Sis seeing to the cooking. Annie and I went to church with the men folks.'

O come all ye faithful
Joyful and triumphant . . .

In *Silas Marner* George Eliot has described a Christmas morning very similar to this one: 'The church was fuller than all through the rest of the year, with red faces among the abundant dark-green boughs – faces prepared for a longer service than usual by an odorous breakfast of toast and ale. Those green boughs, the hymn and anthem never heard but at Christmas – even the Athanasian Creed – brought a vague exulting sense . . .'[48]

Even on Christmas Day there was a postal delivery, with cards for both girls. Joe and Louie and their friend Alf Goodall, another butcher, arrived for Christmas lunch of hare and sirloin beef.

> We had dinner rather late. Gave Mrs D's maid her dinner, Mrs D had hers from Rectory. After we had cleared, (Sis made fire in parlour) us girls washed and dressed and put on our best. Sis and I wore our jewellery presents (Annie gave us a pair of mittens each, and to the boys she gave two pretty boxes of matches). Annie helped us get tea, all the 'boys' went up to Joe's to see after the cattle before tea; Louie, Alf, Sis, Tom and John went to church, Father went with Joe to his house. Annie and I washed up and cleared away, then came upstairs and she read 'The Letters' to me. LL came before the others were back . . . Later on the mummers came, and we had them in the kitchen to act, I did some writing in D. the while . . .'

And after the mummers, the local band! On Boxing Day morning 'the Toddington band came, and played several tunes. Annie and John had a dance or two, I tried, and Alf and Sis.' There was much music, to Ann's delight. Annie gave her, and occasionally John, long music lessons. They were after all a sizeable group of musicians – Ann, Annie, John and Louie all played the piano (Charles sometimes played but from Ann's comment on another occasion, not very well: 'Pap opened piano and said he'd have a tune, hadn't tried for so long, so he made a noise for a bit'). In addition, Tom, Annie and Louie sang solos, and all joined in singing the hymns and songs.

New Year's Eve 1882 was a Sunday, as Christmas Eve had been. Ann and Annie went to church with the boys, where they listened to a sermon on a text familiar from the funerals they had attended 'So teach us to number our days' (Psalm 90:12).

Annie played and sang till supper-time . . . then us two went aloft and did a lot of talking, and I wrote a bit. Boys came up for bed, and pushed in to see what we were doing, and we had a rare 'scrimmage' and shouting. They tried to get at desk, but Sis came to the rescue, and we beat them. Father and Mother followed the boys to bed, us four sat up and read till the bells began ringing Old Year out and New One in. Some men came to the back door wishing us Happy New Year, but we put out the light till they were gone, then went to bed after drinking healths and exchanging good wishes.

1882 had been a year of sharp contrasts. It had begun with Ann a barmaid in a busy town close to London; it ended with her sequestered again in a small village remote from any city. Despite the sadnesses of the year – the deaths of Annie's father, Louie's brother, Louie's baby, Sarah Young's bridegroom – it had been a happy and healthy one for Ann and her family and it ended in an ideal way, Christmas spent among family and friends.

* * * *

Robertsend and Round and About 1883

What are those blue remembered hills,
What spires, what farms, are those?
A.E. Housman

For anyone wondering how the unmarried Victorian girl filled her time, with no career and no husband and children to occupy her, Ann's diary for 1883 provides a revealing insight. We have already seen that she is fully employed at home, an essential cog in the wheel of the family business. In addition to her 'regular work' at home, she is invited and expected by relatives (her mother's family the Pearts were of clan-like proportions) to help them in times of illness or at particularly busy periods in the farming calendar. After her long stay at Enfield Ann's relatives could hardly demand her services immediately. But by the beginning of 1883 she had been at home for six months . . .

During 1883 Ann made numerous visits to help out – to Kemerton, to her octogenarian Peart grandmother, to Broadway where her Aunt Moseley was seriously ill, and to Longdon near Tewkesbury where her Uncle John Peart required help at Robertsend Farm. Sarah never went on these errands of mercy: was she considered too indispensable at the Villa, or did she claim she could not leave her poultry? Sarah, in any case, lacked Ann's patience with the patients. It is Ann who goes, every time, and without complaint. She was a good nurse, and she had plenty of practice.

But at the beginning of the year she was still enjoying the Christmas visit of Mrs Biscoe and Annie. The New Year had opened very early, as was the custom, with small boys singing at the door at dawn ('Sarah went down, gave them 2d, then went back to bed') and a few days later the old Christmas Day was celebrated with 'roast sparib [sic] and plum pudding. (Old Xmas Day.) Annie in shop a good bit . . .' Annie spent much time in the smithy with the boys, often taking her crochet in there. In the evenings she played cards with them, whist or crib, besides sampling village society, a Glee Club meeting, a sewing class at the Rectory: 'Mrs WJ talked a little and read a little. I began a little African shirt.'

One Sunday Sarah cooked kidneys for the visitors' breakfast. This is the only mention of kidneys in the diaries – and food is mentioned a good deal. The family eat other offal – liver, tripe, sweetbreads, brains – but not kidneys. Joe the butcher believed if there was anything wrong with an animal it went straight to the kidneys, and he did not like Louie to have them for this reason (she had to wait till he was out for the day before she could indulge her fondness for them). After her kidney breakfast, Annie began a new diary. She too was still diary-keeping, and would have much to write in it the next day on receiving a long letter from her fiancé, an event marked *in Ann's diary* by the heading *Red-Letter Day*. Friendship expects of us some degree of interest in our friends' other relationships, but this vicarious sharing of Annie's love life displays in Ann a disquieting abnegation of self, and provides a sensitive register of her emotional development at this time: a late developer, her intense relationship with Annie is more like one between young adolescents than women in their mid-twenties. There had been flutters of interest in men at Enfield, and occasionally at Dumbleton – Mr Reeve, Mr Cook – but they are of small significance beside Annie.

Annie began a long letter to her fiancé, but it was unfinished when she set out the next day to accompany Sarah and John to Kemerton. They never reached Kemerton, never left Dumbleton in fact, only getting as far as the Brickworks. Brickworks sound remarkably industrial for this rural setting, but brickmaking was still a highly localised occupation with a kiln in most parishes to produce bricks for the estate and for local needs (Robert Wedgwood's Rectory, for instance). James Taylor's brickworks were off the road which

102

connects the village to the Cheltenham–Evesham main road, and at the opposite end of the village from the Villa.

When Ann went indoors after feeding the fowls

Father came out of shop and told me Jas. Taylor [James Taylor of Dumbleton Brickworks] had sent one of his men up to say old 'Tommy' fell down and threw them all out just past the Brickyard, but not much hurt. We didn't tell Mrs B or Mother. I got Mrs B to lie down, Tom went up to tell Joe. Very soon after, Sis, Annie and Joe came down orchard, and John driving 'Tommy' in Taylor's little trap. The shafts of Joe's [trap] were both broken, horse not hurt. Annie fell out first, John on her shoulder, Sis the other side cut her forehead and hurt left hand. Annie's shoulder and back stiff and painful, John's left leg scratched down and bruised by the horse's shoe. Sis ran to Brickyard for help and the Taylors and their men helped them, gave them brandy, and Sis washed dirt off her face. Mother sent for Grandma a bottle port wine, that wasn't even cracked nor a small bottle cream Louie sent. Father told Mother about it just as they were coming home. (We heard afterwards that Annie Taylor was lying dead at Hawker's, Teddington Hands.) Thinking Mrs B would hear their voices, and be alarmed, I went and told her they had turned back, it was so cold, so she lay comfortably till tea-time nearly. We attended to their bruises, and put their clothes a bit straight . . .

I have quoted Ann's account of the mishap in full because it shows her once again in a familiar ministering role, not only 'putting straight' the disarray around her but careful also to allay the anxiety of the older womenfolk, even allowing herself a mild deception in order to do so.

That evening Annie was recovered enough to accompany Ann and Tom to the Glee Club, only to practice a glee with the title 'Softly Falls'! Their own falls had been sufficiently unsoft for them to visit the doctor in Tewkesbury the next day. He 'pronounced Annie much stronger than when he last saw her [a year earlier, after her father's death], Sis he told to wear her hand in a sling, one of the arteries had broken and bled internally.' John tried a home remedy, lily leaves, on his leg.

Christmas lasted well beyond Twelfth Night in Dumbleton. The Rector's wife invited the girls to go to see The Tree at the School on January 17th, and the Christmas evergreens were not removed from the church until January 18th. Mrs Jones lent the Staights the glees to practice – it was, after all, in her interests for *them* to be in good form as they formed the nucleus of the village singers at the village concerts. The first of the year was held at the school on January 22nd. 'Sis picked us some snowdrops, violets and heath and did up for us to wear. Louie down about 7 and we soon started, Annie and I left our hats and ulsters in classroom, I wore best black dress, silver ornaments, and watch and chain. The concert passed off well. Annie helped sing both glees, and Tom. The hand bell ringers performed twice . . .' Even a concert did not satisfy the family's appetite for music. At home afterwards there was supper and more singing.

John was ill again at the end of January and this time there were three girls to nurse him. Ann made him beef tea, 'Annie put a strong mustard plaster on his chest, and linseed meal after . . . Sis went to the shop for oatmeal and butter, she made him some gruel . . .' Charles Staight helped Tom in the shop, which continued to fascinate the Rector: 'Mr W. Jones in shop long time talking, and blowing bellows, this morning', and Annie spent time there with Tom, when she was not reading to John in bed. Charles Staight again looked about for a substitute: 'A young blacksmith came from Tewkesbury (heard Father wanted a man) he was soaking wet. Gave him some refreshments etc. but didn't engage him.'

Wednesday, February 7th 1883. Fine morning, but rained fast in night, and wind high. Joe brought his bacon down here to dry. John up about 11. Very nice day. The Ordnance Surveyor called to look round, Father took him in kitchen to see our old Map . . . Annie in shop with Tom and Father. Went to church with Tom, Sis and Annie at 7.30. Being Ash-Wednesday there were two services but we didn't go at 11.15 a.m. This evening we had a very nice sermon . . .

Wednesday services, taken by local clergymen during the Rector's many absences, seem to have been frequent occurrences, but poorly attended. 'Feb. 18. Mr Robeson, Vicar of Tewkesbury preached. A very nice sermon, very few there . . . Feb 28. Strange clergyman preached, from Littleton, very few there.' With church such an integral part of village life, it is not easy to assess its significance for Ann, but her attendance exceeded any required norm and indicates that it was more than just habit, social occasion, or a chance to dress up, though it was undeniably these three things as well. With her need for rites and rituals, her love of order, of books and of music, church offered obvious inducements, but I do not think she turned to it for comfort, like those whom the Psalmist describes: 'Blessed are they that dwell in thy house . . . who going through the vale of misery use it for a well' (Psalm 84). Ann attended to the sermons, often quoting subject or text in her diary. Recent sermons had covered 'the shipwreck spoken of in Acts' [Acts 27, 28] and the parable of the sower [Matt.13]. 'Sunday 18 Feb 1883. I put on my "best" and went to church, Mr WJ gave us a nice sermon, text "How old art thou?" (Genesis 47.8).' She noted when there was no sermon or when it was too long:

Feb 11. 1883. Sis, Annie, Father and Tom went to church . . . They were longer than usual at church. Collection today, and Sermons preached by Mr Lowndes on behalf of mission in Central Africa . . . Annie and I lay down (bell passed out at 4 o'clock for G. Grinnall's youngest daughter, not been ill a fortnight). Went to church with Sis and Tom, very long sermon again.

Just occasionally she lapsed: 'We all went to church except Sis . . . I was very sleepy, especially during sermon time.'

* * * *

Valentine's Day brought no letter or card for either girl, but on February 19th 'Annie went to meet the postman, had nice cheerful letter from PP and good news, also two lovely cabinet photos, one for Annie and one for me . . . Had supper, got my album down and we put PP photo in, had to cut it top and bottom.' The following evening, when Ann showed the album to Cormell Morris, 'he saw PP's photo, said it was like Sir G. Wolsey.'

With Ann's penchant for mis-spelling surnames, she has to be referring here to Sir Garnet Wolseley, later Viscount Wolseley (1883–1913), then at the very peak of his fame as military commander. As recently as 1882 he had quashed rebellion in Egypt, routing Arabi Pasha's troops at Tel-el-Kebir. For this he was immortalised in poetry by Tennyson –

> And Wolseley overthrew
> Arabi, and the stars in heaven
> Paled, and the glory grew[49]

and also in the expression 'Sir Garnet' or 'All Sir Garnet' (meaning 'All Right' or 'All's well'), a further endorsement of his highly successful career. Having studied in the National Portrait Gallery Albert Besnard's romantic, idealised portrait (1880) of Wolseley and his horse in some foreign field (Wolseley does not look in it like a man of nearly fifty) I turned to Ann's albums hoping to identify the elusive Mr Paul. Moustache, no beard, fair colouring, lean figure, a definite presence. But all the men had moustaches! and there are a large number of young men in the albums. The photograph of the young man most closely resembling Sir Garnet has not been trimmed. But there are eight empty pages in the album, and it is possible that when Annie married someone else – or for reasons of her own – Ann removed the offending photograph.

Mrs Biscoe had returned to London in mid-January. Annie left Dumbleton at the end of February, 'Annie very lowspirited at last . . . (we talked on a fresh topic for short time)', to face an uncertain future. Ann's sixth diary ends soon after, with ten lines of script written across, at right angles, the previous day's entry. This writing-over is sometimes found in 19th-century letters. In Ann's diary it is just about legible, but the effect is out of character after the neatness and regularity of the rest. Clearly Ann had no new diary ready, no spare paper, and she also felt ill 'Had neuralgia in my head badly . . . Head very bad, came on to bed about 9 and Sis made me some gruel . . .'. She was impatient with the business, but not able to sacrifice the entry, so deeply entrenched, so compulsive, had the writing habit become.

* * * *

March 1883 was bitterly cold, and there were casualties in the animal world as well as inside the house.

> March 8th 1883. Sis up at 7, I lay till 7.30, my neuralgia quite gone. We had a little snow fall, wind very cold still . . . Father went up to Joe's, soon back for bottle of whiskey, big old cow very bad, had two calves, both died, boy fetched Haines from Broadway. Daisy, too, very bad, but got better, and her calf lived . . . Father brought Mr Haines down with him to ask Sis for recipe for St Vitus' dance, he has a little boy ill with it . . . LL came soon after 8, brought John some books. 10 chicks hatched today, 1 nearly dead with cold but Sis brought it round . . .

John was still confined to the house, reading and playing the piano. Ann had not yet read either of the books given her for her birthday five months earlier, and now she chose *The Mill on the Floss* before *Martin Chuzzlewit*: on March 11th she 'read the beginning of "Mill on the Floss"'.

> March 13th 1883. John up to breakfast (first time). Nice day, not quite so cold. (Mr W. Jones in shop this morning, he was speaking of apricot blossoms, so Father brought him in garden to see ours . . . I changed dress and went with Tom to the glee practice, very few there. Mrs W Jones [had] dreadful cold, could hardly sing at all. We practised the new glee several times, but it did not go well. Belfry Tower better. Mrs WJ very amiable . . .

Though it was hardly ideal weather for travelling, Ann went next day to Kemerton, then in Gloucestershire but now across the county boundary in Worcestershire. It is an extremely long village on the south-west slopes of Bredon Hill, one of the villages along with Grafton, Ashton-under-Hill, Overbury, and others which encircle the hill. Ann's grandmother Sarah Peart lived with her unmarried daughter, another Sarah, in Lower Kemerton at the Villa, a smaller, more compact house than the Dumbleton Villa. At a small green the road forks, the right hand going alongside the Villa's small orchard towards Caleb Baylis's mill (now in ruins) which was one of Kemerton's three mills. The Villa is dwarfed by two of Kemerton's grand mansions, the Court and Upper Court; between them, shielded by yew trees, is Kemerton church.

Ann enjoyed her drives with Joe in the trap, but not this one. 'We started soon after 2, had the colt, it went nicely. I felt very cold, Joe had to call at so many places,' and it was so cold that Ann found her grandmother and aunt rearing two baby ducklings and a chick indoors by the fire.

> *When Bredon Hill puts on his hat*
> *Men of the Vale, beware of that.*

Men might heed such meteorological warnings, but Ann could not. When she returned home a few days later, walking away from Bredon Hill and across wet fields, the journey lasted two hours. The consequence was soon clear.

March 21st. Very cold, piercing wind. Mother and Sis did baking. My cold very bad. I lay in bed all day, read a good deal of 'Mill on the Floss'. I did my D., got up at dusk, and did crochet, nice bit.

While Ann recovered from her cold and continued reading the history of another unfashionable family,[50] Sarah 'finished her garment' at the last sewing meeting of the Rectory, the final meeting marking the end of the winter. Her next task, appropriately, was to collect greenery for the church's Easter decorations. Mrs Biscoe and Annie had returned to Enfield for Easter and for another anniversary, and by a strange coincidence while they were there, Mrs Biscoe's sister died and was buried there, as Mr Biscoe had been the previous year, on Good Friday. Annie's cousin Sarah Young had reached, but without a husband, her first wedding anniversary on March 16th and three days after it gave birth to a baby girl.

There were no personal anniversaries to sadden Easter for the Staights at Dumbleton but Good Friday, itself a sombre anniversary,

Above, William and Hannah Moseley at the time of their marriage; left, a formidable character in Ann's album, possibly Grandmother Peart or Aunt Sarah

was marked by meatless meals. Although Sarah kept poultry, eggs are not often mentioned, and Good Friday is one of the rare occasions when they are: 'We had eggs, bread-and-butter and buns for breakfast . . . eggs and bread-and-butter for dinner.' Ann, who had spent the whole of the previous Easter behind the bar at Enfield, made up the omission by going to church *three* times on Easter Sunday:

> *O sons and daughters, let us sing!*
> *The King of Heav'n, the glorious King,*
> *O'er death to-day rose triumphing.*
> *Alleluia!*

The church was fuller than usual in the morning; the children's service followed at 2.45: 'such a number of children, a lot of people too, a collection was made for the mission in Central Africa,' and Ann was there for Evensong too. 'Went to church with Tom and Sis, a lot of people there, Marjery Mann, her husband, Fanny Mann and another gent. came in late, the two sisters came in our pew, the gents sat on boys' seat.'

Her father and Joe, meanwhile, were currently engaged with church politics:

> March 27th. Father and Joe went to the school to parish meeting to choose church wardens. Mr Corbett and C. Grinnall appointed, the latter not there. CM (Cormell Morris) was proposed, but would not agree, said he was a strong Nonconformist.

Visitors to the Villa that Easter included Ann's brother Charley who came from Swindon for Winchcombe Fair, and 'Mr and Mrs Thurstan Holland and their eldest boy called in afternoon, stayed a little while talking to Father and Mother (visiting at Mrs Wedgwood's).' It was Thurstan's last visit to his childhood village, for a year later Ann would record 'September 27th 1884. Mr Thurstan Holland died very suddenly while walking in London not far from his own home.' His unusual Christian name lives on in one of his mother-in-law's novels: the kind and caring Dissenting Minister in Mrs Gaskell's novel *Ruth* was given the name of Thurstan Benson.

*   *   *   *

The weather was beginning to be more springlike when Ann was summoned to Broadway, most famous of Cotswold villages, where her Aunt Moseley was critically ill with bronchitis and erysipelas.

Aunt Moseley was another Peart, Ann Staight senior's much younger sister Hannah, now approaching fifty. Hannah had married late (at thirty-five) the twenty-eight-year-old William Moseley, and they had one son. An enterprising and energetic young man, William had begun his career in Paris, learning the tailoring trade. Later he changed trades, and was now well-established as a grocer in Broadway. Joe was driving to Stanton, which is from Dumbleton halfway to Broadway and a miniature version of it, so Ann rode with him and his new horse. 'Smith's [steam] engine at work close to Wormington road, the horse seemed frightened, turned round and wanted to bolt, but they stopped the machine and one of the men came and led the horse by.' (Both horse and steam engine would cause more trouble a few days later. When Joe drove to Tewkesbury, 'he was going to take a pig, but the horse was so frightened and wild, had to leave pig behind . . . John bruised his left hand dreadfully this afternoon while working at Mr Smith's engine, got it in between wheel and engine while it was in motion, Sis put on Cure-all and bruised parsley with butter . . .'.)

After hearing the cuckoo for the first time that year in the Villa garden on April 19th, Ann returned to Broadway for a longer visit: 'Lovely morning. Sis put my things in large bag, and carried it up [to Joe's] for me. We started at 8.30, went to Sedgeberrow first to take meat to 3 or 4 places, then on by Hinton through to Broadway. Enjoyed the ride very much. Found Aunt still in bed, and certainly worse than when I left her before.' Ann began by sleeping in her cousin Charley's bed and putting him in with his father, but when her aunt did not improve, she decided to sleep in her aunt's room in order to keep the fire in during the night: 'I got out two or three times to it, and gave Aunt beef-tea.' In the daytime she thought up tempting delicacies for the invalid: 'Cooked nice sweetbread and asparagus for her lunch . . .'. A week later a letter from Sarah arrived 'saying I can stay longer *if they wish me to*' [my italics]. While at Broadway, Ann consulted the doctor about herself, the first time this has been reported in the diaries, for she appears to have been exceptionally healthy: 'I was in the room when the Dr came. Uncle brought him up, so I left the room soon after, but they called me up again, and I showed the Dr my neck. He asked me endless questions respecting my health and so on, and advised me to paint the place with iodyne.' When the doctor called again a few days later, at the end of Ann's visit, she asked what she owed him, and was told 'nothing'.

*　　*　　*　　*

110

When Annie had left Dumbleton in February, the Biscoes had no idea where they would settle. Since Mr Biscoe's death a year before, she and her mother had moved between friends and relations, with the Minories as their base. There was nothing to keep them in Enfield and Mrs Biscoe, born at Nunney in Somerset, showed no inclination to return there. Annie consulted Mrs McGlinchy, Ann's friend in Stoke Newington, about settling in that neighbourhood, and they were deliberating over a house there (roughly halfway between Enfield and the Minories) when Mrs Biscoe's son Henry proposed Brighton. A letter to Ann at Broadway reported that she had not heard from Mr Paul recently and that she and her mother were going to have a look round in Brighton. Nothing was resolved there – little did Annie know she would settle there after her marriage – and in May she returned to Dumbleton for a short visit. Every day the girls walked, into the park to see the deer, along the Short Ground, down Nutmeadow to Hogsleasow wood, round Hall's hill and up to Cuckoo's Pen, and finally to Bulman coppice to gather primroses and bluebells for Annie to take to London.

Sarah had mentioned to Annie a small property in Cheltenham, being offered for sale by her friends the Bodleys. There were obvious inducements here – a pleasant spa town, a fresh start, stalwart friends near at hand. The Biscoes travelled from Chatham to Cheltenham early in June to view the property at Bath Parade, Cheltenham, but nothing was decided. It is not surprising that a decision was difficult: after the Rising Sun the little terrace house was miniscule. The name is misleading: the names 'Bath' and 'Parade' both separately and together conjure up a much grander location. Bath Parade is a quiet side street linking two busy roads, Bath Road and College Road; the centre of the town is close by, with its two principal shopping areas, the elegant Promenade and the bustling High Street. The house itself, with its small rooms and low ceilings, is typical of the modest middle-class terrace houses built in Cheltenham in the early 19th century and is not dissimilar to the one to the north of the town where Gustav Holst (1874–1934) spent the first eight years of his life. The little house is a far cry from the tall, elegant Regency houses of Cheltenham's heyday; nor does it resemble in any way the Rising Sun with its several storeys and its large billiard room.

The Biscoes had left Chatham for Cheltenham at eight in the morning, and arrived at Ashton station, where Ann met them, at eight that night. The Villa was full, as Aunt Moseley was convalescing there, nursed by Ann who slept with her aunt in the spare room.

'Letter from Uncle M. expressing surprise Aunt had not written, and asking me to go and stay while they did haymaking . . . After dinner I wrote to Uncle M., told him Aunt better today, and I couldn't promise to go there.' Two days later 'had another letter from Uncle M. a ditto to the other'. Ann could not go back to Broadway because she was already promised to another uncle in the opposite direction.

While Mrs Biscoe and Annie went to and fro to Cheltenham and bargained for 21 Bath Parade (bringing back delicacies not available in Dumbleton – salmon, oranges, gingerbreads), the June days were sunny and peaceful. 'Very warm day. The swarm of bees rose again and settled in apple tree, stayed there till boys came home,' and there was warmth of another sort at church: 'Mr W Jones preached very *warmly* about something that happened last Sunday evening as he came to church. We spoke to Nellie Walker as we came out, she told Sis some of the Dissenting members spread tracts in the church path last Sunday, that was what upset Mr W. Jones' (June 24th 1883).

It was a year since Ann had returned home from Enfield and now, as then, it was haymaking time:

Monday June 25th 1883. Our people helping Joe nearly all the day getting up his hay. Mr Alf Brain came in afternoon and had his horse shod, Father took him in front room to have some cider. Joe hurt his right knee in the evening, was leading the horses, slipped in an ants' hillock. Sis went up and stayed some time seeing about it, LL called in as he went by, and Father took Mr Corbett in too to give his advice, and finally Joe went to Dr Fulcher (drove old Knacker).

Joe's great size and weight made falls no light matter. The doctor advised him to lie in bed a week. He was up next day!

A counterpoint to the human dramas, Sarah's poultry enact their own tiny subplots:

Only 1 little duck from our batch, the hen killed 2 or 3 (pecked them to death).

Sis had 9 little ducks first thing, but before dinner a hen killed one of the best, trod on it, and the weakly one died

and

When Sis went to let the old ducks out, found one duck dead and stiff. She began picking it, but had not time to finish, as she decided to go to Cheltenham with Mrs Biscoe to have a look round, ask about lodgers etc.

112

Later Sarah conducted a postmortem on the duck: 'Sis finished picking duck, and opened it, liver and intestines very swollen.'

* * * *

At the end of June 1883 Ann went to Robertsend Farm for the first of three visits that year. Situated south of Longdon, Robertsend lies away from the main road which links Tewkesbury and Pendock. (Today the M50 passes very close to it.) To the west are the Malvern Hills. Not far from Robertsend, at another End, Hope End near Colwall, the poet Elizabeth Barratt Browning had spent her childhood, and some of her later verse evokes this orchard country in the shadow of the hills:

> Hills, vales, woods, netted in a silver mist,
> Farms, granges, doubled up among the hills;
> And cattle grazing in the watered vales,
> And cottage-chimneys smoking from the woods,
> And cottage-gardens smelling everywhere,
> Confused with smell of orchards.[51]

Set amidst its own orchards, Robertsend was the home of Ann's uncle, John Peart (one of her mother's five younger brothers) and his wife Mary who, at sixty-eight – she was six years older than her husband – could give him only limited assistance. The farmhouse was not an 'easy' one. It was, and is, a long, rambling building, a child's but not a housewife's paradise, full of steps and staircases, hiding places, thick, sloping walls and sloping floors. The house has two utterly dissimilar faces. A black and white timber-framed house faces the barns and farm buildings and beyond them the Malvern hills. The other side of the house, facing garden and orchard, is of a soft red brick. The front door opens into the garden from the hall and around the door frame are bricks inscribed with initials and dates, EB 1776, IB 1776 and again IB 1776. Against the pinky-red bricks white roses and white stocks bloom in summer-time, and beyond the garden gate is the pride of Robertsend, a square timber-framed pigeonhouse or dovecote, a listed building today though the house is not! (John Peart used it, not for doves, but for his chickens.) There was once a moat beyond the garden, but it is not mentioned in the diaries and there is no trace of it today. Although the front door is here, on this side, it is seldom used. Everything happens at the back door, which links kitchens and farm buildings, as if gardens and leisure and formality are irrelevances on a busy farm.

Just before leaving Dumbleton there had been heavy thunder-storms, and now at Longdon Ann's first nights were disturbed ones: 'Saturday June 30th. Woke up last night before 12, by the heavy thunderstorm, the lightning very pretty, lay awake some time. Uncle had to go down and let Boxer loose, he was so frightened.' The following night was disturbed for a different reason: 'Sunday (Wake) July 1st 1883. Had a very bad night, awake for some time before it was light, and afterwards dreamt very much about PP and Annie (made me feel quite uneasy all the day after).' As the nearest Sunday to St Peter's Day, this particular day was celebrated as the patronal festival (Wake Sunday) at Dumbleton. After washing the milk pans Ann and her aunt prepared to go to church at Longdon. They set off on foot, arriving nearly half an hour too early at the church, which is a curious mixture of architectural styles. A flight of steps lead up into the churchyard from the road, the other side of which is the Plough Inn. 'Aunt slipped down on the top step into the churchyard but soon up again. Enjoyed the service very much. We managed the journey back pretty well, both tired. Lovely day, 1.30 when we got in . . .' The churchgoing soothed Ann's unease, and the next night she dreamed of Philip, her Enfield friend. More violent storms raged on July 3 and 4 'Heavy thunder and storm and hail about 4, lightning and thunder dreadful (mare and colt killed not far from here at Pendock Bank). Uncle home about 5 [from Tewkesbury], had escaped the rain each way.'

At Robertsend Ann worked mainly in house and dairy. She was not experienced in dairywork. The Villa had no dairy, its milk, butter and cream all supplied by Joe. While she was not expected to do the milking at Robertsend, there was plenty to do in the dairy, always the responsibility of the womenfolk on any farm. Near the cheese room in the farmhouse a perilously steep flight of steps lead down to a large cellar with white-washed walls and a brick floor. The cellar can also be reached, less steeply, from the farmyard, but this entails a long walk from the kitchen to the outside entrance. Nearly every day Ann mentions the carrying of pans up and down, and this was visibly no small chore. The milk pans were large and shallow to allow the maximum amount of cream to rise to the surface. Morning and evening the cream would be skimmed from the milk in these pans and scalded in hot weather to keep it fresh for butter-making. (Milk was used much less for drinking than it is now. It was saved mainly for butter and cheese making, and for calf-rearing and pig-feeding.) The butter churn was a barrel on a stand with a handle at one end. When the handle was turned, the

114

churning motion turned the cream to butter, which then had to be salted, washed, cooled, and patted with wooden butter pats into half pound shapes. To begin with, Ann just watched, but she learned quickly: 'Watched the woman salt the butter, I washed some of it, weighed nearly all of it, and did up 3 pats, managed it much better today.' In the evenings, she would sit making buttercloths in the house-place, that feature of farmhouses where almost every activity except sleeping takes place – living-room, dining-room, work-room.

The dairy context recalls another dairymaid, another tenant farmer's niece, *Adam Bede's* pretty and proficient butter-maker, Hetty Sorrel. While she made and packed the butter, Hetty's head was full of dreams and reveries, fuelled by the very real attentions of the local squire. Ann, we know, had her strongly romantic side (all those *Family Heralds*), but she managed to inhabit the world of work with more concentration and resignation than poor Hetty could contrive.

Apart from the dairywork there was the poultry, housed in the historic dovecote. Ann never killed the fowls, as Sarah did so matter-of-factly, but she was used to feeding chickens, to collecting and washing eggs. Her diary lists her other work, warming skimmed milk for the calves, picking raspberries and currants, cleaning the silver, skinning a hare, and she is candid about her smaller achievements: 'did a very little gardening'. Even in the night she was not idle. 'Woke at $\frac{1}{4}$ to 5, darned at Annie's stockings, read and did D.' It was at Robertsend that she read *Martin Chuzzlewit*.

Annie and her mother arrived in Cheltenham on July 11th to begin their new life at Bath Parade. Annie's birthday was a few days later and Ann spent it with her, taking a kitten for them in an old basket on the train. Tom made a poker and a large shovel for them in the smithy and these and other items – clothes, butter, flowers, feathers – were dispatched from Dumbleton by Wood the carrier. After buying Annie a jet brooch Ann arrived at Bath Parade where she 'found them very poorly, Mrs B looking really ill . . . Mrs B lay down in afternoon, seemed worse afterwards.'

Another widow was ill, too. Mrs Dunn at the Villa Cottage died at the end of July. An invalid for several years, she had been cared for by her maid Annie Richardson and by the Staights next door. Almost every day one or other of them called in there with a meal or a pudding or with a bowl of onion porridge or onion broth (there was great faith in the medicinal powers of onions), beef tea, or arrowroot. Mrs Dunn's end shows how a village could look after its old people in the days before widows' pensions and welfare states, though of course not all villagers fared so well: a few days earlier Ann reported the bell tolling for 'Old Ed. Nash, died yesterday in the Union aged 86'. As widow of a former agent of the Estate, Mrs Dunn could not be allowed to languish in the Union Workhouse at Winchcombe six miles away, and she enjoyed a privileged and cushioned existence in the cottage by the smithy. While the Staights, because of their proximity, cared for her in a regular way, the Hollands and Wedgwoods honoured their former connections. Mrs Wedgwood wrote to Tom now to say she would pay the funeral expenses. Ann missed the funeral as she returned that day to Robertsend via Tewkesbury: 'August 1st . . . waited on Severn bank till Uncle came . . . Mrs Dunn to be buried today, our 3 boys to help carry her, Father and Mother to follow.' In one respect at least the death was well-timed. Mrs Biscoe was able to buy a good deal of Mrs Dunn's small-scale furniture '6 chairs, best table and old ditto, blankets, bed, bolster' which Wood delivered to Bath Parade. Soon the Biscoes would be settled and ready for lodgers. After a lifetime in public houses, hospitality would come naturally to them and though the lodgers were probably an economic necessity, they would provide social as well as economic benefits for strangers in a new town.

Ann spent two weeks at Longdon on her second visit, returning home in time for John's birthday on August 15th (Annie had sent him the song 'Jack's come home' – not an apt title as John had never left it) and for Dumbleton Show the following day. Sarah did not exhibit this time, but the family made the most of the occasion: 'We went home with a rare lot, most of them the same who were here last year, and other fresh ones, about 20 to tea, and more to supper. We had dancing in kitchen and court (tuned for ourselves), singing and playing, the last lot stayed till nearly 1.' Among the company was Nellie Drinkwater and a friend Miss Richards, who had been mentioned for the first time in April 1883 ('Miss Drinkwater and Miss Richards came from Ashton, came in with Sis for a short time, had been to see Mrs Dunn . . .').

Elizabeth Easter Richards (she was born on Easter Day) was 'certificated schoolmistress' of the village school at Ashton-under-Hill, and with her high neck chokers made of stiffened net she would still look very much the 'schoolma'am' long after she ceased to be one. Eleven years later, Elizabeth Easter Richards would become John's wife, the imposing name sadly contracted to Elsie Staight. Elsie came originally from the New Forest, and one unsolved minor mystery is *why* she ended up in this small village on Bredon Hill. Her

Hampshire village, South Baddesley, is five miles east of Lymington, and consists of a large estate, Pylewell Park, farm, school, church (small church, large churchyard) and a handful of houses. The estate is the focal point of the village and looks over the Solent. Elsie's father was a gardener in South Baddesley and presumably worked on the Estate, the only large garden in the district. Pylewell Park had passed by sale to Mr Ingham Whitaker in 1875 and Elsie had greatly admired his son, another Ingham. It is possible she left Hampshire to escape an unrequited, an impossible, love. In later years she would blush at the mention of his name, murmuring enigmatically 'Old memories . . .'. Years after Elsie's death, her daughter-in-law recalled the Hampshire squire. *Sir Ingham*, as she referred to him, had been ennobled by time and romantic association.

From now on there are numerous references to Miss Richards in Ann's diaries. She called at the Villa frequently, always with her friend Nellie Drinkwater (she boarded with the Drinkwaters), never alone. On numerous occasions they attended Dumbleton church, calling afterwards at the conveniently placed Villa – lured perhaps by the attraction of two bachelor brothers. None of the Staights ever seem to have reciprocated by worshipping at Ashton church where the church is dedicated to St Barbara, patron saint of all who work with metal – miners, gunners, *blacksmiths*. Very occasionally, Tom and John would escort the girls home to Ashton after, for example, a concert at Dumbleton, and in February 1884 they escorted Ann to an Ashton concert. On the whole, though, there was surprisingly little contact between the two villages, and though blacksmiths were traditionally expected to enjoy a drink, the Staights did not make use of Ashton's inns – it had *three* in 1885, the White Hart, the Plough and Harrow, and the Star – preferring beer or cider or a homemade wine at home. Ashton *station*, rather than the village itself, was important to Ann. The Midland Railway's Ashchurch–Evesham branch line which ran through Ashton and Beckford was opened in 1864 (closed 1963) and Ann used one or other station once or twice a week to go on her local expeditions. The reader of Fred Archer's books about Ashton-under-Hill in the 19th and 20th centuries will observe that Dumbleton, despite its proximity, is seldom mentioned. Barely three miles apart, they were separated by effective barriers – a main road and a railway line (and later on a county boundary too: Ashton was transferred to Worcestershire in 1931), and while villages do form miniature alliances, Ashton is invariably linked with Beckford (they shared the railway line then, and now they share a Rector), and Dumbleton with Wormington. So an alliance of Ashton and Dumbleton residents is less likely than would at first appear. While John met Elsie at the Flower Show in 1883, there is no hint in the diaries of a relationship developing between them. Ann seldom writes explicitly about Sarah and Leslie, but we glean enough. (More about them presently.) The acquaintance of John and Elsie, hindered by mutual shyness, only developed into something more years later. At this stage Elsie had, predictably, more contact with Sarah than with any other member of the family. She and Ann (Elsie was two years younger) did not progress to Christian name terms.

*   *   *   *

Ann was back at Robertsend at the end of August and while her uncle 'hauled his barley, a man called (Ordnance Survey) to ask about the name of this place . . .'. Earlier in the same year an Ordnance Surveyor had called at the Villa in Dumbleton. Were Robertsend and Dumbleton to be 'put on the map' at last, literally? In fact, the Ordnance Survey was no new phenomenon, having been founded as early as 1791. The 19th century was a time of rapid industrial and urban expansion which necessitated constant revisions to the Ordnance Survey maps: the railways, for example, were first added to the maps in the 1860s. Rural areas did not require so much attention and the second edition of the one-inch maps did not appear until the 1880s. It seems more likely though that the Surveyors Ann speaks of were working not on these one-inch maps but on the much more detailed six-inch and twenty-five inch ones. A tricky task for these men was to ensure the accuracy of the field names and minor place-names used on these large-scale maps, and this meant spending time with farmers and householders. It is a pity that Ann does not give the Peart version of the name Robertsend. This part of the county has numerous placenames ending in -End (Drinker's End, Palmer's End, Piper's End, Guller's End), all signifying an end of the parish. Gilbert's End commemorates a keeper of part of Malvern Chase back in the 13th century, and Robertsend may refer to a Robert de Hanley mentioned in 1234. The local legend, told by a recent owner of Robertsend, however, is more colourful, and tells how Robert *sold* the right of way across his land (the track is visible today) and was hanged from a tree by his angry neighbours.

The early Ordnance Survey maps depict extensive orchards which do not appear on today's multi-coloured editions. When I visited Robertsend, the cider press stood, unused, in its brick outbuilding,

118

and there were empty cider barrels in the cellar where Ann made butter. The fruit trees had been 'outed', the orchards where Ann had spent many pleasant hours accompanying her uncle to inspect his fruit had vanished. Here is an irony of time, that as cartography becomes increasingly sophisticated, the topography is simplified.

At the same time as John Peart made perry and cider, supplying some of the local inns at Longdon ('September 3rd. The man from Plough came to order 1 tun cider'), the shooting season was underway. Robertsend was on the Pull Court estate, and it was natural for the landowner to make use of his tenants' land for his shooting parties. Pull Court,* named from the Pull stream which feeds the river Severn, was built close to the border of Worcestershire and Gloucestershire by a distinguished family who now rest in Bushley church. Many of the Dowdeswells served in Parliament (the praises of the most famous one, a Chancellor of the Exchequer who died in 1775, are sung on his monument by his great friend Edmund Burke) and the William Dowdeswell whom Ann met at Robertsend was Member of Parliament for Tewkesbury. 'Sept. 1. Mr W. Dowdeswell and 6 or 7 other gentlemen came here to have their lunch quite unexpected about 2, the footman came with the lunch just before, the keepers stayed out in the sheds and had theirs. Mr William stayed behind all the others, talking to Uncle till 4 o'clock, then he and footman drove off home in the carriage. We had our dinner after . . .'. (Ann, with her healthy appetite, could not fail to note the delayed eating hour!) 'The Pull Court gents' appeared again ten days later, and on September 30th 'Bunn (the keeper) called to ask if the gentlemen could bring their lunch here tomorrow.' On this occasion Mr Dowdeswell and his three male guests lunched in the farmhouse, 'I spoke to Mr Wm. before they came in.' Ann's relations with the local squire do not quite match Hetty's in *Adam Bede*, but relations between landowner and tenant were clearly most cordial. It was Mr Dowdeswell who restored the pigeonhouse at Robertsend, a fact noted by the *Victoria County History*.

Highlights at Robertsend were letters from Sarah and Annie, and parcels of stamps and crochetwork from Sarah which were transmitted by Joe to John Peart at the weekly Tewkesbury market. Posting letters was more complicated at Robertsend: 'Wrote to Annie after late dinner, put on best drab dress [Ann is obsessive about accuracy as well as about order] and went to meet postman. A gentleman came riding by, said he was gone, but offered to post it for me.' The

* Today it has a new name as well as a new function: Bredon School.

Above, Robertsend Farm near Longdon; below, Pendock church,
'the church in the fields'

diary-writing was fitted in at odd moments: 'Did D- while water warmed for washing up.'

Churchgoing, like correspondence, was more difficult, too. At the beginning she had looked to her uncle: 'Thought of going to church, but couldn't get Uncle in the mind, so gave it up', but once she realized his churchgoing was more sporadic than her own she pressed on alone. Church here was not just across the orchard. The farm was about mid-way between two churches, Longdon and Pendock. Ann preferred Pendock. In the nineteenth century, and well into the twentieth, there was no access road to Pendock church. 'The church in the fields', as it is called, was originally a monastic church, attached to Little Malvern Priory, and so was built deliberately remote from any settlement. Good weather and dry ground were thus essential for a woman in long skirts to attend church there. Crinolines were out of fashion by now and being replaced by the bustle, though Ann – hardly well-placed to keep level with the latest fashion – still wore them. (She mentions taking the steels out of a crinoline in April 1883.) Her entry 'Thought of going to Pendock Church, but was afraid of the weather' is not an excuse but a real deterrent. The church, which has no known dedication, is two miles outside the village of the same name, and stands at the old boundary of Gloucestershire and Herefordshire. (The Pendock villagers, tired of the rough walk to church, were to build a modest wooden church within the village not long after.)

> Sunday September 9th 1883 . . . Put out my things ready to put on, was winding up watch, forgot to stop at the right time and broke something. Dressed in my best and started at 10.15 for Pendock Church. Lovely day and nice walk (overtook Mr and Mrs Knight by church gate and spoke to them, sat a little behind them in church.) Very nice old-fashioned service, and I enjoyed it much . . .

The Rector at Pendock was the Rev. W.S. Symonds. His love of the past, which may explain the 'old-fashioned service', found expression also in various historical novels, one of which, *Malvern Chase* (published 1881), was set in this part of the country at the time of the Wars of the Roses. His own church features in the story – 'this little monastery at Pendyke' – and so does Prior's Court, the large mansion a field away where until recently one applied for the key to the church. (In 1985 it is the headquarters of a stud farm, and mares and foals graze in the fields Ann walked across.) Mr Simmonds is commemorated in the west window of the church, where red, white and blue hyacinths – not a usual Christian emblem – are incorporated into the stained glass design. Mr Simmonds' wife and daughter were both named Hyacinth (an unusual name which also occurs in Mrs Gaskell's last novel, *Wives and Daughters*) and his daughter would, most appropriately in view of her floral name, marry a botanist – Sir Joseph Hooker of Kew Gardens fame.

* * * *

By mid-September, Annie wrote to announce the first lodger – 'gent came in on Sat. suits very well' – and enclosing a letter she had written for 'Goat' but hadn't sent. Was it something in this letter which prompted Ann to go to Cheltenham at once from Robertsend? The next morning, dressed in her best hat and dress, she set out with her uncle for Tewkesbury. It was raining so hard that she abandoned her shopping intentions and hurried to the station where she had to wait an hour and a half for the next train. Having packed her crochet in her basket along with the butter, eggs and pears for the Biscoes, she worked at it while she waited. 'Sarah Martin from Crowle was waiting there too, we did not recognise each other at first, but after a time she guessed who I was, and we had a long talk together, parted at Ashchurch . . .' Ann arrived, unannounced, at Bath Parade, where the Biscoes were 'very surprised and pleased to see me.' During her two-day visit, she met the new lodger and had her photograph taken. The studio, at Royal House, Cheltenham, was not that of a mere photographer. Mr Suter called himself 'Artist, Miniature Painter, and Photographer', offering portraits finished in water-colours, oils or crayons, which could be enlarged on porcelain, paper, or canvas. Mr Suter (who liked alliteration) was 'sole licensee for Cheltenham for the new patent permanent processes'.

A few days after her visit Annie would post one of the photographs to Ann at Longdon. 'Annie sent me one of my photos to look at.' She looks, but does not comment. That she was plump and buxom, as the picture suggests, a subsequent entry confirms.

> Uncle busy amongst the thrashers today, thrashed all wheat, peas and barley in the barn . . . Uncle weighed his wheat this morning, and sent a load to Tewkes-. He and I weighed, he was 11st 5lbs., I was 10st. 10lbs.

Annie herself visited Robertsend at the end of September, walking from Tewkesbury and going two miles off course by turning up the wrong side road (towards Bushley). The girls explored house, farm and garden and accompanied John Peart on his regular Wednesday drive to Tewkesbury. No wonder Annie wanted to explore Tewkesbury. There is a lot to see there. Like Evesham, which it resembles in

122

several ways, Tewkesbury has a battle field ('the Bloody Meadow'), the River Avon, and fine black-and-white timbered houses. Annie would probably have known about the place long before she moved to Cheltenham, for it had become well-known through literary associations. Mr Pickwick dined so well at the Hop Pole Hotel there (*Pickwick Papers*, Ch. 50) that he slept afterwards for thirty miles on the way to Birmingham.[52] But this is only a passing reference. Tewkesbury had been made famous in 1856, thinly disguised as a town called Norton Bury, in Mrs Craik's *John Halifax, Gentleman*. Inspired by a visit to the town, Mrs Craik transformed the Bell Inn into Abel Fletcher's house and the Abbey Mill into the tanyard. Called a Gloucestershire idyll, the novel has, like *Adam Bede* which followed in 1859, a *tradesman* hero. John Halifax rises, as the title promises, by hard work and good living, to be a gentleman, though its author does cheat a little, for John Halifax, though he has to work his way up from poverty and obscurity, was already the son of a gentleman. The novel, and the town it depicts, were famous by the 1880s. When Mrs Craik revisited Tewkesbury in 1886 she was warmly received; she died the following year, and as early as 1890 a commemorative plaque would be placed on the transept wall in the Abbey.

The Abbey, with its massive square Norman tower, is of course the most important single sight in Tewkesbury. Tewkesbury Abbey survived the Dissolution of the Monasteries, whereas the nearby abbeys of Evesham and Winchcombe did not, because the towns-people purchased it, for the sum of £453, from King Henry VIII. It was the first place that Ann showed Annie. After exploring it and the town and the Fair, Annie returned to Cheltenham as she had come, by train. She had first to travel on the branch line from Tewkesbury to Ashchurch, a village two miles to the east of the town, and then by main line to Cheltenham. Before the railways, Tewkesbury had been an important road link between West and North (as Mr Pickwick knew), and the town would have expected to retain this role when the Gloucester–Birmingham railway was built. But the line went instead through Cheltenham, developing rapidly at this time and four times bigger than Tewkesbury, which acquired only the small branch line from the junction at Ashchurch. As a result, it is one of the few towns in the area to have seen virtually no development during the nineteenth century. The nucleus of ancient buildings, already confined by the Abbey, the Abbey estates, and the meeting of the two rivers, Avon and Severn, is ringed by twentieth-century development.[53]

Ann, a regular user of the railway, both at Cheltenham and Tewkesbury, used it again for a final excursion before she returned home. At the beginning of October she accompanied her aunt to Crowle, where Sarah Martin, her aunt's younger sister, was housekeeper to the wealthy Caleb Baylis. From Worcester the road leads straight from the station to Crowle, five miles to the east. Around Crowle the villages have particularly colourful, double-barrel names – Upton Snodsbury, North Piddle, Flyford Flavell – and there is even a triple-barrel one, White Ladies Ashton, its name, like the Minories in London, inspired by a sisterhood: Ashton belonged to the nuns (the White Ladies) of nearby Worcester. Crowle itself was a small gloving village, *handy* for the gloving industry at Worcester, where a year earlier Ann had seen glovemaking demonstrated at the Exhibition. It was considered better to be a girl than a boy in Crowle: gloving was preferable work to labouring. To begin with, technology helped the cottage industry: sewing machines, which replaced handwork, hummed through the village. Then the humming stopped as advanced technology removed the industry from the cottage to the factory floor.

Saturday October 6th 1883. We started soon after 11, Uncle put us down before we reached the bridge, and we walked on into Tewkesbury. I bought a bottle scent for SM at C– [Sarah Martin at Crowle], and we went on to the station, had ½ hr to wait. Got to Worcester very comfortably, I got Aunt some wine and cake. Paul M. there with carriage to meet us, and we had a most enjoyable ride to Crowle.

The carriage, a novel ride for Ann after the usual butcher's cart or farmer's trap, pulled up at an imposing red brick house near the church. This was Kemerton House, the home of Caleb Baylis and his wife, both in their eighties. Mr Baylis had been a miller and baker at the watermill (now in ruins) at Lower Kemerton, not far from the home of Ann's grandmother. He had named his house in Crowle, which had no mill, after the village in which he had spent most of his life. Ann was clearly fond of the Baylises and had stayed with them before.

Mr B looking much as when I last saw him, Mrs B very much stouter, and so infirm. We sat and talked till tea-time, I helped clear, and went to the church with Sarah and Mr B. Tried the harmonium while they put altar-cloth and cover on. Sarah and I gathered some dahlias afterwards in their garden to go in vases. Later on Mr Baylis started the musical-box going. All to bed before 10, and I slept in the same little room again. (Uncle paid my fare there and back.)

124

The next day, Ann went twice to church with Caleb Baylis and her aunt. 'Mrs B gave us 1/- each for the collection . . . I gave Mrs Baylis my new photo, and she gave me hers and Mr B's, they all put their names in my book.' On the final day of the visit, Ann accompanied Mr Baylis, a principal landowner in the village, on a tour of his orchards, an activity in which she had some practice; she clearly enjoyed both the male company and the talk of farm matters.

Ann's Mr Baylis was a kind old man and genial host. *My* Caleb Baylis, researched locally, is a village benefactor. He presented the pulpit to the church just before Ann's visit in June 1883 (did he point it out to her?) and appropriately for a baker, he would endow charities in both villages known as *the Baylis Bread.*[54] On St Thomas's Day, December 21st, bread was distributed to any villagers in need of it; there was no means test. (Now the applicants receive from the Rector not bread, but vouchers to be spent at the village shop.) *Our* Caleb Baylis was a generous man for whom charity did begin at home: as Ann's visit shows, he treated his housekeeper's guests as his own. God-fearing and bountiful, he is almost a biblical figure – and indeed there is an Old Testament Caleb, in the Book of Numbers, who even speaks, obligingly, about – *bread!*[55]

> Monday October 8th. Gave Aunt a short ride in Mrs B's [wheel] chair, and I went with Mr B to his fields and through the orchards (trees loaded with fruit) . . . Said good-bye soon after 2, (Paul M. driving us to the station) we had ½ hr to wait, Uncle did not meet us at Tewkes. station, so I missed my train, found him at Black Bear . . .

Having located her uncle in Tewkesbury's oldest pub, Ann herself went back to Dumbleton. She had noticed the change in Mrs Baylis and sensed she would not see her again. In November she heard from Sarah Martin that Mrs Baylis was sinking fast after a stroke, and by the time she received this news Mrs Baylis had already died ('in the faith of her redeemer' affirms her gravestone) and was buried in the churchyard just behind Kemerton House. On a subsequent visit to Crowle, Sarah presented Ann with 'two very nice pocket handker-chiefs in memory of Mrs Baylis, and sent Mother some caps. Also a very pretty fan, I gave that to our Sarah.' She would see Caleb a few more times, at Crowle and at Robertsend, before his death in 1888. After the Baylis era, Sarah Martin stayed on at Crowle, where her brother Paul was churchwarden, and she continued to arrange the church flowers. Her solution to the problem of the single aging woman finding an emotional outlet in a small village was a novel one – 'parson-gazing'. She would sit at an upper window of the house 'parson-gazing', I was told by Crowle's oldest resident as if this were the most ordinary, most usual, of activities. From her window she had an excellent view of the Rector's route along the path linking the church to the parsonage a field away. Sarah lived with Paul and his wife at 'the big house', then moved to the black-and-white cottage in the village street, which is now called 'Martins' after them. Sarah, her brother and his wife, share a grave alongside that of the Baylises. The servers and the served lie side by side.

PART THREE
The Last Diaries

The Last Diaries

I

A Birth, a Will, and a Mystery 1884, 1885

The eighth diary ended soon after Ann's return from Crowle. The last entries were scrappy, the final three written untidily in purple crayon. The ninth diary is headed *1883 November*. But something has happened. This diary is different, totally unlike its eight predecessors with their small cramped script. The entries are no longer daily ones, and they are much shorter. In the first eight, Ann recorded every activity, every little task. The material at her disposal was limited, of a domestic or family nature, about house or garden or village, but it all went in. Now the diary entries become short and perfunctory jottings, set down at irregular intervals. The ninth diary and the next, final one, though identical in shape to the earlier ones, are much thicker and cover much longer periods. The first eight diaries covered less than two years. This ninth diary covers nearly three years (November 1883–August 1886). The last one runs from 1 September 1886 to 28 December 1891 (5 years) and is only half-filled.

There has to be some explanation for this change. It is not as if Ann gave up keeping a diary at this point. That would be easier to understand for it is something that often happens: adolescents, for example, often grow out of diary-writing, as the obsession with self and the need for self-expression and self-discovery recedes. Ann carried on, but in a different gear. A possible explanation might be her health. In the early diaries she had been exceptionally healthy, the robust country girl alongside the more delicate Annie Biscoe. Now there are occasional references to ill-health, the first one coming early in the ninth diary:

> December 11, 1883. Wind very high all night, regular hurricane. We had wretched night, I was very bilious, had some brandy.

The most likely explanation, however, seems to be that the *exchange* of diaries with Annie had ended, which meant the incentive to write fully, to account for and share every moment's activities (though not its thoughts and feelings) was lost, the imaginative impetus gone.

Annie's life had changed drastically in the past year – she had lost her father, become engaged, moved to a new home in a new town – while Ann's had remained static, remarkably unruffled, and it is not surprising that Annie, in amongst the disruptions, tired of the old girlish pastime. A joke heard on a television comedy show 'Only dull girls keep diaries; the others don't have time' is unkind but may have some application here. The taciturn Ann makes no reference to the marked change in diary-writing. The diary-exchanges may have stopped, but the friendship certainly had not.

February 1884 saw very rough weather, snow and hailstorms and rain. Ann paid two visits to Longdon (where her uncle was busy ploughing) and enjoyed seeing Caleb Baylis who stayed overnight at Robertsend after visiting his tenant at Castlemorton. In March she went to the doctor in Tewkesbury, but does not say why. 'Uncle and I locked up, and went to Tewkesbury for short time. I went to Dr D's,' and she went again two weeks later, from Dumbleton.

Went to Tewkesbury by 9 train, back by 1.30 to Beckford. (Dr gave me bottle medicine). Saw Uncle J [John Peart] for few minutes. Letter from Mrs McG., her nephew John obliged to be put in Hanwell Asylum.

Her previous entry had recorded the death of the Duke of Albany: 'Prince Leopold (Duke of Albany) died suddenly abroad (28th March 1884).' The haemophiliac son of Queen Victoria injured his knee in Cannes and died the following day from a brain haemorrhage. He had been there awaiting the birth of his second child.

At Dumbleton, another birth was awaited with the same sort of nervous anticipation. Unlike the birth of Louie's last child Joseph Harry, Ann gives no details of waiting for the confinement, only the result.

April 6th 1884. Louie's little daughter born about 3 a.m. (Tom fetched Mrs Hall [the nurse] from Broadway the previous evening.)

The expertise acquired at Longdon now came in useful. Ann could help at Joe's with the butter-making: 'I was up at Joe's all morning, made up 16 lbs. butter'; 'Up early, did the butter at Joe's', and she helped in the butcher's shop itself, writing out the price tags for the meat. She was thus more than usually busy when a plea arrived from Annie on April 17th, asking Ann to go to her at once. John had spent a very cold Easter weekend with the Biscoes. On his return he took to his bed, and the same day 'Wood brought at night the basket from Chelt. and John's clothes, also a note from Annie, asking me to go over; was very poorly herself, taken ill the evening John left (14th), had kind of fit, left her terribly weak, and eyes very bad.' Next day a letter from Mrs Biscoe arrived by post, 'telling me of Annie's illness, and asking me to go. I went by 12 train from Ashton. Found Annie looking very very sadly, Mrs B fairly well. Went to chemist's for Annie in afternoon and evening.'

Annie convalesced at Dumbleton, and Ann went to Cheltenham to keep Mrs Biscoe company and to help her with the lodgers in Annie's absence. One of the lodgers, Mr Luntz, invited the women to Gloucester, where he showed them over the cathedral and the town and gave them tea. Years later, Ann would view the cathedral in very different circumstances, and also another Gloucester building, close to the station, which she may have glimpsed from the train: a crescent-shaped building partly hidden by trees, its elegant façade belying its grim function, and in its grounds, a small redbrick chapel.

Ann was in festive mood, and so was Cheltenham:

May 15th 1884. The Yeomanry headed by Lord Fitzhardinge came into the town today for a week, flower show and great demonstrations in honour of the event, town decorated gaily.

While in Cheltenham, Ann tried out the different churches, not just the nearby St Luke's, but also the Parish Church (Cheltenham's only medieval church, and the one in which her parents had been married), St Matthew's and the Congregational Church, besides having 'a look at the Salvation Army'. She explored locally, going on foot to the fringe areas of the town, to Charlton Kings and to Pittville. One Sunday she and Mrs Biscoe walked out of Cheltenham, pausing at the cemetery 'to have a look round' there before walking on to Prestbury, at the foot of the Cotswolds and close to Cheltenham racecourse. Then a separate village, Prestbury is now virtually a suburb of Cheltenham, though it has managed to retain its village identity and its old buildings. Naturally the walkers gravitated towards the church, where Evensong was not quite over:

Recessional hymn sung, and incense burned at the close (Rogation Sunday). Very pretty church, every window painted, fine oil paintings too of scriptural subjects hung on walls.

Ann clearly liked the church, appreciating its richness and colour after the relative austerity of Dumbleton's walls and windows, but she may not have cared for the incense. Prestbury was, and is, High

131

Church, unlike most parish churches in the area. It had been restored in the 1860s (by the same G.E. Street who designed Toddington Church) at a time when there was a restoration of catholic practices. Ann with her reference to incense touches, quite unaware, on a particularly 'burning' issue. The Anglo-Catholic leanings of the Prestbury vicar were resisted by a minority of parishioners afraid of 'Popery' – their fears would not be allayed by his Irish wife and seven children – and in 1881 he was deprived of his living. He disregarded the sentence of the court, and did not resign till 1884, the year of Ann's visit.[56]

Ann returned home on May 21st, met by Annie 'looking much better', in time for the christening of Josephine Louisa Staight on Whit Sunday, June 1st. Joe and Louie had named their first two children – Louisa in 1881 and Joseph Harry in 1882 – after themselves. Both children had died one day old (in registration terms, 0 years). It was common practice for favoured names to be used again if a child died (remember Robert Staight's repeated use of the names 'Thomas Pitman'), and the new baby combined both parents' names. (Joe's names would be perpetuated in full when Josephine had *her* son, thirty-three years later.)

There was a lunch party for ten at Joe's that day, and the baby was christened after the children's service. 'Baby had lots of presents. Silver knife, fork and spoon in case, pretty little white frock, 5/- piece from Alf G., another from Aunt M., 6d from Charley [Moseley], some little chemises, a gold chain and seal for her ready when she is grown up.' Everyone at the Villa, and Cormell and Leslie from the mill, went to supper at Louie's. After the sad antecedents, there was relief and thanksgiving for the much-wanted, long-awaited baby.

Presents for her also arrived from the Wedgwoods. Although they were no longer in Dumbleton, they were in close touch with the old village and with the Staights, especially Joe, who regularly delivered meat and fruit to them at Stanton. The Wedgwood-Staight connection, largely commercial, partly social, refutes the notion that Gentry did not call on Trade, for after the Eyres at the Hall the Wedgwoods were undoubtedly next in the social hierarchy. Annie Wedgwood had been friendly with Sarah, often calling at the Villa to talk to her. Anne Sophia (always called Annie Wedgwood in the diaries) married Wilfred Baugh Allen in December 1883, coming to the Villa on December 12th 'to say good-bye'. Sarah Staight went to see her presents, which included 'a pretty table toilet set' from Joe and Louie and 'a pair of flower pot vases' from Ann's parents (who also gave

her some of Mrs Dunn's things, a toasting-fork and six china plates).
Now, with baby Josephine's christening the Wedgwoods responded
with their presents, Mrs Wedgwood sending 'a complete bassinet' on
April 16th, and her daughter Henrietta sending 'a pretty robe' even
earlier.

The youngest Wedgwood daughter, Eliza (who was just younger
than Ann), was one of the soloists at the June concert in Dumbleton:

Annie played twice Schottische* (Bon Soir) and Sleigh Race Galop, and sang
'Jessie's Dream'. Miss Eliza Wedgwood sang twice. Mrs W. Jones's brother
brought two young gents from Oxford, who caused much amusement with
their comic singing. I wore my new dress . . .

Eliza would spend the rest of her life at Stanton, first at the Court and
then, after the death of her 'extremely handsome and demanding
mother', at a cottage higher up in the village. At her mother's death
she came into her own, and is depicted as 'A Cotswold Character' in
the memoirs of Lady Cynthia Asquith[57] who grew up at nearby
Stanway House. Eliza became a well-known local figure, kind and
eccentric, nicknamed the Queen of Stanton, where 'she was as great
a benefactor of the local people as of the birds she also loved.'

*   *   *   *

Wake Sunday on July 6th introduced a time of holidays and
excursions, with almost everyone making use of the railways and the
good weather to visit relatives or to have a change of scene. John
combined business with pleasure, going by excursions to a Wol-
verhampton exhibition, to the Royal Show at Shrewsbury and to the
Birmingham Onion Fair. Mrs Biscoe went by excursion to London.
Annie could hardly remain alone in the little house with two male
lodgers, so Ann stayed with her at Bath Parade. August 4th was the
Bank Holiday, and the two girls planned an excursion for themselves:

August 4th 1884. Bank Holiday.
We were up at 6, started at 7 to Lansdown Sta[tion], thinking to go to
Weston-super-Mare, but there were such crowds of people, train crammed
full, so we waited till 9.30 and went to the Forest of Dean, saw the excursion
for Tewkesbury Regatta start while we were waiting, a lot of people went

* The Schottische, a piano solo, was originally the Germanic idea of what a Scottish dance was
like. In the 19th century it was a popular dance.

there (Tom and John went from home). We went to Lydbrook Junction, tried to reach Symond's Yat (a hill)* but it was so hot we rested in fields instead, had dinner (we took with us); by 3.30 train went to Speech-house.† lovely place, had nice tea at the hotel and afterwards walked back to station through Forest, reached Bath Parade at 10.

The two girls have acquired greater freedom since the day when Mrs Biscoe rebuked them for going off to London with a man in his carriage. For one thing, the railways had transformed travelling – and travelling conventions. The excursion, two girls going off alone, is perhaps less surprising than their being left alone in a small house with the lodgers, though both men were away for the holiday weekend itself. Other excursions by railway took Sarah to an inland port and to a regicide's castle – to Sharpness on the Severn Estuary and to Berkeley Castle where Edward II was murdered. Louie took her baby to Dorking to see friends and family; the Rector took the choir to the Tewkesbury Abbey Festival. The holiday period was rounded off by a good harvest but a poor Dumbleton show: 'not a very good Show, nor large company . . .' Harvest Festival and Ann's birthday ended the festivities and the summer.

Winter began early that year, with Grandma Peart ill at Kemerton, Uncle Tom Staight 'very sadly indeed' at Childswickham. Mrs Smith at the Bank Farm died a month after giving birth to a baby daughter: christening followed funeral.

November 30th. Miss Eliza Wedgwood, her little nephew and governess, and some of the servants drove to our church this morning. (Small-pox at Stanton.) Very wintery day, snow and rain afternoon and evening . . .

* * * *

It seems likely that Annie Biscoe derived spiritual sustenance from her friendship with Ann, from the Staights generally, who all shared, like most country people, a simple but unwavering Christian faith. Or perhaps Cheltenham deserves some credit. It was enjoying a religious revival – its many churches, except for the medieval parish church of St Mary's and one or two modern ones, are all Victorian – largely due to the influence of one man, the Rev. Francis Close (commemorated today in the name of one of Cheltenham's public schools‡) and this is probably why Tennyson, who came here often in the years 1846–50 to visit his mother, had dismissed the town as 'a

* More accurately, where the River Wye flows between a break or gateway in the hills.
† The Speech House Hotel, in the centre of the Forest of Dean, so named because it was the Verderers' Court. The railway no longer exists.
‡ Dean Close School. The Rev. Close later became Dean of Carlisle.

polka parson-worshipping place'. Cheltenham, elegant, affluent, leisure-loving, with its spa, its expensive shops and hotels and racecourse – racing started at Cheltenham in 1831 – seems an unlikely spiritual centre (I do not think it can be said to have remained one) but even George Eliot alluded to this centre of religious fervour in *Middlemarch* (published 1871–2) where the troubled Bulstrode proposes a visit to Cheltenham to his wife: 'We will make a journey to Cheltenham in the course of a month or two . . . There are great spiritual advantages to be had in that town along with the air and the waters, and six weeks there will be eminently refreshing to us.'[58] From the Staights, from Cheltenham, or from both, Annie Biscoe assimilated some of these spiritual advantages. She was baptised in Cheltenham in March 1885 in St Luke's church, one of the batch of new Victorian churches in the town, and situated only a few hundred yards from her home in Bath Parade. The following day she was confirmed there.

Ann had left her mother ill in bed to witness these ceremonies, and she hurried home after them. Unfortunately, and not for the last time, Ann Staight Senior had to endure a major bereavement while she was ill herself. 'March 27, 1885. Grandma Peart died about 1 pm, aged 89 years and 9 months. Jas. Goodall rode over to tell us after tea. She was as well as usual early same morning, but changed for worse after . . .' She was buried, not at Kemerton, but over the hill from Dumbleton at the tiny Norman church of Great Washbourne where she had spent much of her life. Ann's mother was slow to recover, not coming downstairs till mid-April and it would be mid-June before she went to church again.

Before then there was to be another murmur of Dissent in the village. In May 1885 two funerals on consecutive days were organised rather differently:

> May 6th 1885. Mrs Dudfield buried at Dumbleton this afternoon. Father and Tom, Mr Burge, and the bailiff were pall-bearers. I went with Nellie Walker. Sis made a cross.

Next day

> May 7th. Wm Green buried this afternoon by some Dissenting Minister, they did not enter the church.

Most country parishes, as Professor Mingay[59] observes in his book *Rural Life in Victorian England*, came to have two ministers, an Anglican and a Nonconformist. The former's 'origins, education and

135

tastes were those of the gentry, [while] the latter sprang from a lower level in the social scale. The Anglican dined with the squire, while the Dissenter went to tea with the tenant.' Dumbleton was a village of tenants, yet there is no evidence of a Dissenting minister residing in the village. Ann's attitude to Nonconformity – made clear in her dismissive reference – was a typical one in the village, and is not fair to the Dissenters, some of whom were most distinguished people: Mrs Gaskell is a notable example.

* * * *

Meanwhile, at Bath Parade, the two male lodgers had left, and in November there were new arrivals: 'A widow lady (Mrs Thomas), son and daughter came in to stay.' By mid-December the news was grave: 'Their inmates left previous week, behaved *very* badly.'

The Biscoes did not last very long in Cheltenham, not strong enough, either mentally or physically, to deal with lodgers without the help and protection of a man. Annie's fiancé was the obvious person to assist her and her mother, but he was elsewhere (and Ann had ominously made no mention of him in recent entries). In this predicament, there was only one solution. Male protection was what was needed, and although Annie's brother Henry had not been entirely adequate on previous occasions, he fulfilled at least their basic requirement. His mother and sister had been in Cheltenham for less than two years. In April, the little house was sold by auction, the furniture and luggage despatched to Kent. Ironically, as the Biscoes packed up to go to Henry's protection, Henry himself was very ill with congestion of the lungs. After a farewell visit to Dumbleton, they set off for Chatham to Henry, who came himself to Dumbleton in June for a few days' holiday or convalescence, bringing his camera with him – the only one mentioned in the diaries (everyone was still going to the studios to have their portraits taken).

23rd June. HB took photographed front of house, also shop, brought his 'machine' with him.

Ann's inverted commas and uncertain wording convey the newness, the strangeness, of this phenomenon.

There was another sale by auction in June, that of Grandma Peart's property:

Uncle John bought house etc. for £300; our Joe, Kemerton field for £330, and Mr G. Mumford, Overbury, field for £400.

What prompted Ann to make a Will at this time? Her grand-mother's death did not materially affect her circumstances; probably her sole gain was a gold ring set with a large coral stone which she mentions receiving. The large number of recent deaths may have made her think about her own. Did she have some premonition that she would die young? On August 10th, 1885 she made her Will, using one of Joe's blank invoice forms. Apart from the novelty of an illustrated Will – and the novelty of a symbol of male strength (a large steer) adorning a document concerned, after all, with female frailty – the Will holds no surprises. The principal beneficiary is Sarah. Legally, the Will was invalid, as it was not witnessed. However, as we shall see later, its chief request was honoured at Ann's death, though in circumstances vastly different to any envis-aged by Ann when she made it. The writing is more laboured, less assured, than the fluent script of the diaries, and this is not surprising, for the document was written by Joe, in a new role as Ann's amanuensis. He wrote it down at his sister's dictation, and kept it thereafter, for it passed with his papers to his son and surfaced not with the diaries at the remote Herefordshire farmhouse, but at the home of Pitman Staight's daughter in Stow-on-the-Wold.

There is no mention of the Will in Ann's diary, no mention of self at all on that day. The following night was a sleepless one, not because of the Will-making, but because there was a rail excursion to London at dawn the next morning:

> August 11th. Had no sleep all night, up at 2. Tom called Joe, we had breakfast, packed up and drove to Ashton by 4.13. Tom brought trap back, Joe, John and self went to London (St Pancras) a very roundabout way, but pretty country. Arrived there 9.45, Mrs McG. met us, we called on Fanny [Staite], left our luggage and went on to the Inventions.

This international exhibition of inventions and music at South Kensington had been formally opened by the Prince of Wales on 4 May 1885, and it would close in early November. The Staights were among the three and a half million people to visit it. (Sarah and Louie would also go, by day excursion, in August, and Tom went on a choir outing, all of them rising at 3 a.m. and returning at 2.30 a.m. the following morning.)

That evening, Joe returned home while Ann and John stayed on with the McGlinchys. While Mr McGlinchy took John to Blackwall 'to see the ships', Ann went to Enfield to visit her old 'particulars' and, of course, the cemetery. On her return to Jenner Road she found a letter from Annie 'asking us down, Mrs B. very ill'. She

M.

Bot. of J. H. STAIGHT,

Family Butcher,

DUMBLETON, near EVESHAM.

PRIME OX TONGUE.   CORNED BEEF.

My Will. August 10th 1885

I should wish to be buried at Dumbleton, & the expenses of my funeral to be paid out of what money I have, & also a nice gravestone [set up], & besides my own name put on; those of my brother Edward & Uncle Henry too; &, after this is paid for, any money should remain, I leave it to my only sister, also my clothes, books, jewellery, &c. except the Guinea I wear to Annie Bisvoe & anything else my sister may choose to give her, my silver brooch with pebbles to my Mother, my other silver

brooch to little Annie Chidley (Mark Attwool grand child).

My brother Tom to have my new Bible, John my Dictionary & small Album, my dear Father to have anything he may choose of mine, & Baby Josephine some of my toys. my sister must give my little Reynolds divide not named, very little Reynolds divide

Signed this 10th

August 10th 1885

Anne Straight

Ann's Will, 1885

went at once and stayed overnight, while John went back to the Inventions, and to the Globe Theatre. Mrs McGlinchy's niece Fanny called again (was she pursuing John?). There will be more news of Fanny later.

In Dumbleton, Mrs Eyres called in person from the Hall to borrow the Villa's cake tins for the next festivity. Here is a nice cameo – the lady of the manor needing to borrow kitchen utensils from the village blacksmith – and shows a surprising instance of interdependence between the two private householders in the village.

August 21st. Miss Eyres' birthday (4 years old)
Tea treat for all schoolchildren, mothers, widows, teachers, choir, ringers, etc. Miss Tyrrell and I went. The tent was put up near the Hall. Toddington band in attendance; a Punch and Judy show; some balloons were sent off by Mr Sharpe, and a lot of prizes given to the children, dancing for the older folks.

Ann and her Aunt Sarah set off for Longdon after the Flower Show, driving themselves there with old Polly. At Robertsend Ann found her old friend Boxer 'very bad with distemper'. Not a stranger to underdoggery herself, Ann always made friends with the dogs – Gypsy at Enfield, Boxer at Robertsend. In September, back at home, she recorded laconically –

Letter from Aunt S., her foot worse, and the dog dead.

Aunt Sarah was soon to be very ill with erysipelas in her face and foot (Ann would be summoned back to nurse her), but she was tougher than Boxer, and lived.

*　　*　　*　　*

It is around this time that an element of mystery creeps into the diary, in amongst the wholly unmysterious entries relating to family and to village life.

October 21st. Joe went to Gloucester on the Jury.
[He returned home late the next night with two other Dumbleton jurors, C. Grinnall and James Taylor.]

October 29th. Liberal meeting in the school-room this evening, passed off quietly.

Nov. 5th PP) (Nov. 1st. Sunday.) (Dec. 2nd.)

Nov 7th. My jacket came by parcel post (quite a *miss fit*).

Letter from Mrs Drinkwater (late of College Farm) to Father and Mother about her son, who was struck dead by lightning in America a short time ago.

Nov 11th. Father hired Wood's van and horse to take them all to Tewkesbury to receive the money from Kemerton property. Uncle and Aunt M. [Moseley] left their horse and trap here, and went on with Father and Mother, Aunt Sarah and Lizzie Peart. All the Uncles Peart met them there. Finished cider making today. *Sent to Annie . . .*

There has been no mention of Annie's fiancé for a long time. A letter had arrived for Annie from Iowa in February 1884, forwarded from Enfield. In April she had written to Ann with 'still better news from A- this week' (presumably A- is America, where Mr Paul was known to be). Ann herself had written to him on April 6th, straight after hearing this 'better news'. After that, there is silence about him until this cryptic November 5th 1885 entry, a year and a half later. This is the last mention of PP. When had the engagement ended? The dates alongside November 5 (November 1st, and December 2nd) are quite unexplained.

There is another set of unexplained dates beside the November 20th entry.

Nov 20. Had Budget from 54. (*Nov 23rd,*
                 Jan 17th, Dec 24th)

and shortly afterwards a date underlined twice, normally a sign of an extra-special occasion.

Dec 3rd. John went to Birmingham show, and bought some ironmongery.

Dec 4th. Voting day. Mr Yorke successful. Father would *not* vote.

<u>Dec 9th.</u> Sarah went to Tewkesbury. Very cold and frosty. Mr Witcombe of Childswickham killed in afternoon while unloading some straw at his house, some of the boltings on which he was standing gave way, and he fell on his head, and w~~as killed~~ died in a few minutes.

Dec 10th. Sarah in bed to cure a cold. *Very* sharp weather. Boys *full* of horses *all* day. Rev. Barlow, wife and son called with a pair going to Tewkesbury, couldn't get along. They waited in front room.

There is a lot to look at here. Just as the Liberal meeting in (ultra-Conservative) Dumbleton is followed closely by unexplained dates and underlinings, so here the political is again juxtaposed with the personal, as Mr Yorke's election success is followed by a date twice-underlined. Mr Yorke's success warrants amplification. He was Conservative candidate for the Tewkesbury division (which includes Dumbleton), and won by a small majority of 182. Apart from Cheltenham, which was and is notoriously Conservative, all the other Gloucestershire constituencies went to the Liberals. This was the first occasion on which the 'counties' as opposed to the 'boroughs' had the vote, and was thus a historic occasion. Tewkesbury had been the scene of ugly scuffles on the evening of the polling. The *Evesham Journal*,[60] appalled by the goings-on, had a drastic remedy to propose: 'An election without politics is not to be thought of . . . an election without excessive drinking can be practically secured by the temporary closing of public-houses.'

Ann alludes to the election but is clearly preoccupied by other issues. It is December 9th, not December 4th (Voting Day) which is doubly underlined. It does not seem likely that either the weather or Mr Witcombe's sad end at nearby Childswickham (where, incidentally, the Reverend Barlow, who called at the shop next day, was Vicar) provide the answer. For the first time in her diaries Ann is making notes which have meaning only for her. The intials PP and the dates alongside suggest some relationship between him and Ann – a connection sustained by letters rather than meetings. Was he explaining to her the breakdown of his relationship with Annie, or trying to renew the old one with Ann? This is pure conjecture, and the dates could refer to something quite different – to a series of illnesses, a menstrual cycle. Ann, like any diarist simple or sophisticated, does not tell all. Between the lines of the open, public record are signs of another, secret, private life.

*   *   *   *

II
Two Weddings 1886

'Woman, before marriage, is a delightful anticipation;
woman, after marriage, is a fact, and facts are stubborn things.'
(Source unknown)
Written by a Peart relation in Lily Staight's album

Ann is no help at all in charting the relationship between Sarah and Leslie Legge. In the early diaries she cited his every visit, and his interest in Sarah was quite undisguised, as he followed her outside to shut up the poultry for the night, sat alone with her in the kitchen or front room, and so on. He had continued to visit regularly with his friend Cormell Morris, but these visits were often to see their friends Tom and John. By the ninth diary, by 1884, all such details go unrecorded.

How Leslie came to be in Dumbleton at all is something of a mystery (like Elsie at Ashton) but Louie is a likely link (two Legge relations witnessed her London wedding). Leslie came from Fulham (he was christened in Walham Green church there in 1856) and in 1873 he was apprenticed to Charles Morris of Dumbleton Mill for four years to learn 'farming, millering, and baking'. Leslie's apprenticeship had cost eighty pounds, paid in two instalments. The *Indenture* document, which prohibited among other things fornication, marriage, and the setting up of dice tables during the apprenticeship, was signed by Charles Morris, by Leslie and his father. Legge was (and is) the family name of the Earls of Dartmouth, but Leslie's origins were less illustrious: his father Joseph was an upholsterer, but must have been moderately well off for he could afford to buy a private plot in Brompton Cemetery for the family grave (he is buried in it with one of his children).[61] Joseph was married at least three times. One of his wives was a Miss Leslie from Scotland, after whom his son Leslie was named. Of Joseph's thirteen children, only three boys (Leslie, Joseph and Willy) grew to adulthood. A photograph shows Leslie standing arm in arm with brother Joseph. Their stance would seem to indicate a certain levity, but there is absolutely no levity about their expressions. With their long faces (in both senses) and best Sunday suits, they are differentiated only by Joseph's walrus moustache; the clean-shaven Leslie looks more like a clerical worker than a miller.

Leslie stayed on at Dumbleton Mill when his apprenticeship was ended, and was clearly very happy there. The mill is about a mile from the Villa, down Nutmeadow and set back from the Sedgeberrow–Winchcombe road, nearer to Wormington than to Dumbleton. The mill-race waters are drawn from the little River Isbourne, which flows north – something rivers rarely do – through Winchcombe and Toddington to meet the River Avon right in the middle of its great curve through Evesham. Between Evesham and Winchcombe (where at different times the little river fed silk and paper mills as well as corn ones) there were four corn mills. There has been one at Dumbleton since before the Domesday Book. The mill was partly rebuilt in Victorian times and is still standing though the adjacent bakery building has gone. The machinery inside the redbrick building, though inactive today, is structurally sound, missing only some of the cogs (made from local apple wood) in its great water wheel.[62]

Charles Morris was an old man, and much of his work – farming, milling and baking – was undertaken respectively by his son Cormell, Leslie, and by a baker who like Leslie boarded with the Morris family. Leslie and Cormell were contemporaries, and inseparable. Leslie's courtship of Sarah Staight was almost inevitable: the friendship of the two men at the Mill with the two blacksmiths made contact with her easy and frequent. Village courtships were usually long ones, and this one was no exception, protracted and not without turbulence. As the number of young unmarried girls in Dumbleton was extremely limited, the marriage was a case of propinquity.

During 1884, Leslie made occasional entries in a tiny (5 × 8 cm) paperback diary. Much smaller than a regular pocket diary, *The Reading Calendar* was published as publicity material by the Reading biscuit manufacturers Huntly and Palmers. Each month occupies a double page, with one line for each day. By necessity, Leslie's entries could not be lengthy ones, and provide a sharp contrast to Ann's early home-made diaries.

The entries are only occasional ones, but despite their brevity, the progress of the relationship is economically conveyed. Sunday was a good day for developments (and is indicated by an S below):

January	
15	S.E.S. v. M.A.M.
March	
20	A visit from Sarah
May	
25 S	Saw S. Savage
26	Spoke to S in a serious manner
June	
1 S	Christening
15 S	Went to Toddington Church with J and T Staight
22 S	Wrote to Mrs B and to JH
July	
20 S	Fell out
August	
3 S	Toddington
9 S	Wrote to Mrs B
September	
1	Fell in again
7 S	Doubtful
11	Went to Cheltenham

14 S	Wrote to Mrs B. Very promising S
December	
7 S	Spiffin
8	Hair cut
14 S	Mrs B

The miller in literature has been depicted as roguish and philandering – 'crafty and dusty and powerful . . . much too successful with women, even – or especially – married ones.'[63] Leslie was not at all like this (whoever Mrs B is!), lacking the temperament necessary for a life of intrigue, whether in mill or bedroom. High romance is reduced to 'falling in' and 'falling out', and rates the same space as a hair cut! On the day he 'weighs' the two women against each other, there was a concert at Dumbleton and possibly he could view both women together at that event. The same day Sarah had visited his employer's wife at the Mill (Mrs Morris was ill with bronchitis), and this would have been a point in her favour. Sarah's visit to Leslie in March was not mentioned by Ann, who was more concerned with illness than romance that day: 'Grandma suffering with bronchitis. Prince Leopold (Duke of Albany) died suddenly abroad.' Ann made *no* entry in her diary on the day on which Leslie presumably spoke of marriage to Sarah. So the year had ended well for Leslie. *Spiffin* (or spiffing or spiving), a colloquialism in general use by 1879, has the same meaning as 'super'.

At the end of the little diary there are three blank pages for notes and Leslie used part of this space to record some 1885 happenings. The first few entries make no mention of Sarah, then there is a crisis: 'Ceased to visit April 19–June 7.' Ann (who has not mentioned him since the Christmas Day festivities of 1884) reported that he was at the Villa for tea on June 21st 1885, confirming that the breach was healed by then. In August, after more letters to Mrs B and more hair cuts, Leslie broke the news: 'Wrote to Mrs B Aug 10th telling her of S.' Mrs B, whoever she is, is mentioned no more.

1885 was a good year for weddings. In April Joe's friend Alf Goodall married Miss Day at Eckington; Sarah's friend Nellie Drinkwater married Harry Panting at Ashton. On July 23rd, Ann recorded the marriage of Princess Beatrice, the ninth and youngest child of Queen Victoria, to Prince Henry of Battenburg: Tennyson,[64] the Poet Laureate, marked the occasion ('The Mother weeps / At that white funeral of the single life / Her maiden daughter's marriage') with a poem which makes *dizzyingly* clear the princess's predicament, common to so many Victorian girls, the conflict between personal fulfilment and family obligation:

144

But moving thro' the Mother's home, between
The two that love thee, lead a summer life,
Sway'd by each Love, and swaying to each Love,
Like some conjectured planet in mid heaven
Between two Suns . . .

In August, Alice Anderson, a childhood friend of Ann's, wrote to say that both she and her brother were shortly to be married. (She, like Sarah Young, would be a widow within a year.) From Leslie's point of view, by far the most significant wedding was that of his friend Cormell to Miss Augusta Cole at Sedgeberrow in November, which no doubt expedited his own intentions.

On January 3rd, 1886, Ann recorded Leslie's presence at breakfast at the Villa. This was unusual, and there were more unusual happenings in February.

Feb. 5. Sis and I went to Tewkesbury to do some shopping, by 3.30 train and back by 8, put old Polly in at Beckford Inn.

Feb 6. Sis and I went to Cheltenham by first train and back by last to see about dresses and bonnets etc . . .

The sisters never shop together: one stays at home when the other goes out. *Two* consecutive shopping expeditions *together* leave one in no doubt about the special nature of the purchases. The first wedding present arrived on February 12th: Mrs Biscoe sent by rail a pair of 'handsome tapestry curtains'. On February 14th, St Valentine's Day, Sarah and Leslie go out together publicly for the first time, driving to Broadway to see the Moseleys. The same day their banns are published for the first time in Dumbleton church – the first formal reference we have in the diaries to the forthcoming marriage.

Ann's reticence about the engagement (we never learn how long it lasted) shows clearly her resistance to it: she did not like Leslie (though she never says so), and did not want to lose Sarah. While she could feel no great delight, her family do not appear to have been enthusiastic either. The Legges maintain that the Staights did not regard Leslie as good enough for their Sarah. On top of the instinctive wariness towards anyone who was not local, there was also a suspicion of town people still shown today in rural areas. (Although I live in a city, because of my Ann-like origins I am not regarded as a 'Townie', and on Ann's territory I have been exhorted: 'Beware of Townies!' or 'It don't do no good marrying a Townie!') Leslie's London origins, capping his lack of wealth and his lack of drive (he was a placid, unambitious man) made him appear unpromising husband material. There was also a political difference: while the Staights were staunch Conservatives, Leslie was a Liberal – that is, until, years later, Lloyd George offended him.

Whatever else marriage to Leslie would entail, it meant leaving Dumbleton, for he could hardly take his bride to lodge at the Mill where he had lived with the Morrises for so many years. It was necessary to find another mill. In February 1886 Leslie finalised a rental agreement with a Worcestershire baronet, Sir Francis Salwey Winnington, of Stanford-on-Teme, for 'a malt house and water corn mill' on the River Teme between Martley and Clifton-on-Teme.

Ann's diary space for February is devoted almost exclusively to Sarah's wedding presents. In this triangle – Ann, Sarah, Leslie Sarah is the only one for whom no diaries survive. All we have of hers (appropriately for such a practical person) is a small notebook containing various lists, of presents, of glass and crockery, of books, besides the contents of Leslie's trunk and his Gladstone bag. It is interesting to compare the two versions of the wedding presents, the different emphases and details showing the sisters' different predilections. Where Sarah writes down 'Pincushion Mrs Fisher', Ann is more lavish: 'A very pretty pincushion, velvet and beads.' Amongst the presents were *five* brackets. These strange objects were small, often ornamental, shelves on which the vast collection of knick-knacks common to all Victorian households could be accommodated. These could be quite plain, or elaborate in different ways: Mrs Morris's bracket had a bevelled mirror and small coloured glass vase attached, and Mrs Fawdry's pair of brackets were in 'cardinal plush and green plush'. Amongst the bracket-givers were Mrs Wedgwood and Eliza; her two married daughters had also sent presents (a fancy mirror from the former Annie Wedgwood, and a gold brooch from Mrs Hoskins).

The most interesting of Sarah's presents were two pictures. These were reproductions of two popular paintings by John Everett Millais, then at the very height of his popularity (in 1885 he was the first artist to be made a baronet). Sarah's description of the two paintings is her own version, and not quite accurate.

Mrs Howlett two pictures.
(Hussar taking leave of his sweetheart,
& French lady tying white scarf round Hugionot's arm)
& Photos of herself and Mr Howlett.

(Sarah does not always cross her 't's, and doesn't cross them here, so *The Huguenot* in her version looks like 'French lady lying while scarf round Hugionot's arm'.) Its correct title is 'A Huguenot, on St Bartholomew's Day, refusing to shield himself from danger by wearing the Roman Catholic badge', and Sarah's 'Hussar taking leave of his sweetheart' was in fact *The Black Brunswicker* (1860), a later painting than *The Huguenot* (1851) but a deliberate attempt to repeat its success by using threatened lovers in a historical setting, their passion made respectable for the sensitive Victorians by their remoteness in time *and* place. Mrs Craik had been highly impressed by the *Huguenot* painting, and allows her Tewkesbury-based narrator, Phineas Fletcher, in *John Halifax, Gentleman* (published 1857) to have seen it and to refer to it at some length:

> He [John Halifax] *spoke gently, laying his hand on his wife's shoulder, and looking down on her with that peculiar look which he always had when telling her things that he knew were sore to hear. I never saw that look on any living face save John's; but I have seen it once in a picture of two Huguenot lovers. The woman is trying to fasten round the man's neck the white badge that will save him from the massacre (of St Bartholomew) – he, clasping her the while, gently puts it aside – not stern, but smiling. That quiet, tender smile, firmer than any frown, will, you feel sure, soon control the woman's anguish, so that she will sob out – any faithful woman would – 'Go, die! Dearer to me than even thyself are thy honour and thy duty!'*
> *When I saw this noble picture, it touched to the core this old heart of mine – for the painter, in that rare expression, might have caught John's.*[65]

And not only Mrs Craik. The painting was already so famous by 1875 that Robert Browning could incorporate it without annotation along with other famous pictures into a description of an inn's parlour

> On a sprig-pattern-papered wall there brays
> Compliant to sky Sir Edwin's dripping stag;
> His couchant coast-guard creature corresponds;
> They face the Huguenot and Light o'the World.[66]

The two Millais pictures make apt wedding presents in that both portray handsome couples and ardent young love. Less appropriate is the doomed quality of that love, the life of the man in both pictures, in both situations, being at risk. Sarah was not a romantic person (she was too practical for that) but she would enjoy the analogy of the handsome young lovers, and would particularly appreciate the garden setting of *The Huguenot*, the detailed flower painting of nasturtiums and canterbury bells at the foot of the ivy-clad wall. Ann was less interested in paintings than in books: she would have preferred to *read* about the Huguenot. She dismissed the gift in her diary as 'A pr. of pictures', and was more appreciative of

Miss Meyer's book rack, 'a nice, useful little present.' We have not hitherto associated Sarah with books, but that she had some to fill the rack we shall see presently.

It was a pre-Lenten winter wedding. The winter of 1885–6 had been a severe one, with heavy snowstorms and freezing temperatures in January and February. 'The old woman picking her geese' is an old country description of a snowstorm. Did the poultry-picking Sarah murmur the local variant (recited by her niece Josie years later)

> *Old Mother Goose is a-picking her geese*
> *And selling the feathers a penny a piece*

as she watched the snow and waited for her wedding?
It was still snowing on the eve of the wedding.

> March 1st. 1886. Bitterly cold snowy day. Annie sent me by post a very nice writing-case at my request, as a present from myself to Sis (with stationery etc. inside). Sis went to Evesham in afternoon (had pony to Beckford station), brought back wedding-cake from there (Willis from Tewkesbury made it and sent by rail); she bought herself some little bronze low shoes, and silk stockings for the wedding, and brought and gave me a nice gold brooch. Joe and LL here in the evening, the latter left the mill that day, and stayed at Joe's all night.

At this stage in the diaries we have ceased to expect detailed information. The entry for Sarah's wedding day is in fact longer than usual, more than half a page, but there is no big heading or underlined date to mark its importance.

> March 2nd 1886.
> Fine day, but very cold and dirty. Sis and LL were married by Mr W Jones at 9.30. The fly came at 9.15, Tom, Sis and self rode up in it to church, LL waiting in church, and Joe outside, for us; a lot of the villagers there (Mrs WJ away at her mother's). The bells rang most of the day.
> Sis and LL left at 10.50 for Evesham station, thence to Reading and Bournemouth. Postman not here till after, brought a letter from Mrs Goodall, and 6 lovely little salt-spoons. (LL gave Sis (Monday night) brooch and earrings, gold set with pearls). Mr W. Jones sent Sis (just after the wedding) a nice book (The New Testament with Commentary). I took Betty Millen a bit of cake etc. in afternoon, and Mrs Fisher. Joe took Mrs Walker some as he went home after dinner . . .

The entry continues with more present-listing. Donors did not worry too much about getting their presents to the couple before the ceremony. Joe and Louie would buy their present on March 4th, Tom and John not till March 22nd. 'John went to Tewkesbury in afternoon, bought 4 electro-plated table-spoons and 4 dessert spoons to give Sarah from Tom and himself.' Here is an early instance (buying silver plate and not silver) of the trait which would later earn John the nickname of Pincher Staight.

Charles Staight recorded the marriage (Ann, Tom and Joe had been the witnesses) in the *Evesham Journal*,[67] where it appeared on March 6th:

> At the Parish Church, Dumbleton, by the Rev. F. Willoughby Jones, rector, Leslie Legge, to Sarah Elizabeth, elder daughter of Charles P. Staight.

Two other Dumbleton residents featured in the same issue, not in a nuptial context, but *on charges of cruelty*. James Taylor of the Dumbleton Brickworks was charged by an officer of the Society (not yet a royal one) for the Prevention of Cruelty to Animals with working a horse in an unfit state (he was better with humans, having been helpful when the Staights' trap had overturned nearby); and Helen Green, formerly a servant at Mr Corbett's, was caught beating and torturing a cat.

Sarah and Leslie returned from their honeymoon a week later. The weather continued to be severe.

> March 16th. Very cold snowy day. Sarah invited a lot of folks to tea and spend the evening, but nobody came except Mrs Goodall (came by 1.30 train to Beckford and walked up in all the snow and dirt) . . .

It is tempting to picture Leslie and Sarah going off together to their new mill and their new life in the same way as Tennyson's miller:

> *Arise, and let us wander forth*
> *To yon old mill across the wolds;*
> *For look, the sunset, south and north,*
> *Winds all the vale in rosy folds . . .*[68]

The reality was very different, and much more prosaic. The business of moving involved nearly everyone. It was, after all, no mean feat moving from one rural area to another. From Dumbleton to Ham Mill is about 26 miles. It took most of a day to do the journey with horse and cart. Indeed, on one occasion the journey took *twelve* hours, but this was an exceptionally slow one, explained to some extent by Ann's diary entry: 'Leslie came here with the old mare and heavy cart, fat pig alive, and 6 grown-up chickens. Left home at 9 a.m., reached here 9 p.m.' The obvious solution was to use the railways. But Ham Mill, although it is only ten miles from Worces-

Left, Leslie Legge (with his brother
Joseph); below, Dumbleton Mill

Right, Ham Mill; below left, Sarah; below right, Nancy and Ruth Legge (*c.* 1891)

ter, is remote from railway services. This fact is strikingly apparent on any map of the city of Worcester, where one observes at once the inverted Y-shape formed by the railway lines: one line goes north-east to Droitwich and Birmingham, the second south-west to Great Malvern and Ross-on-Wye, the third south-east to Cheltenham and Evesham. There is no line going in a north-westerly direction, the direction of the mill.

Sarah saw her new home for the first time on March 22nd. She and Leslie went by train to Worcester where Joe, who had left earlier with the dog cart and Leslie's new horse, met the train and drove them on to the mill. From Worcester to Martley the land is flat and thick with fruit orchards. (A mile along this road, at Upper Broadheath, is the modest brick cottage where the composer Edward Elgar had been born in 1857.) After Martley with its *red* church the landscape changes to one of rolling hills. From the Cotswolds and the Vale one looks across to the Malvern Hills to the west, where they look expected, familiar, forming a distant hilly backcloth. From the high ground near Martley the perspective is utterly different: you see the Malverns end-on, away to the south, varying shapes and heights, in differing, darkening shades of indigo and violet. They rise suddenly, mysteriously, out of the flat plain. The effect is so startlingly different that they scarcely seem to be the same range of hills as that wavy blue line seen from the Cotswold heights.

Leaving behind this spectacular sight, the road drops down to the river Teme at Ham Bridge. Just as it is difficult to think of Louie's Surrey Wotton without the Evelyn family, in the same way the River Teme is inextricably linked with the name of Elgar, born not far away, and who would one day write of it 'Surely the most beautiful river that ever was . . . I love it more than any other.'[69] The 'strong and lusty Teame' (so Michael Drayton saw it in the 17th century) rises in the Clun Forest, flows south through Shropshire (Ludlow stands on it) to join the river Severn south of Worcester at Powick, close to the site of the 1651 Battle of Worcester. Sarah, about to see her new home for the first time, would not be thinking about Charles II's difficulties as she crossed the river. From the bridge the road continues upwards to Clifton-on-Teme, but the travellers in the dog cart turned off it for a muddy track which runs alongside the river for a short way. This rough track – now updated by concrete surface and cattle grid – leads to the remote mill and, beyond it, to the even more isolated Ham Farm. Ham Mill makes Dumbleton seem like the very centre of civilization. One arrives at the side of the house, its walls covered by a vast

Pitmaston Duchess.* The house itself is not ugly, but its isolated position and its yellow-grey bricks create an inordinately bleak impression on a grey wintry day. The house's best aspect, the front, looks down to the river meadows below and beyond them to the site of the former water-mill and the river itself. At Ham Bridge the river is quiet; here at the weir it is fierce and noisy, 'strong and lusty'.

Sarah's first visit was short. There was a sale of goods at Ham Mill on March 23rd, and Leslie began trading there two days later. Sarah went back to Dumbleton to begin the packing. Her notebook gives details of the glass and crockery she took with her, and one list reflects her sewing and gardening interests –

pruning knife
watering can and trowel Father and Mother gave me on my 13th birthday
3 strawberry baskets
1 marketing basket
tiny reticule basket
Case needles from Father (Redditch)
ditto from Aunt Moseley
Workbox engraved SES
Knitting basket Aunt Peart gave me

besides the usual paraphernalia of femininity – 'gophering irons,† curling ditto, glove stretchers.'

The most interesting section of Sarah's inventory is that devoted to her books and magazines.

9 Queens newspapers
12 complete for one year of Young Englishwoman
Jan Feb and March Myra's Journal 1882
Shakespeare
Kingsleys Westward Ho
Cassells Magazine from June to November inclu.
The uncommercial Traveler (sic) by Dickens
Bible from Aunt Moseley
Reference bible from Mother
Dictionary of Daily Wants Nos. 5 and 10 missing
Lesson Book
Beetons Cookery Book and Dictionary of Gardening
Cabbin by the Wayside a tale
two Hymn books
Language of Flowers
Views of Malvern Hills.
Ann Davis old Cookery book
Homes and Haunts of Bri. Poets.

* a pear tree which produces very large pears.
† irons for crimping edges of fabric.

A book list tells quite a lot about a person, and Sarah's confirms that she was not a bookish person. Apart from the obligatory Bible and Shakespeare, the reference books again reflect her gardening and sewing interests (Myra's Journal was a cheap fashion journal which included paper patterns). The novels are clearly random possessions. The Kingsley novel, first published in 1855, recounts the adventures of a Devon knight, and the Dickens (1860) consists almost entirely of London sketches. Cassell's Magazine had been described as 'a penny periodical appealing to the more respectable members of the working class, those who would find congenial its message of thrift, temperance, industry and contentment.'[70]

At the other end of the notebook Sarah listed the contents of Leslie's trunk and Gladstone bag, revealing his fondness for mauve accessories:

Tie white	gloves mauve
do. mauve	do. 2 pr. black

(a miller in mauve gloves?) and including a black-bordered white handkerchief for funerals. Sarah began to catalogue her own clothes – 2 new flannel petticoats, cream fancy wool shawl, black silk bodice – but then gave up. She did not share her sister's fondness for writing (her writing is more difficult to read and more spattered with spelling mistakes). Sarah was happier with cooking spoon, trowel, or needle than with pen.

Having packed up her possessions, Sarah, Ann, Tom and John were up at three a.m. on March 27th for the big move. There was livestock to be shifted – three geese and eight fowls – as well as luggage. A Sedgeberrow man, hired to take the wagon as far as Worcester, set out at four o'clock in the morning. John took 'old Polly' by train to Worcester, where Leslie met him and the hired man. When John returned home on March 30th, he left Polly and dog cart at Worcester for Sarah (who stayed there overnight) to drive herself home to the mill. It was not a good time for a move of this magnitude. The severe winter had turned into a wet spring; the day of Sarah's lone drive was 'a very windy, rainy day'. A note home from Sarah next day told how it had taken her till mid-day to drive the ten miles from Worcester to the mill. The road near Ham Bridge was flooded (it floods easily). Polly was 'up to her knees for a short distance but had gone through it well.' It was a long, wet, solitary journey, a long way from Tennyson's miller and his wife strolling together into the sunset.

* * * *

A little miss
A little kiss
A little bliss
A wedding that is splendid
A little jaw
A little law
Back home to Ma –
And so my story's ended.

Written by a Peart relation in Lily Staight's album

The second bride of 1886 was Annie Biscoe. But in one respect at least, her 'story' could not match that of the rhyme. Only a fortnight after Sarah was installed at Ham Mill, news of Mrs Biscoe's death reached Ann. The last time they had met (in August 1885) Mrs Biscoe had been 'very ill'. Only sixty-one, she had outlived her husband by only four years, and like him she died just before Easter. Ann, as always, responded with flowers, posting them to the Logsdons at Enfield for the funeral next day.

And what of Annie? Annie wrote on May 3rd 'with fresh news', and arrived in person a week later. Ann drove the reliable Polly, unscathed by her recent flood experiences, to meet her friend, who brought wedding presents for Sarah and mementoes of her mother for all the family:

> She brought Sis a nice view of Rochester Castle and Gardens (in frame), black satin cushion cover with handsome crewel work, and antimacassar to match, also a pretty little gold brooch in memory of Mrs Biscoe with a little plait of her hair in. Annie brought me a little gold brooch, too, very like Sarah's, also Mrs Biscoe's purse, and some gloves, Mother nice cameo brooch, Father spectacles and case, Tom black silk beaded watch-chain, and John gold solitaires [shirt studs].

Annie stayed till June, then returned to Rochester, just missing the birth of Lilian Mary, Louie's fourth child, on June 4th 1886. From what we know of Annie, she was not the type of woman to be alone for long, for reasons of health and temperament. Soon after returning to Kent she was ill, but wrote in July to say she was better and 'enclosed photographs of herself and Mr G'. Mr G's photograph is still in Ann's album, twice in fact (in two different sizes). The immediate impression, of an older man, is created by various signs of ageing – the receding hairline, the lines under the eyes, and the many layers of clothes betraying an old man's concerns of health and warmth – and he is heavily bearded. But though much older than

155

Herry Gibson

Annie

Annie – certainly not young and dashing, and not very robust either – he looks to be a kindly man. The arrival of his photograph is the first mention of Mr G in Ann's diary. The relationship, while not as sudden as might appear from Ann's record, would certainly be expedited by Mrs Biscoe's death. On July 27th Annie left Rochester, having warehoused her possessions there, and after spending a night in the Minories with her aunt Young, she accompanied Mr Gibson on a visit to his relations in the north. Ann had not yet met the new man in Annie's life, but she soon would. After the visit to Darlington, Annie brought her fiancé to Dumbleton for a three-week visit in August 1886.

> 'Aug. 4th. Annie B. and Mr G. came from London to stay with us, walked from Ashton.'

The 'B' suggests a shift in attitudes, a new distancing. Ann expressed no opinion of Henry Gibson. There is no entry at all for the next four days while she adjusts to the new situation, then a purely innocuous one:

> Annie and Mr G drove Polly to the Jam Factory, bought some Jam, went on to Gretton . . .

During their visit they went out for drives, on their own to Cheltenham, with Joe and Louie to Evesham, with John and Ann to Wormington church. Ann's private relationship with Annie had now passed into the public domain: the couple are friends of the whole family and the exclusive relationship of the two girls has to adapt itself. No longer can Ann keep her friend under her own life's key.[71] During this period the private girlhood intimacy is successfully transformed. Mr G becomes Harry and is accommodated within the friendship.

Ann was at Ham Mill when she learned the date of Annie's wedding.

> October 23rd. Aunt Sarah and I went to Ham Mill, left Beckford 11.40 train, waited at Worcester station some hours before Leslie arrived for us, not at Ham Mill till quite dusk.

Leslie is perpetually late, which cannot have improved Ann's feelings towards him. Not the man to worry about such things, his calm disposition complemented Sarah's sharp tongue and fiery temper. Sarah was older, and gave him plenty of 'jaw pie':[72] not only in his work did he 'go through the mill'. In answer to Sarah's harangues, he would murmur soothingly 'Very well, Sarah, very well'. When the pigs escaped and ran away, Sarah panicked, but Leslie was unruffled. 'Never mind, hunger will bring them to knowledge' he said sagely, and it did: the pigs returned to be fed. Sarah worked as hard as Leslie, or harder, to build up the business, and her visits to Dumbleton were not only to see her family but to try to rustle up orders. (One diary entry mentions her going to church at Dumbleton on one of these visits: 'Wore her best clothes that were here,' and certainly she would have no use for her finery at Ham Mill.) On returning from one such visit home ('she was unsuccessful at College Farm and Mill') she brought Ann a letter from Annie to say 'they had decided on shop at Brighton, and wedding to be on the 1st prox.'

Ann underlined the date twice:

<u>Monday November 1st 1886.</u> Harry Gibson and Annie Biscoe married at Darlington. Lovely day. They went straight to York, and on the 2nd to London.

3rd. We received a parcel of wedding-cake for ourselves, Sarah, Aunt S and Aunt M(oseley).

Nov. 8th. Annie and Harry reached their new home at Brighton.

Nov. 11th. We sent money presents to Brighton for Harry and Annie G. to choose what they like best (Registered letter).

The new initial (Harry and Annie G.) suggests the adjustment had been made. Ann clearly liked Harry, and she calls him by this name from now on. The contacts continued unbroken. The couple had remembered her birthday in October, and she received a Valentine as usual in 1887 ('a short letter from Brighton and pretty pin tray for Valentine'); she reciprocated with snowdrops, heather and violets for Harry's birthday in March. There is never any mention of a present for Leslie Legge.

* * * *

III
Golden Jubilee 1887

'A happy people'

Pigs make an unlikely introduction to Queen Victoria's Golden Jubilee. Just before it, Joe presented Ann with her own piglet: a

Jubilee present? Pigs played a large part in country life. The poorest cottager had his own pig, which would be killed around November to provide good food for Christmas and supplies for the hard winter months. Cobbett in his *Rural Rides* mentions pigs in Gloucestershire:

> *The Gloucestershire people have no notion of dying with hunger . . . The people seem to have been constantly well off. A pig in almost every cottage sty; and that is the infallible mark of a happy people.*[73]

There are other local connections with pigs. One explanation for the name Evesham is that it was named after Eoves, a visionary swineherd. An Anglo-Saxon charter, earlier than Domesday, tells how Adelsige forfeited the land at Dumbleton because he stole a fat pig! Fred Archer, rather more recently, has written of Ashton-under-Hill 'this was a land of cider, fat bacon, and bread pudding' and this is equally true of Dumbleton across the valley from Ashton.[74] Pigs and apples, roast pork and apple sauce, the two go well together.

Charles Staight regularly bought pigs, or more usually half-pigs, sometimes from Joe, sometimes from local farmers ('Father bought $\frac{1}{2}$ a pork pig from Joe . . .') and such purchases led to a flurry of activity for the women, described by Ann in the earlier diaries. 'We had ½ pig in from Mr Smith, I cut the leaf and melted': this odd-sounding process involved removing the doily-like part of the pig's intestine which was melted down for lard. Nothing was wasted. The pig's feet, ears and head were cooked for brawn. The diaries mention collecting 'the fry' from Joe's, a dialect word for various internal parts of the animal (which might include the 'products of a lamb's castration'[75]) which were fried and eaten. An early entry mentioned giving Mrs Dunn her dinner out of *griskin* – and this unappetising meal was not, as it sounds, a mixture of gristle and skin, but the lean part of the loin of a bacon pig. A better-sounding joint was *sweetbone*.

Joe, as a butcher, kept pigs as a useful source of ready meat. Young pigs (below six score,* for example) would be killed for immediate consumption for pork; the rest would be allowed to grow large and fat and were killed for bacon. The very large pig would give large quantities of fat bacon, for which there was much more of a demand in the nineteenth century than there is today. After Joe's infant son was buried in October 1882, Joe's very next act concerned bacon: 'Joe came down at 7 with small flitch of bacon to dry in our chimney.' And now, just before the Jubilee:

---

* Score: a weight of 20 or 21 lbs. used in weighing pigs or oxen.

June 9th. Joe gave me a tiny pig.

With regard to animals, sentiment and sense had to be kept separate. Once the animal was fully-grown and ready to be eaten, it was killed. Similarly, if it ceased to give service. In March, Joe's horse Tommy ceased to be useful. Ann's entry is almost callously unsentimental. In our own age we have the paradox of sensitivity in an age of violence: the same facts about a favourite horse today would be worded quite differently:

> March 31st. First thing this morning Joe found 'old Tommy' down in the stalls with his leg broken (supposed he slipped up), so they killed and skinned him, our boys and Bob busy helping.

When Ann's Jubilee pig, seven months later, was ripe for slaughter (it was a bacon pig, not a pork pig), Ann did not waste her words:

> Jan 23rd. 1888. Killed my pig. It weighed 12 score.

At least with Joe doing the killing, we are spared references to pigstickers.

Three brief entries separate the gift of the pig and Jubilee Day itself. Ann's account of the celebrations in Dumbleton is brief. Her one-word sentences give no indication of what part of the festivities she herself witnessed: the signs are that she was not much involved.

> Tuesday June 21st 1887. Jubilee Day.
> Service at 1 pm. Dinner at 2 in tent near school, nearly the whole village assembled. Children's tea at 4, others at 5. Sports. Dancing. Ending with procession to the top of the Park. Bonfire. Fireworks. Dancing, and then a procession back, cheering, and singing National Anthem.

The bonfire at the top of the park (there was one too on Bredon Hill) does not quite match Tennyson's injunction to 'Set the mountain aflame tonight'! The very next entry shows the Jubilee euphoria was still rampant and London still full of visitors for the celebrations; it shows also why Ann was not concentrating much on Dumbleton activities:

> Thursday June 23rd. Went to Brighton.
> Joe drove me to Evesham, went by 2.37 train to Paddington, cab to Victoria, could not get along for the crush of people and vehicles, missed 2 trains, reached Brighton 9.30, HG meeting me at station.

Ann stayed with Annie and Harry for a week, going to the beach

160

with them once or twice every day, as it was easily accessible from their rented accommodation. St James's Street, where Harry had a tobacconist's shop, runs parallel to the Marine Parade, well-placed for visits to the Aquarium and the Pavilion and for church at St James's. Harry escorted Ann (Annie was expecting their first child) to the West Pier to see 'Miss Louie Webb's clever performances in a tank of water. She could eat, drink, sew, write, pick up shells in basket, and open and shut her eyes all under water!' and for a sail in the *Skylark* '4 or 5 miles out, enjoyed it much.' Other visits included one to Preston Park, about two miles away, and to the Swimming Club.

> Saturday July 2nd. We went and watched Swimming Club before breakfast for last time. I left by 1.50 train for London, Harry saw me off. Intensely hot journey, reached Mrs McG's about 4 . . . Melting hot.
>
> July 3rd. Fanny [Staite] came to dinner, after dinner I went to Enfield, called on Mary at Miss Hobbs', and chatted for ½ hr. then went alone to Cemetery and loitered about, reached Logsdon's about 6. Went to church with them, did not stay many minutes after . . . When I reached Jenner Road, Fanny was ready to start, so Mrs McG and I went some of the way with her. *Very* hot day.

Next day, appropriately for this Jubilee year, Ann saw the Queen.

> July 4th/87. Mrs McG and I went by [underground] train near to Hyde Park, walked into the Park, saw the Queen and others of the Royal Family go and come back to lay foundation stone of the Imperial Institute. The 2nd Life Guards looked very pretty as they kept guard.

The Imperial Institute of the Colonies and India, established as a memorial of the Jubilee to represent arts, manufactures and commerce, would not be opened to the public until 1893. Since that time it has changed its name and its location: it is now called the Commonwealth Institute and is sited in Holland Park. Imperial College, part of the University of London, occupies the Imperial Institute's original site close to Hyde Park. The foundation stone laid by the Queen on that hot summer's day is still visible at the foot of the tower:

> *This stone was laid by Her Majesty Queen Victoria Empress of India on the 4th day of July 1887 in the 51st year of her reign.*

161

The intention was, as the Poet Laureate proclaimed, to

> *Raise a stately memorial,*
> *Make it regally gorgeous,*
> *Some Imperial Institute,*
> *Rich in symbol, in ornament,*
> *Which may speak to the centuries,*
> *All the centuries after us,*
> *Of this great Ceremonial,*
> *And this year of her Jubilee.*[76]

Today the Queen's Tower stands, aloof and alone, surrounded by green lawns and twentieth-century university buildings. If the building 'speaks to the centuries' at all (do those science students pay it much attention?) it speaks of a long-lost Victorian optimism and imperialism.

After Royalty – Cowboys and Indians.

> We went by bus to the American Exhibition, met Mr McG and his brother there . . . we stayed to see Buffalo Bill and his Americans and Indians perform, some of them wonderful riders and shooters.

Ann was clearly taken with Buffalo Bill and his Wild West Circus at Earl's Court, for in December she would go to see him again, when a rail excursion took her with Tom, John and Louie 'to Birmingham Cattle Show, and to Ashton Lower Grounds where Buffalo Bill's Wild West were performing . . .'.

After the long winter of 1885–6, culminating in the wet March of Sarah's wedding, the summer of 1887 was exceptionally hot and dry, to the extent that there was severe drought between June and mid-August, followed by a very early harvest. Outdoor celebrations demand good weather to ensure their success, and the Golden Jubilee was indeed a golden one, but both Queen and subjects suffered from the excessive heat. After the Queen had laid the foundation stone she wrote 'The heat was quite terrific and I felt dissolved'.[77] Ann, similarly, had found it 'melting hot' and 'felt the heat very much', and she was relieved when July 5th was cooler for her journey home.

*　　*　　*　　*

IV
Godmother 1887, 1888

'I count myself in nothing else so happy
As in a soul remembering my good friends'

(Bolingbroke on arrival in Gloucestershire)
Richard II, II.iii.46

Annie's son was born in Jubilee Year, in September 1887. Ann received the news almost at once, for the birth is not recorded out of sequence:

> Sept 5th 1887. Dr Allard came about 1, was anxious to know how the fresh medicine (he sent last week) suited Mother.
> Annie's son born very early in the morning at Brighton.
> (Aunt M. went to Ham Mill from Evesham Station . . .)

Ann herself was fully occupied, not only with a sick mother but with two visiting nieces, Charley's daughters Frances and Amy, so busy that she did not get to church that Sunday nor to the mid-week Harvest Festival. For one local farmer, fire and drought made thanksgiving difficult –

> Sept 12th. Early in the evening a fire began near Little Buckland, a barn full of corn destroyed and 5 or 6 ricks; lasted many hours (no engine and very little water) could be seen for miles around.

> Sept 14th 1887. Our Harvest Festival. Father, Mother, nor I did not go. The others did.

> Sept 16th. Charley's two girls went up to Joe's to stay and sleep. A lad dreadfully hurt at the Brickyard at the pipe machine in afternoon and died there same evening.

Annie's son, William Henry Biscoe Gibson, was christened in October. Although Ann was godmother, she was unable to be present.

> Sunday October 9th . . . Christening at Brighton today, Harry and his friend (Bert) godfathers, and Annie for me.

Sarah's first child was born two months after Annie's, on 2 November 1887. She was now thirty-six and the family must have been anxious for news, particularly after Louie's difficult early

163

confinements. In view of the lavish care bestowed upon Louie by all the family on those occasions, it is curious that Ann did not go over to be with her sister at this time. Was it because Sarah, ultra-capable, scorned offers of help? Or having cast in her lot with Leslie's did the family leave her to fend for herself? What is more likely is that Ann wanted to go but was needed at home by her ailing parents. That she was anxious for news is conveyed by her entry:

2nd Nov 1887 Sarah's little daughter born about 11 a.m.
We did not get the letter with the news till 4th.

The same day there was a letter from Annie with photographs of herself and her baby. There is no doubt about which couple were better at keeping in touch. Sarah's news had to wait till she surfaced and could write herself. Her baby was christened in December and this time the godmother was present. After a rushed visit to John Peart at Longdon – 'Uncle better. He had a slight stroke on 6th, which left him very ill', Ann went with Tom to Ham Mill to be godparents at the christening at Clifton Church.

Clifton-on-Teme, an uphill drive from Ham Mill, is a small, pretty village of black-and-white cottages. It is not *on* the Teme at all, but about six hundred feet above it. After the steep climb from Ham Bridge, all Clifton's important buildings – church, inn, forge – are conveniently located at the entrance to the village. Opposite the forge (a large inverted horseshoe of dark-coloured bricks is set into the redbrick wall) is the church, dedicated to the child/king/martyr St Kenelm, a 'local' saint for Sarah, for he was buried outside Winchcombe. Inside the church are plaques to the Winnington family, the patrons of the church, and Leslie's 'patron' too at Ham Mill.

Sunday December 11th. Sarah, Tom and I drove to Clifton Church in afternoon, and had Baby christened (Ann Catherine). We were very late, so there was an empty church.

The baby, named Ann after aunt and grandmother, was always known as Nancy.

Ann returned home next day with Leslie, who was going to Evesham's Monday Market. Rendezvous with Sarah in Worcester after this were not over-successful either because of long delays –

I went to Worcester to meet Sarah, waited at the Bear till after 2 before she and Leslie came

164

or because of weather difficulties. On one visit, Ann determined not to rely on the tardy Leslie for transport. She walked part of the way from Worcester, then sat down by the roadside and waited for the carrier, reaching Ham Mill at six. While Leslie delivered his bread round Martley and Hillside, Ann sat beside him nursing the baby. Various baby items travelled between the two counties, by post, by train, or cart: in February 1888 'we sent the child's chair to Sarah by goods train' and later, Leslie took over the old baby carriage, repaired and painted in the shop. Despite the distance, he continued to make use of the shop and the skills of his brothers-in-law: when his water-wheel broke he did not use the Clifton forge but fetched John from Dumbleton.

In between being godmother to Nancy, and godmother yet again in June 1888, Ann reported local news items – deaths and fires and fears. The year began with Mrs Morris of the mill dying from dropsy less than seven months after her husband. At the funeral, Leslie's friend Cormell was on crutches, having cut his leg with an axe while felling a tree. A few days later there was another big fire.

Jan 24th. A large fire at Sedgeberrow. Mr Tredwell's barn burnt down, broke out about 6 pm. Tom went down to see it. Mrs Coldicott died from the shock, went out in to the court to look at it, fell down, and never spoke again. There had been two fires previous to this in less than a fortnight in Sedgeberrow, one from a chimney being on fire, the other a mystery, like the last.

and not long after, a suicide

April 20th. Mr Arthur Smith of the Laurels Broadway shot himself through the head in his saddle-room this morning. He kept livery stables, and is supposed to have been in difficulties. Inquest 21st, Verdict Temporary Insanity.

Most of Ann's news came via her brothers' shop, a more immediate source than the weekly paper. One entry at this time was not derived from that source. Ann was the least self-dramatising of people, but one entry reveals a personal concern.

Went to Chelt by 9 train, Joe drove me to Beckford. Sharp frost. Went to see Dr Ker about bruise on my bosom (which I did 15 months back when roost ladder nearly upset me). He said there was nothing to fear at present, only take care not to hurt it again. Called at Mr Howlett's shop and left eggs, did other business work . . .

In June 1888 Ann was godmother for the third time, when she drove with Louie and John to Stanton to be 'sponsors' at the christening of the Chidleys' infant daughter Lilian Maud. But it was a short sponsorship, for on July 2nd 'Mrs Chidley's tiny baby (our god-child) died after several days illness aged 7 weeks (inflammation of the bowels).'

Meanwhile, in Brighton, the Gibsons faced various vicissitudes. Annie had been ill, and was nursed by her good Aunt Young from the Minories. Harry had given up the tobacconist's shop and became a traveller, within Brighton, for a local firm in February 1888. But in October Ann was writing 'Harry out of berth, not business enough', just when Annie was expecting her second child. (Her daughter was born in February 1889.) The last news of Harry is not promising; his brother had recently died, and he was ill, 'obliged to give up situation, Dr ordered him to rest 2 months'. Annie still had a little money of her own after the death of both parents, but things cannot have been easy for her. Illness and unemployment, however, did not hinder (and nor did the Post Office) the regular and speedy transmission of gifts and greetings between the two families – usually eggs and apples from Dumbleton, sometimes home-cured bacon, a duck or a chicken ('sent 2 chickens, 1 for birthday present for Annie, the other to settle with her for making Nancy Legge a little coat'). To mark her thirty-sixth birthday, Ann received from Brighton a night-dress case from Annie, sweets from Harry, and more from the two children. Despite the distance between them, the friendship, after more than ten years, flourished as strongly as ever.

*   *   *   *

The two weddings of 1886, especially Sarah's, had greatly affected Ann's life. Her two closest companions were removed. Sarah's removal from the Villa could have had a liberating effect upon Ann, who had lived in her sister's shadow for a long time, but this does not seem to have happened. She acquired greater responsibilities within the household, but the new status in no way compensated for the loss of her sister. During the period covered by the two final diaries, she slipped quietly into her role as maiden aunt. There are no mysteries now, no dates underlined to suggest a secret life or clandestine letters. We have no indication from this private person about how she felt about being man-less, at having slipped into the spinster's traditional role of looking after ageing parents. It would be facile to say that her life was unhappy, but a certain zeal is missing.

And her world is shrinking. There were, however, many things to be enjoyed, an unexpected pleasure being the children appearing on the scene. She had been adamant earlier in not wishing to take a Sunday School class, and this might suggest an antipathy to children, but it is not borne out by her relationship with her nieces, Joso and Lily, of whom she saw a great deal, and Nancy. *This* circle was increasing. On Easter Monday 1889 'Joe's little son was born'. This was another Thomas Pitman Staight ('Baby Pitman' would as an adult be known simply as 'Pit') perpetuating the tradition begun by Robert Staight with his sons. And a year later, Sarah's second child was born.

Feb 12th 1890. Sarah's second child (another daughter) was born about 6 pm (Wed.)

Feb 15th. Letter from Sarah to tell us the news of another daughter, the letter was two days coming, had been to Malvern.

Ann took Josephine (called Joso), just six years old, to Ham Mill on a visit, but she seems to have developed a special relationship with Joso's little sister Lily. (One entry mentions taking Lily to Cheltenham, where they had their photographs taken together, another of driving to Willersey Wake) and one can draw parallels here between the lively and attractive older sisters, and the quiet, gentle younger ones. Playing with the children had its disadvantages –

Sunday 13 May. In evening called at Joe's, was playing in court with Lily when my best winter hat tumbled off into water tub, the water was greasy and quite spoilt my hat

but it was light relief after running the household, now a bigger task with Sarah gone, her parents ageing and her brothers to be waited on:

July 13th 1886. John went to Liverpool by Cox's trip for two days. Met Uncle M[oseley] at Evesham at 5 a.m. I got up at 2.45 a.m., got his breakfast and started him. Mrs Morris and Miss Chard came in afternoon but would not stay tea as we were washing . . .

A washing machine had been purchased in August 1884, and Ann was pleased with it: 'Using machine first time, answered well.' Pictures of washing machines at this time show cumbersome contraptions with heavy handles on each side. Without electric power, washing was still heavy work, often prolonged by bad weather ('I had month's wash about, and could not get much dry, bad weather (9 and 10 November)).' In addition to the washing machine, Ann

Joe's family: left Joe and Louie with Josie and Lily (1888); right, Pitman and Emma (1895)

now had the help of a young servant. First Agnes Richardson, aged fifteen, who left in August 1888 to move to a post in Malvern ('Father gave her 5/- as a present'), then her sister, who left after a few months ('did not consider wages enough'); thereafter a woman came in on an occasional basis to wash and clean.

There was never, of course, any washing on Sundays, set apart from the rest of the week not only by the no-work rule but by church services, special Sunday clothes, special meals, hymn-singing after supper. This traditional view of the sanctity of the Sabbath is expressed in one of the Staight autograph albums:

> *A Sabbath well spent,*
> *Brings a week of Content*
> *And Wealth for the toils of the morrow!*
> *But a Sabbath profaned,*
> *Whatso'er may be gained,*
> *Is a certain forerunner of Sorrow.*

That Ann upheld this idea is clear from an 1888 entry. After recording the burial of a villager after a fit in the harvest field, she indignantly wrote of a villager succumbing to temptation:

Sunday 9 September 1888. Mr J.W. Smith and his men busy wheat carrying and ricking all day, just as on a week day.

Apart from Sunday leisure, Ann's opportunities for recreation were necessarily curtailed. She was still as mobile as ever, getting herself to Evesham and the nearby villages in Joe's trap – or his dog cart:

July 5th 1886. Joe and I went to Evesham after dinner. Joe bought a dogcart by auction, and we came home in it.

Apart from visits to Worcester to see her sister, she went regularly by train to Tewkesbury and Cheltenham to shop and visit friends. Amongst her Cheltenham circle were the Howlett family, who had given Sarah the Millais pictures for her wedding-present. After one such visit

Went to meet last train, just missed it. Telegraphed Joe at Beckford Station to that effect, and then Mr and Mrs Howlett and self went to the theatre 'The Fugitive'. I stayed all night at Andover House and till 4 pm next day. Got back 5.30 train, Joe met me and told me they never had the telegram and did not know whatever was the reason. Mr Howlett told me Mr Edwin White died in the Asylum some time ago.

In place of the absent Sarah and Annie, Ann's usual companions were likely to be her Aunt Sarah, in between housekeeping stints, or Louie's maids, Miss Pullin (who 'came to live at Joe's as Useful Help' in December 1888) or her successor Miss Tyrrell. An old stalwart, Mrs McGlinchy, came from London to stay in August 1889. Outings included a drive with old Polly to the Grange gardens at Wormington, to the jam factory at Toddington, and further afield by train to Tewkesbury and Ripple, from where they walked to Queenhill churchyard, set within the Pull Court park of the Dowdeswells. At Bushley Green, not far from Robertsend itself, the two women had tea. Mrs McGlinchy's relations had lived in this area and so, before she went to work in London, had her niece, Fanny Staite.

*   *   *   *

V

Attempted Suicide, Accidental Murder 1889, 1890

Fanny Staite had recently been very ill (Ann noted this in October 1888) and during Mrs McGlinchy's visit Ann would certainly have enquired after her health. Fanny was not one of Ann's closest friends, but they had met often at Mrs McGlinchy's home, and exchanged cards every Christmas. Fanny was one of the few girls of Ann's acquaintance who had to work.

Shortly after Mrs McGlinchy's return to London – the same month – Fanny hit the headlines. News of her came to Ann from an unexpected quarter, the local paper. Amongst such diverse items as the London police receiving a Jack-the-Ripper letter (the multiple murders happened in the winter of 1888) and an advertisement for the forthcoming Dumbleton Garden Show was a subheading under the Tewkesbury news: *Attempted Suicide of a Tewkesbury Woman.*

Francis Staite, a lady-like person, who is said to have left Tewkesbury, her native place, 13 years ago, to become manageress at one of Spiers and Pond's establishments, but had lost her position through tippling, was charged at Dalston Police Court, on Thursday, with attempting to commit suicide at Clissold Park, one of the recent additions to London's recreation grounds. The evidence was that prisoner was found by a parkkeeper over the rails within two feet of the New River, which runs through the park. The officer caught hold of her, and she struggled; and said she wished to drown herself. With assistance she was got from the water and to the station. A half-pint bottle, half-filled with gin, was found in her pocket. Prisoner now said, in an agitated manner, that she did not intend to commit suicide. She would swear she did not, and if *the magistrate would let her go she would swear never to touch spirits again. The water had a strange fascination for her as she stood in the park, but she did not intend to destroy herself. <u>An aunt of the prisoner was present in court, but would not undertake to be responsible for the accused</u>, and her landlady's daughter thought her mother would not take her in again. – The magistrate: under these circumstances I cannot let you go. You must find somebody to be responsible for you. – Prisoner: Oh, aunt do! The Aunt: No, I cannot. – Prisoner again assured the magistrate and her friends that she would be better if allowed another chance; but she was put back. <u>The aunt told the magistrate that prisoner had brothers in good positions, but they would have nothing to do with her.</u> Prisoner was then remanded for a week, Mr Holmes of the Church of England Temperance Society, saying that he would arrange to get her into a home for inebriates.[78]**

Poor Fanny. The 'ladylike person' is now reduced to 'prisoner', not even allowed the courtesy of the definite article, and deserted by her family when she most needs them. Mrs McGlinchy had been a sterling friend, hospitable and generous to Ann over a period of many years, but she, like her nephews, disowns Fanny in this crisis. The park, in Stoke Newington, and close to Mrs McGlinchy's home in Jenner Road, had been open to the public barely a month when Fanny made use of it.

Ann's entry for August 31st, the day the paper appeared, was a brief précis of the article.

August 31st 1889. Account in Evesham Journal of Mrs McGlinchy's niece Fanny attempting to drown herself in the water in one of the London parks, and being brought before the magistrates and remanded, and afterwards sent to a Home.

Ann makes no mention of Fanny's let-down by her family, or of the drink problem – the tippling at work, the half-full bottle of gin in her pocket, and the nature of the Home to which Fanny was referred are quietly omitted. As a non-drinker herself, Ann could have been censorious of Fanny's weakness, and an ardent advocate of Temperance, but she was not.

The Temperance movement, which belies its name – temperance is *moderation*, whereas the Temperance movement advocated total abstinence from alcohol – has its origins in the early 19th century. Ann's diaries pinpoint its arrival in Dumbleton.

July 28th 1886. Church Temperance Society started here, first meeting in schoolroom this evening, lecture by Mr John Abbey of Oxford. A lot of villagers went, but none signed the pledge but Mr W. Jones.

* My underlining.

September 28th 1886. Rev W. and Mrs Jones had a magic lantern at the School this evening for the especial benefit of the Church Temperance Society lately started here. A lot of children there, as well as 2[? edge of page torn] little abstainers. I went, and afterwards called at Mrs Walker's to inquire after Bessie who was ill. I got lost in the orchard for ¼ hr, then Joe found me, and put me right.

'Little abstainers'? Child teetotallers? It might appear that the Dumbleton children were particularly vulnerable or depraved. In fact, having failed to win over the adults in sufficient numbers to their cause, the Temperance movement did deliberately try to win over, to 'catch' the children before they were old enough to acquire a liking for alcohol.

Three years later the Rector was still trying his best, but interest had waned:

June 12, 1889. Temperance lecture on Rectory lawn in evening, very few there. A Mr Edwards lectured.

A temperance lecture given at Winchcombe was titled 'The House we live in and how to treat it.' Fanny would be subjected to many lectures on the abuse of her 'House' in the Home for Inebriates.

*   *   *   *

The danger with village life is that events on a national or international scale seem comparatively insignificant beside local affairs. Sir Garnet Wolseley is mentioned, not because of his military triumphs abroad, but because he looks like Annie's boyfriend. The different Liberal and Conservative governments of Mr Gladstone and Lord Salisbury come and go, unrecorded. It was just the same in the *Adam Bede* village, where Napoleon fails to make much impact: 'the news that "Bony" was come back from Egypt was comparatively insipid, and the repulse of the French in Italy was nothing to Mrs Poyser's repulse of the old squire.'[79] This is always the case with village life, but even allowing for this, Ann's focus has narrowed alarmingly with the passing of time. Her diary covers a smaller and still smaller circumference. Even the references to the Royal Family ended with the wedding of the youngest royal princess, Princess Beatrice, in 1885. She still read the local paper regularly, along with the rest of the family (the avid desire for newsprint is a family characteristic: even today those members who do not read books, any books, read eagerly any newspaper that comes their way), but the *Evesham Journal* is cited in her diary only when something or someone very

172

local is involved, like Fanny Staite. Similarly, Jack-the-Ripper goes unrecorded, but not, in March 1890, the Boswell brothers.

March is generally associated with severe weather and with end-of-winter illnesses, and March 1890 was no exception. At the Villa, both Charles and his wife had been ill with bronchitis in January and February. And in March –

> March 1st. Self caught fresh cold yesterday, today cough troublesome. Very winterly wind, *too* keen, and snow in morning.

and a few days later

> Uncle Moseley brought Aunt Sarah back after dinner with a cold as bad or worse than she took with her.

Against this bleak, cheerless background, the family read each Saturday of the 'progress' of The Lenchwick Tragedy.

Lenchwick is one of a cluster of villages and hamlets north of Evesham, all bearing the name Lench: Rous Lench, Abbots Lench, Church Lench, Atch Lench, Sheriff's Lench. Lenchwick is the one furthest south, nearest to Evesham itself, though the incident happened just west of Lenchwick at Wood Norton, the estate of a French nobleman. Such an exotic personage seems curiously out of place in this rural setting where (even today) foreigners are rare. Here the Duc d'Aumale and later his great-nephew the Duc d'Orleans resided. The proximity of 'royalty' was not overlooked by the local tradespeople: on the back of one of the photographs in Ann's album are the words 'R.A. Reeks of Evesham, Patronised by his Royal Highness the Duc D'Aumale'. A gamekeeper on the Duc's estate, Frederick Stephens, was attacked one evening in November 1889 when he surprised three poachers, Joseph and Samuel Boswell and Alfred (Lovely) Hill. Stephens was seriously injured, but lived on for twelve days, cared for by a local Evesham doctor. Then he died, and the ugly question of murder had to be raised. The case came up for trial at Worcester Assizes early in 1890. Because the protagonists – attackers and attacked – were all local people, there was great interest in the case, both suspense before the sentence was passed, and after it also: would there be a reprieve? The jury found all three men guilty but recommended mercy for Alfred Hill.[80]

The *Journal* for March 8th 1890 was devoted, almost exclusively, to the burning issue of the reprieve. Its editorial began 'At the time we write the question whether the three condemned men are to live or die has not been answered.' It dwelt on the part chance had played in the proceedings, the problems with the jury, and stressed 'the growth of public opinion that if these men die, a penalty in excess of the actual crime will have been enacted.' The editor warmed to his subject, writing of the urgent necessity of saving the men from 'the stern doom of the law . . . the shocking and ignominious death, which every pulsation brings nearer.'[81]

It was not just the editor who was pulsatingly eloquent. The Vicar of Evesham also rallied his forces. Above the river Avon in the centre of Evesham two ancient churches, St Lawrence's and All Saints', share a churchyard. In St Lawrence's church that Sunday morning the vicar urged the congregation to pray for the three prisoners 'now lying [note the emotive power of that word] in Worcester gaol' and in All Saints' the same evening he delivered a powerful address, without a text, in reference to the case of the three condemned men, their crime, and some lessons to be drawn from the event. A petition to the Home Secretary for clemency, signed by 2000 people, included more than 1200 signatures from these two churches alone. Elsewhere in the paper the same minister invited readers to send contributions to help support the families of the convicted men. A visit by the two Boswell wives from Evesham to Worcester, and the difficulties they were now encountering, were described in full. The one Mrs Boswell, who had four children and was out of work, found her husband Joseph 'looking very ill; he did not seem to have the same features as he had before'. He begged her forgiveness and she replied that 'she most readily forgave him, and this seemed to ease his mind considerably'. Samuel, the older brother at thirty-nine, looked less ill, but had a wild look.

As if all this were not enough, the paper contained gruesome details about the enlargement of the gallows at Worcester gaol, last used five years earlier. The existing space was insufficient for three men to be executed alongside each other. The pit, which was 7 ft. 6 inches long, was therefore being extended. Berry (hangmen do not appear to warrant the courtesy title of Mr) would officiate as executioner.

Less than a week later it was all over. Hill was reprieved, the two brothers were not. The editorial was censorious, not towards the condemned men, but towards the Home Secretary: 'In a case studded with mistakes it was reserved for Mr Home Secretary Matthews to make the last and by far the gravest . . . .'. The editor considered that 'there was not a pin to choose between the three men on the score of character', yet Hill had been reprieved, 'leaving the two Boswells to the tender mercies of the hangman.' A member of the *Journal*[82] staff was amongst a group of reporters present at the execution at Worcester, fixed for 8 a.m. 'Amongst the reporters, only one had previously witnessed an execution, and all were evidently impressed with a sense of the solemnity of the occasion. It was an ordeal which none would have chosen . . .'. Nevertheless, he did his duty to his readers with a graphic description of the proceedings. When the condemned brothers were brought to the gallows, their faces were covered with white hoods so that they would not see the preparations for their deaths. It was not known if they knew of Hill's reprieve: did they realize he was not beside them at the end? Their fraternal farewells were particularly touching, and they, just as much as Stephens, became victims of a drama as they were handed over to Berry's 'terrible dexterity'. The report of the execution concludes in a manner anticipating the end of Thomas Hardy's *Tess of the D'Urbervilles*:[83] 'the black flag . . . fluttering above the entrance to the prison – the outraged law had been satisfied.'

As she had done with the much smaller saga of Fanny Staite, Ann summed up, as economically as always, these matters of life and death:

> March 11th 1890. Two Evesham men (brothers named Boswell) were hung in Worcester (for the murder of a gamekeeper named Stephens at Lenchwick). The third man (Hill) was reprieved (penal servitude for life).

In fact, Hill did not serve a life sentence. After only ten years, he was released, and did not even have to remake his life elsewhere. He returned to his old haunts, where he left off poaching for an occupation ideally suited to the district, that of market gardener.

* * * *

VI
Maladies and Remedies 1890, 1891

During 1890 and 1891 Ann's parents were frequently ill, often at the same time, and more than once Ann refers to visitors calling to see 'our invalids' or comments 'I did not go off the premises'. Charles no longer worked in the shop. A new smith arrived from Stroud in 1890, but left in mysterious circumstances after two weeks –

Sunday 27th July. Our new 'smithy' disappeared today and did not return. He lodged at F. Lyes, and he got up between 5 and 6, and went off before they were up, taking a parcel with him and leaving his old box. Had agreed to stay on here, and said he liked it very well.

In October a young boy, Bob Walker, started work in the shop.

After several attempts at employment, Aunt Sarah was now more or less resident at the Villa, except for visits to Peart or Moseley relations. She illustrates well the predicament of the single woman rendered homeless by bereavement and forced to undertake employment, in later life, for the first time. She had taken her first post in 1886:

June 3rd. Aunt went to Evesham to meet Mr and Mrs Rimell of Bretforton and engaged to go housekeeper at a lone farm house of theirs

but she was back at the Villa in October. In March 1888 she went briefly to a farm at Mickleton. Ann is nicely ambiguous in an 1890 entry:

April 10th. Aunt went to Chipping Norton to see about a situation, but did not suit.

It is not clear whether she does not suit the job, or the job does not suit her. The former, in view of her record, seems more likely. Later that year, she went to Bishop's Cleeve near Cheltenham to be housekeeper to a schoolmaster there. Shortly afterwards, in November, Joe called on his way home from Cheltenham 'to see how she was getting on.' Not very well, presumably, for she was soon back at the Villa, where she seems to have had a perpetual cough.

Ann's two brothers suffered too from minor ailments, and also from injuries sustained in the shop. Of all the village crafts, the blacksmith must be the most susceptible to accidents – burns as well as blows. Usually it was John who was indisposed, but Tom had his share of mishaps. In March 1889 his eye was badly bruised when the young assistant 'in striking, knocked Tom's hammer, which fled back in his eye, it was bad for nearly a fortnight.' His doctor gave him a certificate for 'Club use' (The Men's Friendly Club was an early form of insurance). And in 1891

March 12th 1891. Confirmation held at D. Church 2.30 pm. Bells rang merrily, nearly 100 candidates there from own and different parishes. I did not go. We had no one call. Tom did not go, for yesterday the lad was striking hot large piece of iron, when it rebounded, and struck Tom on chin and throat,

176

struck his jaw a bad blow, cut and burnt his throat. He stayed in the house two days, and part of two more . . .

Earlier Tom had suffered from boils or carbuncles: 'Joe drove Tom to Tewkesbury to see Dr Turner about carbuncle on back. Dr said we had treated it right, only to use linseed-meal instead of bread poultices.' (Linseed poultices are a favourite remedy: when Aunt Sarah suffers from 'congestion of the liver, Dr ordered linseed poultices, and no solid food (only milk and soda-water)'.)

While Tom suffered from boils, Ann was suffering from another symptom of poor health, of being 'under the weather':

> May 26th. My eye very painful, seemed like another sty (the third lately) coming on it.
>
> 27th. My eye worse, face swelling altogether.
>
> 28th. My eye still worse, Aunt afraid of erysipelas, face much swollen, so Joe telegraphed at Kemerton for Dr Allard. He came in afternoon, said there was great inflammation in eye, and I needed medicine, would send lotion for eye, as well as my medicine . . .
>
> 29th. The gathering in my eye broke.

'Aunt afraid of erysipelas' – the fear of erysipelas was a very real one for everyone, not just for Aunt Sarah. A rapidly spreading inflammation of the skin, it could lead to gangrene and to death. Once pus had formed, the medical books declared, it was too late for treatment. Here is an early (1836) account of it under its other name, St Antony's Fire:

> Saint Antony's fire is a fever, attended with a red and painful swelling full of pimples, which afterwards turn into small blisters on the face, or some part of the body; the sooner the eruption takes place the less danger there is. Let your diet be only water gruel or barley broth, with roasted apples; take a glass of tar water, warm in bed every hour, washing the part with the same.[84]

Usually the disease attacked people who were already unwell or malnourished. Charles Lamb died from it. After injuring his face in a fall at Edmonton, erysipelas developed; he was nearly sixty, worn out and with little resistance, and died quickly (1834). It is strange to think of the Staights as malnourished, with their own supplies of meat and poultry and their home-grown fruit and vegetables. (Indeed, on one occasion the doctor diagnosed 'stomach fever' in Lily from 'living too well'.) But while their diet seems to have been rich and varied, living conditions (heating, lighting, sanitation, hygiene generally) were much worse than now. The house, with its long passages and numerous side doors would be cold and draughty, and it was mice-ridden too: more than once Ann finds a mouse in kitchen or pantry and fetches the cat to dispatch it. Because health was so much more precarious then, erysipelas was a common accompaniment. Today it rarely occurs (one doctor tells me he has never seen a case) and this success story is explained by vastly improved living conditions and healthier humans, as well as the ease with which it can be treated since the introduction of sulphonamides (1936) and penicillin (1944).

The dreaded disease reared its head, more menacingly, in October 1890, when it was not only feared, but diagnosed. The doctor was summoned to Charles Staight

> . . . who had been getting gradually worse since Sunday. Dr Allard came in the evening, and said he had erysipelas in his face; painted it over with some strong smelling stuff, and left some medicine.
>
> 2nd. Father not much better.
>
> 3rd. Father no better, Dr came again and dressed his face, and left more medicine, and F. to go to bed. Thought him worse.
>
> 4th. Dr came, F very ill, in danger, medicine and nourishment to have night and day.
>
> 5th. A little better, Dr said.
>
> 6th. Dr pronounced him out of danger if he did not have a relapse.
>
> 7th. Charley's wife and daughter went back home. Dr came in evening, F much better. (Rev. Jones here before dinner to see Father).
>
> 8th. F. better, but not up. No one came to see him all day, but Mr W. Jones called at our shop, and Tom did not ask him in.
>
> 9th. Squire Baldwyn, Ashton, had a sale of surplus stock. Father dressed and sat in his room. Mr W. Jones came to see him. Mrs Chidley, May and baby came down in afternoon – they spent the day at Joe's while Mr C went to Ashton sale, John rode with him. Dr A. came about tea-time. This morning Ashton porter [from station] brought up a basket which had come late previous night with large fowl and 4 eels ready for cooking for F, also some jam [from the Gibsons].

On October 11th, Charles was downstairs for the first time and the next day the doctor said he would not come again. The crisis was over. Ann's diary entries had concentrated almost exclusively on her father, only alluding to other matters as his condition improved, and they illustrate in a worrying way his importance for her. The entries are untidily written and the peculiar syntax further illustrates Ann's

178

distraught state. In her Will he had been 'my dear Father', and life without him was unimaginable. Did Ann wonder what would happen to her if he died? But then her mother would still need caring for, the Villa would still have to be run.

It was with great relief that Ann dispatched apples to the Gibsons and the McGlinchys, and the concert on October 16th was particularly enjoyable, not only because of the absence of Glees.

> Concert in the schoolroom, very good one, no glee singing. A Mr Reeve (nephew of Mr Reeve, Alstone) caused much amusement by his comic songs, as did also a gent from Miss Ashwin's (Sedg.) with his banjo and songs . . . Miss Phillimore before she could finish her song turned faint, and Mr Jones and Dr Cox helped her off the platform.

By March 1891, after a long and grim winter, there were three invalids to look after. Ann summoned the doctor 'to Mother with bronchitis, also Father with bad cough, and John with lumbago . . . the Dr came 4 times in all, and on Sunday April 5th brought a swell friend with him.' (She is not using American slang here! The word formerly meant stylishly or handsomely dressed, of good social position or of distinguished appearance or status.) Ann was not meeting many 'swell' people by now, for the nursing and domestic role made meeting any new people, let alone *swell* men, extremely infrequent.

The high mortality rate has been a marked feature of the diaries, and even when there are no deaths in Ann's immediate circle of family and friends, there is, regularly, a death in the village, so that every few entries in the diaries are punctuated, like a regular refrain, by news of a death:

> Old Farley (the late Mrs Porter's father) was buried at Dumbleton today, brought from Winchcombe Union (February 1891)

> Mrs Smithin, formerly of Dumbleton, died at Lench. aged 65, after a painful illness, cancer. (March 1891)

> Mrs Walker died after being upstairs nearly five months. (April 1891)

> John Clarke's wife died after a short illness of cramp and spasms . . .

Just as in the early Enfield diaries Ann had been taking flowers to Mr Biscoe's grave, now she was going over the hill to the little Norman church at remote Great Washbourne, where her grandmother Peart and Sarah Martin's older sister were buried:

> Sunday Feb 22nd. After dinner Miss Pullin and I went to Washbourne churchyard to take some snowdrops to put on Miss Martin's grave. Tom

went with us as far as W[ashbourne] Hill to put us right. Mrs Oldaker and 2 little girls were at the service there, and Letty Burge and a little friend came into the churchyard as soon as we got there. We were back at Joe's to tea 5.45 pm.

and a few months later they were there again, this time with summer roses.

In June 1891 a relative of the Rector's died from influenza. It seems an odd time for influenza, in summertime, but cases of it reached epidemic proportions at this time in parts of England, in the United States and on the Continent. There was *snow* in May that year (on May 18th, Whit Sunday) and a few days later Ann's mother was seriously ill, though not with flu, and was given an injection, the only one in the diaries: 'John drove down early for Dr, but he didn't come till 12, had another case on. When he found M in such pain he gave her an injection of morphia in her arm, which eased the pain, and she dozed all afternoon and evening.' The next entry is over a week later:

June 7th. Dr Allard came about tea-time (for last time) to see Mother, but sent her more medicine the end of week, and self some more (3rd bottle).

Ann relished a rail excursion with Joe and Louie to Weston-super-Mare, the nearest coastal resort, at the beginning of August, where they met up with Louie's relatives ('We found out their address by inquiring at Post Office'), and in September she was staying with the Moseleys who now lived at Willersey at The Orchard, a house built by William Moseley, when her mother was taken ill again:

Sept 10th 1891. Aunt and I were getting dinner ready and she was making cakes when our boy (Tom Walker) came up to the door with a note, had walked all the way, to let me know Mother was taken very ill. We did not stop for dinner but Uncle had pony put in big cart, and he and Aunt came with us back. Found Mother a bit better, and the Dr with her (but she was still up) and Mrs Clarke here. He (the Dr) said disordered liver was the cause of the attack, and her heart very weak too . . .

*   *   *   *

The final entries in this last diary, for December 1891, record – in the terse manner to which we have become accustomed – a series of illnesses and mishaps. The month opened with a cousin of Ann's own age dying in Tewkesbury Hospital.

December 1st. Lucy Peart (Mrs Lane) died on [the anniversary of] her parents' *wedding day*, left a baby girl not two years old. She was 37 years old.

A more hopeful note was sounded on December 3rd. Ann's parents were both better after 'a fortnight's touch of bronchitis'. But then –

Sunday 13th December. Mother had a bad fall on bricks this morning, caught her clog in a hole, and couldn't save herself. Tom and John helped her into the house, no bones broken or sprained, but bruised (stiff and sore).

The next entry echoes an earlier one: 'Aunt Sarah came back . . . brought her old cough again.'

On December 21st, Ann went to Cheltenham.

I walked to Ashton to meet 11.40 train, very sharp weather and the fields so rough and slippery, I could hardly get along. Nearly missed the train. Mr C Smith from Sedge[berrow] was going by the pike (as used to be) so took my basket and ran on, got the guard to wait, Mr W. Jones was at the station and laughed at me. I did not call on any friends except Prissy Williams. Went to Miss Joyner's first to try dress. Bought myself new jacket at Lance's, and some strong boots at Oliver's. It came on very foggy in afternoon. Young Charley met me at Beckford (8 train) with 'Old Polly', had been to Kemerton.

Even this undramatic entry had a sting in its tail. Before they reached the station gate, the poor old horse (she was called 'Old Polly' six years earlier when Joe first bought her.from James Taylor of the Brickyard)

. . . slipped down on her side, and I went out head foremost, was only scratched a little about head and face, but walked nearly all the way home, and the lad led the pony, it was so slippery.

Ann's shopping expedition had been useful and forward-looking, buying new clothes and new *strong boots* (she gets through a lot of pairs of these, and never mentions dainty shoes in the diaries at all!). Christmas Day was a low-key affair, with very frosty weather and only Joe and Young Charley as guests. Louie was expecting her sixth child imminently, and stayed at home with the children who were unwell. The Rector and his wife were unwell also, so there was no evening church. The last entry in this final diary is for Monday, 28 December, and is a short one:

Tom in bed all day with bad cold and cough (touch of Influenza).

This last page is untidy and blotchy. Ann was busy nursing with little time to spare for writing. She stopped writing when the diary was barely half-filled: the final word 'Influenza' and the many blank pages which follow it tell their own ominous story. The diaries end as Ann's drama begins.

PART FOUR
After the Diaries

Lord, let me know mine end,
and the number of my days:
that I may be certified how long
I have to live.

Psalm 39
(Book of Common Prayer)

After the Diaries

The Epidemic

'The insidious and deadly foe'

The 'touch of Influenza' with which Ann concluded her diary was no light one, though Tom did recover. January is traditionally the flu month, and by January 1892 it had reached epidemic proportions (in London alone there were 500 deaths from influenza that month). Medical history gives October and November 1891 as the height of the epidemic in Gloucestershire. So it was late in reaching Dumbleton – not altogether a surprise, in view of its seclusion and relative lack of contact with a more unhealthy outside world.

The *Evesham Journal* devoted part of a wordy editorial to the epidemic:

> *Another visit of the influenza is about the last thing one would have wished for or even expected at the beginning of the New Year; but here it is amongst us again in almost all its pristine vigour . . . In our own immediate district the visitation is at present partial rather than general . . . a vast amount of sickness, but it is accompanied with a low general death-rate. While the mortality then is not excessive, there are grounds for hope that the visitation, bad as it is, will spend itself within a moderate space of time. It is reported from Berlin that the germ of the disease has been discovered. It is to be hoped that this is the precursor of the discovery of a remedy for a disorder which, in its universality, resembles nothing so much as one of the plagues of the middle ages. The latest notable victim of the Scourge is Tewfik, Khedive of Egypt, whose death is likely to raise questions of difficulty in connection with the British occupation of Egypt.*[85]

But in one household at least the mortality *had* been excessive. By the time the editorial appeared, Dumbleton had its own 'notable victims', as well-known in the village as Tewfik was in Egypt. Charles Pitman Staight died from influenza and bronchitis on 8 January 1892, eleven days after Ann stopped writing. His wife, ill in the next room, could not fail to learn of his passing. She had learned of her mother's death when she was ill in bed – now it was her husband. She has been a pale insubstantial figure in the diaries, and Ann says less about her than about any other member of the family. We have learned little about the relationship between her and Charles, but his death removed the will to recover for a sick woman already suffering from the same illness. She died three days after him, on 11 January.[86]

The next issue of the *Journal* (16 January) would be dominated by deaths, principally that of the Duke of Clarence. This grandson of Queen Victoria, and next heir to the throne after his father (the future Edward VII) was not yet a popular figure, not a known figure at all. (Tennyson speaks of his 'brief range of blameless days' when he was in fact suspected by some of a clandestine life: was he homosexual? did he have an illegitimate child? was he even, though this was asked much later, Jack the Ripper?) His death on January 14th from influenza and pneumonia captured the imagination of press and public because it happened so soon after his December engagement to Princess May of Teck (later Queen Mary). We know from our own times how much the country revels in the prospect of a Royal Wedding. 'Death has suddenly snatched away the expectant Bridegroom', the *Journal* lamented, and elsewhere the Poet Laureate, himself ailing (he would die later that year), struggled to produce a poem to comfort the bereaved family:

> *The bridal garland falls upon the bier,*
> *The shadow of a crown, that o'er him hung,*
> *Has vanish'd in the shadow cast by Death*[87]

and followed this lugubrious beginning by a forced cheerfulness he could hardly have felt himself: 'Yet be comforted . . . the toll of funeral in an Angel ear / Sounds happier than the merriest marriage-bell.' The *Evesham Journal* marked the death by edging its editorial columns of type in black, and beginning its editorial 'The death of the Duke of Clarence this week transcends all other topics . . .', referring to the influenza as 'the insidious and deadly foe'. Elsewhere the paper reported that 'Almost at the same moment as the Duke of Clarence died, Cardinal Manning drew his last breath . . .'[88]

Dukes and Cardinals – and Master Blacksmiths. The Deaths column in the *Journal* that week was much longer than usual, and included the names of Charles Pitman Staight and Ann, *his relict*. Under the local news, where the paper reported that there was no parish in the neighbourhood 'where a large number of the inhabitants are not laid up with influenza', was a report of the Conservative meeting held at Dumbleton school on Thursday 14 January, addressed by the Tewkesbury MP, Sir John Dorington. In his opening remarks, the chairman disarmingly combined expressions of sympathy for the Royal Family with, nearer to home, the Staight family:

The Chairman (C.H. Smith) in opening . . . expressed sympathy for the Queen and the Prince and Princess of Wales in the loss of the Duke of Clarence . . . The Rev. F. Willoughby Jones would have presided in the absence of Mr Sharp but in consequence of there being so many deaths in the parish from influenza and other causes, he felt that he could not do so. In that parish they had lost Mr and Mrs Staight, two very old and respected inhabitants, and he was sure nobody sympathised more with the family in their bereavement than he did . . .[89]

There were no Staights at this meeting. The following day, January 15th, the two 'very old and respected inhabitants' (they were both only seventy-two), having shared nearly fifty years of marriage, shared also a funeral service and a grave. They were buried on the north side of Dumbleton church, near to the cat o' nine tails and the horseshoe tombstone of Charles's forefathers.

* * * *

There had been a great many deaths in the years covered by the diaries – a staggering number, which included Louie's two infants, Will Rose, both of Annie Biscoe's parents, Sarah Young's husband, the Rector Robert Wedgwood and his brother, Grandma Peart at Kemerton, Uncle Tom Staight at Childswickham, Annie Dudfield and her mother, the Morrises at the Mill, the Baylises at Crowle – and many more. But no one very dear to Ann had died, and often her prevailing feeling was sympathy and concern for the bereaved – for Louie, for Annie – rather than grief and loss at the bereavement itself. She had written fully about the death of Annie's father and its aftermath, of Mrs Biscoe's mourning and Annie's low spirits. How would she manage her own bereavements? And how would the new household work at the Villa? Of the large united family there, only three members – Tom, Ann and John – remained. How would the three quiet ones fare together?

There has been nothing in the diaries to suggest any difficulty between them. There had been Glee Clubs with Tom, excursions with John. Within the home they had worked well together – 'Tom and John cleaned out the furnace flue for me, it was got very foul' – and the only rivalries were playful ones, the 'ganging up' of the sexes, curiosity to extract girlish secrets:

I did my D- up, Annie came up before I'd finished and read some of her letters. Boys came to look at us, but weren't troublesome.

John, although the youngest – and the most indulged – seemed likely to assume the leadership of the reduced household, carrying on the business with Tom while Ann cooked and cleaned for them. Once over the sudden shock of her parents' death, her quiet country life could continue. She would visit Sarah and write to Annie and continue to chronicle the seasonal changes and the church festivals as she had done before. There was no reason for the arrangement to fail. If one of the brothers married, Ann would continue to care for the remaining bachelor.

But Ann did not write her diary again. The final diary had become brief and perfunctory as we have seen, and ground to a halt when she was too busy and too tired to write. Once the epidemic was over the incentive to write did not return. It was better to be silent than to be like one of Shakespeare's sufferers:

> Discomfort guides my tongue,
> And bids me speak of nothing but despair.[90]

The attempt at creating a new life was short-lived, and it was not successful. Ann died five months after her parents. After the strain of nursing and losing both parents, did she contract the influenza and die from it as they had done? The reality was worse. She died in the County Lunatic Asylum.

* * * *

The Asylum

> 'Beyond this place of wrath and tears
> Looms but the Horror of the shade'
> (W.E. Henley)

Ann had been fortunate in not being forced by poverty to go out to work, like Fanny Staite or Elsie Richards, but it was also her misfortune. Staying at home, and in such an enclosed village as Dumbleton, had made her dependent upon her own family, emotionally as well as economically. She had never worried about money, a topic seldom mentioned in the diaries. (There had been a list of expenses in the notebook, and later references were confined to 'Put my expenditure book straight' and 'Put 20 in Lloyds'.) Her father had paid her an allowance, and whatever it was, she appeared neither to be short of money nor to wish for more. Under Charles Staight's will, all his children were equally provided for, but after her parents' deaths Ann must have worried about her future, and wondered if she would be assured of a home with her brothers if they married. Or would she become suddenly redundant, suffering the double calamity of the Victorian spinster, of emotional loss and sudden homelessness? It was unusual for a single woman to live well at that time, unless she was an heiress: the very state of singleness suggested poverty. Eliza Wedgwood enjoyed a good (if eccentric) life at Stanton, but she had at least a vestige of the Wedgwood money. The other single women featured in Ann's diaries had not fared too well. Fanny Staite, to put it baldly, was drunk and suicidal; Annie Dudfield, daughter of Joe's predecessor at the butcher's shop, 'declined' and died. On visits to the Villa Ann noted this decline: 'Annie D. looked very ill, I made her a cup of tea, she wouldn't have anything else' (May 1883), and 'Annie D. called, looked very sadly' (June 1884). She died in 1886, aged thirty-four. Of the older women, Sarah Martin would resort to the odd habit of 'parson-gazing', and Sarah Peart lasted in none of her housekeeping posts and fell back on the goodwill of her relations. Would Ann fare any better? In rural areas, and even today Gloucestershire is nine-tenths rural area, the choice of available jobs was extremely limited. In Dumbleton, apart from field labouring and teaching positions (at the school or as private governess on a local farm[91]), there was only domestic work. There was no cottage industry, like Crowle's glove-making. The maids at Dumbleton Hall were recruited from outside the village to ensure the privacy of The Family, which left the farms (most farmers had servants of some sort) and the more well-to-do tradesmen (Joe's 'Useful Help', for example). If Ann had to work, her opportunities were already extremely limited by reason of her location and her lack of training. And her health was deteriorating. If it worsened, she would not be able to work at all.

She had nursed both parents and one brother (possibly two) with influenza, and may have succumbed to it herself. But quite apart from the epidemic, she herself was unwell. She had been taking, over a long period, medicines for an illness she does not describe in much detail. Only by sifting through the last diary do clues to her medical history emerge:

May 1886 Self very middling with bilious attack

August 1887 Saw the Dr, had medicine for self

Dec 1888 Had bad bilious attack in evening, head bad all day, did not go to church

May 1889 Did not go to church, my head very bad

June 1891 (3rd bottle of medicine from Dr)

September 1891 Self very poorly all day, head terribly bad.

Earlier still, in April 1884, one entry had alluded in uncanny premonition to her health and to an asylum:

. . . (Dr gave me bottle of medicine). Letter from Mrs McG, her nephew John obliged to be put in Hanwell Asylum.

Collating the diary data about bilious attacks and headaches with that supplied on her death certificate, it is clear that Ann had been suffering, over a long period, from kidney trouble.

Little was known about kidney trouble then, and it was frequently not recognised as such. The mysterious and sensitive workings of the kidney had been recognised by Joe who, though a butcher, actively discouraged his family from eating it. The kidney is one of the body's 'painless' organs: you don't hear people complain of kidney pains. We can't feel our kidneys, only the effects they have on the rest of the body when they malfunction. It was during the Victorian age that advances were made in the study of kidney disease. Lord Annan has observed[92] that while much Victorian medicine seems to us today to belong to a prescientific age, it was then that doctors – Bright, Addison, Hodgkin and Parkinson – gave their names to diseases which they had isolated. Ann's headaches and bilious attacks were caused by Bright's Disease (named after Dr R. Bright who died in 1858), but she did not know this and her doctor probably did not either. (As late as the 1930s the disease remained mysterious and unpredictable, as can be seen in the case of the writer Winifred Holtby.[93]) The condition, also called acute nephritis, is caused initially by a reaction to another infection, such as a sore throat, quinsy, scarlet fever, erysipelas, and Ann had nursed relatives with at least three of these illnesses. It can be cured if the patient rests and if the intake of protein, salt and water is controlled. In Ann's case there was no rest and no dietary restrictions (these were not introduced till the 1930s), only bottles of medicine, and so the acute nephritis developed over the years of the last diary into the much more serious chronic form. By the late spring of 1892 the sickness and headaches became more frequent, more severe, or both.

All through the diaries, men and women, friends and relatives, had been shown going to Dumbleton in or after illness to recover their health. Sometimes they had failed in this, like young Will Rose. Ann, who had nursed parents, brothers, aunts, friends and relatives of friends, was now in need of nursing herself. Why did Tom and John, the two brothers with whom she had been on such excellent terms, allow her to be committed to the Asylum, in an act which mirrors the earlier rejection of Fanny Staite: 'the prisoner had brothers in good positions, but they would have nothing to do with her'? Is this another glimpse of that harshness amidst harmony which halts any rosy idealizing of the past, a harshness earlier sensed in the slaughterhouse alongside the parlour, in the cruelty charges alongside the wedding proclamation, in the favoured daughter left unattended in the isolated mill-house at her first confinement?

There had been no signs of madness in Ann's diaries, though there had been premonitory signals which made breakdown of some kind possible, even likely, after the traumatic double bereavement. There had been the buttoned-up emotions, the emotional dependencies; there had been signs of inner disturbance in those upsetting dreams over the loss of Annie; there had been the obsessive desire for order and regularity: 'I put my things in places . . . finished putting my things in place.' Now things were out of place, and she could no longer put them straight.

Ann was stricken. Sad and sick – and strange. With hindsight it is clear her mental distress had pathological as well as personal origins. As her condition deteriorated, as toxins accumulated in the bloodstream, she would have suffered increasingly from vagueness, lapses of memory, mental confusion. To her brothers it looked as if she were mad, or going mad, and fear of madness is a powerful, potent force. Even at the distance of ninety-odd years I felt a little of its potency. Nineteenth-century records for Gloucester's Asylum patients are lodged at the County Record Office but remain classified information until the patient concerned has been deceased one hundred years. In this way the family of the patient is humanely protected from information which may be distressing. Ann's medical records will thus not become available for public scrutiny until after 1992. I did not want to wait that long, and while I waited to learn her fate through private application – a wait prolonged by changes in Health personnel, for the office to which I was directed to write suddenly ceased to exist – while I waited, I found myself growing apprehensive about the possible nature of her 'madness'.

*   *   *   *

Other brothers, in Victorian life and literature, had coped manfully with insane or invalid sisters. Charles Lamb, that earlier sojourner at Enfield, was one of them and he died before his sister, undoubtedly worn out from worry about her. Mary Lamb had stabbed their mother to death. Charles secured her release from an asylum by undertaking to be responsible for her for life, and he was, living with her when her health permitted and arranging her care elsewhere (not in institutions) when her periods of insanity made cohabitation impossible. And in literature? In the novel which has already been mentioned many times in this book there is a shining example of brotherly devotion – that of the Rector, Mr Irwine, towards his invalid sister Anne. Even when she is stricken with one of her worst headaches and unable to speak, he still visits her and knows, without any words, that she appreciates his solicitude:

> Miss Kate came towards her brother and whispered, 'Don't speak to her; she can't bear to be spoken to to-day.' Anne's eyes were closed, and her brow contracted as if from intense pain. Mr Irwine went to the bedside and took up one of the delicate hands and kissed it; a slight pressure from the small fingers told him that it was worth-while to have come upstairs for the sake of doing that. He lingered a moment, looking at her, and then turned away and left the room, treading very gently – he had taken off his boots and put on slippers before he came upstairs.[94]

Ann had demonstrated the same sort of solicitude to her brother John when he was ill ten years earlier, getting up to him constantly in the night, doing all in her power to make him more comfortable. Did John choose not to remember, not to reciprocate, those ministrations now?

In fact he and Tom coped as long as they were able to, till mid-Summer. Then, perplexed by circumstances they could neither control nor comprehend, the brothers appealed for help to the family doctor, and accepted his solution. It is a curious anomaly, a relic of the former close relationship between asylums and prisons, that an Asylum committal was made, not by the family doctor but by a magistrate contacted by him. On 15 June 1892 Ann was referred to the County Lunatic Asylum by Mr W.D. Stanton J.P., a member of the Board of Guardians of the Winchcombe Union. Eleven years earlier, the local magistrate would have been Ann's own Rector, the kindly Robert Wedgwood. Mr Stanton was another minister-magistrate, Vicar of the neighbouring parish which embraced both the large and lofty church at Toddington and the tiny ancient one at Hailes. Ann had occasionally attended services at Toddington – her blacksmith ancestors had lived there – but she has never mentioned the Rev. William Darke Stanton by name in her diaries, and there was no personal relationship to delay or prevent the committal.

While primarily responsible for the poor of the district (in 29 parishes) the Winchcombe Union also arranged for sick patients to be transferred to the local Asylum. Destitute patients would be conveyed to Gloucester from the Winchcombe Workhouse, purpose-built in 1836 and situated in extensive grounds behind Winchcombe's main street, past the Corner Cupboard Inn and up Malt House Lane. (Today an entirely new building occupies the site and the only hint of the earlier institution is found in the name of the nearby *Union* Cottage.) Ann, who was not destitute, was spared the ignominy of the Workhouse. On 16 June, the day after Mr Stanton signed the committal order, she was conveyed from the Villa to Gloucester, passing through Tewkesbury where she had spent happier days. The details relating to her admission are brief. Her nearest relative is given as *Thomas Staight, Brother*. The form of mental disorder is concise, too: *Melancholia caused by Domestic Troubles*.

* * * *

By 1892 there were two County Asylums in Gloucester. Ann was admitted to the First Asylum at Wotton. There is irony in the name, for the Staights would by association link the name with the Surrey beauty-spot, the welcoming hostelry, of Louie's happy girlhood: the Gloucester Wotton, close to the centre of the city, provided a 'welcoming hostelry' of a different sort. The Asylum is not far from the Cathedral and even closer to the Railway Station. The first impression is of an elegant crescent-shaped building which softens the severity of the institution, giving it a gentler aspect than that of the Second Asylum at Coney Hill, which by its severe redbrick appearance has to be either a mental hospital or a prison (above its entrance an inscription reads, not the 'Abandon Hope . . .' which one almost expects to see in this grim place, but 'Bear Ye One Another's Burdens A.D. 1883').

The First Asylum at Wotton was one of the first purpose-built mental hospitals in the country. There are legends – untrue – that it was built with money from the mad George III (who took the waters at Cheltenham) and that it was designed by Nash, an idea inspired presumably by that crescent. First proposed in 1793, it was opened in 1823. By the 1890s it was a condemned building.* Behind that

* The same building is in use today but it operates under a kinder name, Horton Road Hospital.

The Gloucester Asylum. This 1930 photograph shows the site as it would have looked in the 1890s (very little building work was done until the 1950s). The chapel is on the road to the left of the crescent building

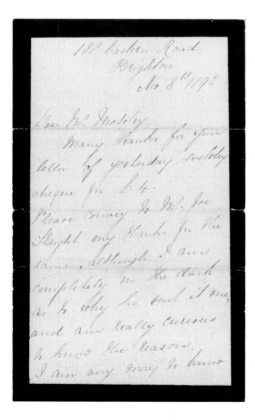

Annie's black bordered letter

elegant facade, there were still vestiges of prison life in some of the attitudes or terminology – 'airing courts for exercise', for example. The Report of the Commissioners in Lunacy (April 1892) regretted the inadequate sanitation and hot water provision.[95] The nurses received no hospital training (one result being that from the records of 100 autopsies, 33 cases were found to have bedsores). But at least local citizens, for weekend entertainment, could no longer pay one penny to walk along the hospital corridor, viewing on each side the lunatics locked into their cells; no longer were patients locked into their boots to prevent self-injury(a boot-with-lock is exhibited in the Administrator's office).

The stigma of insanity remained very strong, however, the institution being regarded with horror by everyone outside it. The Asylum Chaplain was

> . . . sorry to confess that a stigma does attach to anyone who has been confined in an asylum; but it is entirely the fault of the public, and I can see no remedy for it, when, on the frequent appearance of our inmates outside the walls of the Institution, the unthinking multitude designates them, in the vulgar tongue, 'lunies'.[96]

One of the outings 'outside the walls' was to Sanger's Circus – which Ann had seen ten years earlier passing down the street in Enfield. Other entertainments and diversions included concerts (though Gloucester could not, like Worcester County Asylum at Powick, boast an Edward Elgar as conductor of its band*), dances, conjuring and Christmas trees. And there was the chapel.

The Asylum at Wotton had its own chapel, a separate building in the grounds (used today to house hospital stores). The modest redbrick building could boast some advantages over the city's grander churches, advantages not lost on the Asylum chaplain, the aptly named Reverend Box:

> . . . No congregation in our Town or Village churches can surpass our own in reverent behaviour. I might, indeed, go further, without exaggeration, and say, that I do not think there are many congregations whose devout conduct at Divine worship could equal that of these afflicted people . . .
>
> Interruption never occurs, except, it may be, through an occasional epileptic fit. I think I have, therefore, some ground for being proud of my congregation, and doubly so because of the eccentricity of their affliction. Not being affected by any considerations of weather, we always have full congregations. The chapel seats 350, but the space is insufficient to accommodate all who wish to attend . . .

---

* Elgar was first a member, then conductor, (1877–84) of the band. See Kennedy, *Portrait of Elgar.*

From the grounds, the patients could enjoy the sight of another church building, the soaring tower of Gloucester Cathedral. 'In any view of Gloucester from far or near', wrote a 1930s admirer, 'that great and harmonious tower of the 15th century is upreared over the vast Norman building, for all its massiveness, with so infinite a grace that you scarcely need its bells to call you to it anywhere within the radius of its enchantment.'[97] But not all could share this enchantment.

Ann was one of 267 patients admitted in 1892, a year which had begun badly because of the influenza epidemic, from which Asylum servants and attendants suffered as well as patients. In Ann's age group (30–40), only 23 women were admitted; the figures are much higher for the other age groups. On her death certificate she is described as a 'Housekeeper (Domestic) of Winchcomb' (presumably Winchcombe is named, not Dumbleton, because she had been admitted by the Winchcombe Union), and she was one of four housekeepers admitted that year. (There were far more (25) unstable domestic servants.) During the year one man and four women were admitted by the Winchcombe Union. Visits by the Guardians to the patients chargeable to their Unions were commended by the Asylum; included in the commendation for 1892 was the Winchcombe Union, which had paid two visits. The weekly charge to any Union for maintenance at this time was just over eight shillings a week. In some cases, the family chose to pay the sum to avoid the stigma of pauperism, and they would then pay a slightly higher amount than that paid by the Union. Ann's admission notes make clear that she was paid for by the Winchcombe Union. In view of John's 'carefulness', this is not a surprise.

Amongst the various tables in the Asylum's annual reports,[98] available for scrutiny at Gloucester's Shire Hall, is one listing the probable causes of insanity, the reason for admission to the Asylum. These are subdivided into moral and physical causes. Moral causes, besides Ann's 'domestic troubles' (a blanket term which clearly brought in a large number of people), include disappointment in love, intemperance, fright, grief at loss of relatives, overstudy, pecuniary difficulties, religious excitement, solitary modes of life. No sexual problems – or, to be more precise, no acknowledgement yet of sexual problems: the influence of Freud and Havelock Ellis has yet to be felt. In Table XV, Physical Causes, under the subheading *Bad Health and Exhausted Condition* is the entry: Nephritis and Melancholia 1 female. This is surely Ann Staight.

Ann's case notes are minimal (no mention of any treatment)

because her stay in the Asylum was an unusually short one. She died on June 29th, two weeks after her admission. A postmortem examination was peformed by the Asylum's Resident Medical Officer to find out why. Autopsies were not uncommon – that year 106 were performed, the high number demonstrating how often the doctors were baffled by their patients' condition. Ann's death certificate gives the cause of her death as Uraemia and Acute Nephritis (the order is curious as one would expect it in reverse).[99] Nowadays, Uraemia, blood poisoning caused by kidney failure, would be treated by dialysis or transplant. Then there was no treatment, though plenty of medicines were prescribed. Renal failure could be caused by arsenic and mercury powders, popular remedies of the time. We noticed earlier Ann's faith in medicine, any medicine,

> Tom very middling, Dr T gave him some medicine which put him right in a few days
>
> I took some of Annie's medicine in kitchen
>
> Father had two doses of last week's medicine left, he wouldn't have it, so I did, and it seemed to do me good

and it is possible that the medicines in which she had such faith hastened her decline.

Ann's death was recorded in the *Evesham Journal* of July 2nd,[100] her name spelt, oddly, in the old way.

> Staite. June 28, at Dumbleton Villa, Annie Staite, younger daughter of the late Charles Pitman and Ann Staite, aged 36 years. Friends will kindly accept this intimation.

The date does not tally with that (June 29) given on the death certificate. The discrepancies in date and spelling may be due to the shock or haste of whoever reported the death to the *Journal*'s office. The Asylum is not mentioned, nor the illness, and clearly the brothers – who had a double stigma to come to terms with, the stigma of insanity and the stigma of having allowed their sister to be 'put away' – did not wish to elaborate on the circumstances, either in the notice itself, with its mild deception about the place of death, or in sending out 'mourning-cards' to Ann's friends. The final sentence discourages neighbourly enquiries, verbal postmortems.

But a postscript to this matter, in the form of a funeral card, was unearthed amongst Sarah's possessions. So they *did* have some cards printed after all. The pale grey-green cover design depicts a spray of flowers, not the predictable ivy or lilies, but fuchsias, above the words 'In Memoriam'. Inside the card, on the left hand page, a sad little verse. Who chose it? The butcher or the blacksmiths? Probably Louie.

> *A broken heart, my God, my King,*
> *Is all the sacrifice I bring;*
> *The God of grace will ne'er despise*
> *A broken heart for sacrifice.*

. . .

> *Not gone from memory, not gone from love,*
> *But gone to our Father's home above.*

On the righthand page is the expected information:

> *In loving memory of*
> *ANNIE*
> *Younger daughter of the late Charles Pitman and Ann Staight*
> *(of Dumbleton Villa, Evesham)*
> *who died June 29th 1892,*
> *Aged 36 years*

While we know that Ann died from kidney failure, she died another death as well. Besides the medical explanation there is a family one as well, and the verse acknowledges this second dimension. The 'broken heart for sacrifice' (the two nouns repeated for emphasis) is a well-chosen image. Hearts are traditionally broken by unhappy love affairs. Ann's heart was broken not by a love affair (though we don't know what she felt about her failure to marry) but by the deaths of her parents and by what seemed to her the rejection by her brothers. The family had been all-important, too important. When it broke down, Ann broke down too. She was, in the end, a sacrifice, the plaintive verse implies, sacrificed to the family, by the family. It is curious that of the four books* named by Ann in her diaries, two depict powerful brother-sister relationships (Tom and Maggie Tulliver in *The Mill on the Floss*, Tom and Louisa Gradgrind in *Hard Times*), relationships which demand some sort of sacrifice from the sister. Ann had certainly not been a victim of exploitation earlier, but was she now seen by the brothers as the sister they had sacrificed? They had kept her at home up to the eleventh hour; this

---

* *Oliver Twist, Hard Times, Martin Chuzzlewit, The Mill on the Floss.*

198

redeeming fact is clear from the brevity of her time in the Asylum. Could they not have kept her at home to the end? As if the idea behind the verse – Ann herself speaking of her broken heart and her sacrifice – is too painful to pursue, the funeral card concludes with the much more comfortable image of home. Ann, whose life had been wholly domesticated, was again at home, and 'our Father's home above' hints reassuringly at a Celestial Villa, a Heavenly Blacksmith.

* * * *

The fervent desire of village folk (a desire depicted eloquently in *Adam Bede*[101]) was to die in their own beds and to be buried in their own churchyard. This was not, alas, always possible, least of all for Asylum inmates. When patients died in the Gloucester Asylum they were buried nearby in the municipal cemetery. Rarely were their bodies returned home for burial. During the fourteen days of Ann's absence, however, the brothers had time to think about what had happened. Someone (probably Joe, as it was in his possession, and in his nature to be generous) recalled Ann's Will with its unequivocal opening words 'I should wish to be buried at Dumbleton . . .'.

She was, on the same day that the announcement of her death appeared in the *Evesham Journal*. In the burial register in the church only one entry (Mr Smith of the Bank Farm) separates the record of her burial in July from that of her parents in January. She was buried with them. After the horrors of the last six months culminating in that infernal final fortnight spent among strangers over twenty miles away, she was truly 'gathered to her fathers' – father, grandfather and great-grandfather – in the quiet country churchyard.

* * * *

Postscript: 'Our Dear Girl who is Gone'

Ann's diaries had been, in their modest undemonstrative way, a continuing celebration of friendship. Without her ever saying so, it is clear that Annie is important to her while Leslie, for example, is not. There had been nothing, no letter or diary, to reveal Annie's view of the friendship, and it is omissions of this sort which cause the compiler of a story from surviving documents and miscellaneous papers to envy the freedoms of the historical novelist. None of Annie's letters to the Villa survived but – such is the randomness of family archives – something else did. The sole surviving document in Annie's hand is a conventional letter of acknowledgement written four months after Ann's death to William Moseley, Ann's uncle and the family executor. There, tucked between the opening and concluding courtesies, is an unsolicited epitaph for the friend she does not even need to name, an epitaph halted by a broken line which represents the broken relationship quite as much as the black-bordered notepaper on which it is written.

188 Eastern Road
Brighton
Nov 8th 1892

Dear Mr Moseley

Many thanks for your letter of yesterday, enclosing cheque for £4.

Please convey to Mr Joe Staight my thanks for the same, although I am completely in the dark as to why he sent it me, and am really curious to know the reason. I am very sorry to know he has had illness in his house, measles is very prevalent in Brighton but so far we are free, but have all had bad colds and coughs.

I hope dear Mrs Moseley keeps well, I often think of her with feelings of affection and in connection with *our dear girl who is gone, I cannot trust myself even now to write about our cruel loss, it is with me a 'sorrow too deep for words' I cannot realize that I shall never again in this world see my darling friend, who was to me what David was to Jonathan**

. . .

It will be a relief to you all to have finished the legal business, it is such long-winded work as a rule, but I hope everything was settled satisfactorily, I know you would do your best for all parties concerned

I expect Charlie is quite a man by this time, please remember me to him, I hope he is doing well.

With kindest regards to yourself and love to dear 'Aunt Moseley', once more sending my thanks to Joe for his kindness.

I remain

Yours very sincerely
Annie Gibson

My husband sends very kind regards to all.

---

* My italics.

. . . And Afterwards

It was inevitable, once the two brothers were alone at the Villa, the family reduced and the housekeeper gone, that their thoughts should turn to marriage, and it is surprising that their respective marriages did not happen sooner. Tom married in April 1895. At a vestry meeting in Dumbleton church on April 16, 1895,[102] a vote of thanks 'for his services as churchwarden during many years was carried unanimously, and a new churchwarden appointed in his place as he was leaving the village.' His bride, Kate Bryan, came from Tredington, which is just off the Fosse Way on the Stratford-Oxford road. They moved to Manor Farm in Stanton, near the entrance to the village and not far from Mrs Wedgwood and her daughters at Stanton Court. Tom was, at forty-five, an elderly bridegroom – and he died at Stanton, childless and not very prosperous, nearly twenty years later, just before the outbreak of the First World War. Family folklore had it that he was gored to death by a ram, which seemed far too melodramatic an end for the undramatic Tom. John was with him when he died, and registered the death: the death certificate gives diabetes as the cause of death,[103] with no mention of the ram. Of Charles Pitman Staight's seven children, all but two – Tom and Sarah – are buried at Dumbleton. Tom's grave at Stanton, almost hidden today by ivy and briars, is close to that of the two Wedgwood sisters, Henrietta and Eliza, who had preceded him to Stanton.

*　*　*　*

John had married six months before Tom, which may explain why he, the youngest son, managed to acquire the family home for himself. He had known Elsie Richards for eleven years by the time they married in November 1894. Both were 36, and very shy. This was another long courtship, like that of Sarah and Leslie, another marriage of propinquity. It was an odd match and to Elsie John must have seemed disappointingly far removed from her Hampshire squire. The only direct quote we have of Elsie's does not show John in too bright a light. When he set off for Gloucester market, Elsie

Left, Tom Staight; below, John and Elsie Staight with their first child

was heard to murmur: 'May he be gone a long long time.' It is interesting that the happiest marriage, on the evidence available, was between partners (Joe and Louie) who did not meet locally within 'a confined locality'.

Elsie had five children in quick succession between 1895 and 1901. She particularly wanted to name one of her sons after the squire she had 'admired' long before. John ridiculed the name, but when her third (and last) son was born, she had her way: he was christened Ingham. Her second son, Harold Pitman Staight, who later farmed the Mill Farm in Dumbleton, had carried on the 'Pitman' name begun by Robert Staight generations earlier.

The family business continued at the Villa. John always wrote the initials R.S.S. after his name on letters and documents. These did not denote membership of some august royal society: the letters stood for 'Registered Shoeing Smith'. But, like all his brothers, John turned more to farming (in his Will he is called a Farmer, not a Blacksmith) and he took over the tenancy of Cullabine Farm, passing it on in time to his son Ingham. The smith connection continued, oddly, when all three of his sons (none became blacksmiths) married girls, quite unrelated to each other, with the surname of Smith. John was a good businessman, but his 'carefulness' had earned him the nicknames of 'Old Pincher' and 'Pincher Staight'. (If he could, he would have sold the skin off a rice pudding!) He did not like parting with things. He even made sure of his chamberpot by fastening it to the bedleg with a padlock and chain. And he would not willingly part with 'any old iron'; there was always plenty of it, lying in heaps in the Villa grounds. Josie's eldest daughter, as a small child at Cullabine, was frequently put on the back of a horse and told to take it to the Villa for new shoes. When she arrived, having negotiated the piles of old iron, the tall and sinewy smith employed by John would lift her down and send her inside to wait while the horse was shod. She would sit with her Aunt Elsie, who moved quietly, spoke quietly (and not very much), and in season the child would gaze longingly at a gorgeous crop of purple grapes which were grown under glass at the back of the house. She was never offered a single grape.

Elsie did pass on, however, some of her books, including fine leatherbound editions of the poetical works of Tennyson (inscribed 1894, the year of her marriage) and Elizabeth Barratt Browning, the latter bound in maroon with a motif of gold roses. Inside the back cover of the Tennyson, a blackbound, Bible-like book, is a loose sheet of paper, on it a poem entitled *Sins of Omission*:[104]

It isn't the thing you do, dear
 It's the thing that you've left undone
Which gives you the bit of heartache
 At the setting of the sun.
The tender word forgotten,
 The letter you did not write,
The flower you might have sent, dear,
 Are your haunting ghosts tonight.

The stone you might have lifted
 Out of a brother's way:
The bit of tender counsel
 You were hurried too much to say
The loving touch of the hand, dear,
 The gentle and winsome tone,
That you had no time nor thought for
 With troubles enough of your own.

The little acts of kindness,
 So easily out of mind,
These chances to be angels
 Which all we mortals find.
They come in night and silence
 Each chill, reproachful wraith
When hope is faint and flagging,
 And a blight has dropped on faith.

For life is all too short, dear,
 And sorrow is all too great,
To suffer our slow compassion
 That tarries until too late —
And, it's not the thing you do, dear,
 It's the thing you've left undone,
Which gives you the bit of heartache
 At the setting of the sun.

The poem was obviously of some significance to Elsie. She went to the trouble of copying out its four verses, and it was not merely inserted, but pinned securely, at the back of the Tennyson. It was not written by Tennyson but by a minor American woman poet.[104] Its authorship, however, is not important here. What is significant is how peculiarly apt it is in this context. Here is another postscript, as it were, on Ann's story. It could almost be Elsie talking to John. Did Elsie the outsider recognise John's sin of omission, the negative cruelty in allowing his sister Ann to be sent away, in letting the Union pay for her?

John, who had required so much nursing in his youth from his family, lived longer than any of them, and was nearly ninety when he died. While he had not been of much help to Ann in 1892, he was a good brother to Sarah and in his final years his great pleasure was to be read Sarah's girlhood diaries (mainly about her eggs and poultry) by a daughter-in-law. Both he and Elsie died in 1948, and were buried on the *south* side of the church, away from the family group on the north side, and not far from the sundial above the south door with its 'Waste me not' message. John and Elsie had been nursed by their eldest daughter who now – unmarried and in her fifties – met the fate which might have been Ann's: she exchanged the Villa, which was sold by her brothers, for a forlorn bedsitter in Cheltenham. She lived frugally: even at the Villa her god-daughter remembers her going down the garden path to pick dandelion leaves for a salad lunch.

After surviving so long as an island property, the Villa was, not surprisingly, swallowed up by the Estate. But its assimilation was only temporary, and today it is again a private property. Its gardens, covering about four acres, include much of the orchard in which Ann had lost herself a century earlier after a Temperance meeting, and again one dark March afternoon in 1889 when she wrote

> Went to church with Tom and John, left them at Joe's and came on alone, got lost in the orchard, it was so dark, muddled about for an hour before I could find my way home, then it got lighter . . .

The apple and pear trees where Ann 'muddled about' form part of a landscaped garden today, their trunks embellished by climbing roses. The blacksmith's business was discontinued at the Villa, but for several years the 'shop' was the nucleus of a Cotswold Vale cider factory. Not only has the blacksmith's business gone from the Villa, it has gone from the village too, and all that remains is the name of the lane linking Villa to village.

*　　*　　*　　*

The Staight name and tradition were continued at the butcher's shop in Dumbleton, not by Joe but by the son of Charles the publican, Young Charley, who had helped Joe at the butcher's shop for many years and who succeeded him as village butcher. Young Charley had four sisters: Frances (Francie), Maria (Tot), Amy and Louise Letitia (Louie) and all in time came to live with him at the butcher's shop. They became known as the shop girls and the name stuck even when they left the shop and ended their days in a private house in Cheltenham. None married (nor did Young Charley) and all were most circumspect: when Amy was taken into hospital on a stretcher (where she would die the next day) she insisted on stopping to put on her hat.

* * * *

The diaries stopped with Joe and Louie awaiting the birth of their sixth child. Emma Ann Staight was born the day after Charles Pitman Staight died. *In the midst of life* . . . and vice versa. Emma died herself, from diphtheria, four days before her fourth birthday. She has her own grave in the churchyard, which bears the same inscription as that of Louie's first two infants: 'Thy Will Be Done', used also for Louie's parents in Wotton graveyard and, incidentally, on a fictional tombstone too, the wife's grave in George Eliot's first story.[105] Louie struggled for stoicism, but that her grief and rage were still vehement nearly two years later is clear from an entry in a Birthday Book, misappropriated for her own purpose. Against January 4th, instead of a list of birthday celebrants, we find

> Jan 4. Our darling Emma died, Jan 4th 1896 after 9 days' illness ulcerated throat and nose bleeding – A light is from our household gone / The voice we loved is still / A place is vacant in our home / Which never can be filled. O how I miss her – It proved to be Diphtheria – wretched Drs.

and this outburst is dated December 13th 1897. Pitman had also contracted the disease but he recovered, allegedly saved by the burning of sulphur candles in his room.

So Louie had lost three of her six children. The three surviving ones were strikingly good-looking, and none inherited Joe's vast figure. Dumbleton's oldest resident recalled Joso, now Miss Josie, as a lively spirited girl, dashing up the village on her pony, her hair flying in the wind, in the early years of the century. Josie knew everyone in the village and was on 'visiting' terms at every house and cottage there, even dining on occasion with the lady of the manor, as a 1902 invitation from the Agent indicates:

Dumbleton Hall
Evesham.
11.10.02

Telegrams: Dumbleton

Dear Mr Staight,
   Miss Eyres desires the pleasure of your benign countenance and also the pleasure of your wife and 2 daughters – also the Great Pitman – at dinner on Saturday night at 6.30. N.B. not your Beef!!
   Yours sincerely,
   Arthur H. Sharp

In 1908 the pretty and popular Sunday School teacher (she took on the job her aunts Sarah and Ann had declined) married a Worcester-shire man, Harry Curnock Stephens.

Four years earlier, there had been another bride, a much grander wedding. The heiress at the Hall was still a child when Ann last referred to the birthday celebrations. In 1904 Caroline Mary Sybil Eyres married Lieutenant Bolton Monsell, and the bride and groom were toasted by Joe 'as the oldest Tenant on the oldest part of Mrs Eyres Monsell's Estates and the weightiest of any of you . . .'. Like an earlier squire of Dumbleton Hall (Edward Holland) Bolton Monsell entered politics and became Conservative Member of Parliament for South Worcestershire (now the Evesham division). Later he resumed his Naval career, rising to the position of First Lord of the Admiralty – his ensign fluttered from the tower of Dumbleton church when he was in residence – and in 1935 he was created Viscount Monsell for his services to the country.

A glowing picture of him is found in an unexpected quarter, a book by the romantic novelist Barbara Cartland. In a biography of her mother[106] she describes the first meeting of her parents with the Eyres-Monsells at a Pershore Conservative meeting.

Mr Eyres-Monsell spoke extremely well and aroused great enthusiasm . . . [He] had been in the Navy where he had specialised as a Torpedo Lieutenant. He was fair, clean-shaven, with a smile which seemed to illuminate his face and which was inestimably charming. He had married a Miss Sybil Eyres, whose family had made a great fortune in Leeds. They lived at Dumbleton Hall, Evesham . . .

At the time she [Polly Cartland] thought Bobbie Monsell one of the best-looking men she had ever seen and his wife very nice, if a little shy.

Even allowing for a romantic novelist's gloss, the match, the alliance of money with ability and ambition, looked most auspicious; to cement it, the two surnames were amalgamated.

If one asks any question about Dumbleton history at this time (why did Joe Staight move to the Bank Farm, for example) one is likely to get this sort of reply from Dumbleton pensioners: 'I expect Her Ladyship arranged it . . . .'. While her husband pursued his career in public service (the villagers seldom saw him), Her Ladyship was a powerful presence, in almost a medieval way, in the village. In the diaries, Ann had walked freely in the Hall grounds and Mrs Eyres, though regarded with respect, had not featured very much and was not regarded like a royal personage. Now the gulf between Hall and village widened. The Hall grounds were sacrosanct, and no one passed without invitation through the heavy gates. In the church,

Josie as a young wife

Left, Joe and Lily at The Bank Farm
(*c*.1924); below, Josie as a widow with
eight children (1926)

while Josie and her family sat in the second pew (Cullabine) and later in the fourth (The Bank) – just beyond the spray zone, as one of her children put it – the Hall pew was at the back of the church, an unusual location at first sight, but from here Her Ladyship had an excellent view of who was in church and who was not. If anyone missed two Sundays, her footman would deliver a note asking to know the reason. (The south aisle of the church was, and is, known as Beggars' Aisle, but it is inconceivable that beggars would have been tolerated in this well-regulated place.)

The Monsells were extremely wealthy, and lived accordingly. There were at one time twenty indoor servants alone, the maids being recruited from depressed areas like South Wales or the industrial towns. When the Monsells went to their Belgravia home, the dairy produce from their Jersey herd at Dumbleton was considered superior to anything London had to offer, and supplies were sent up daily by train from Evesham. The same herd produced free milk for the school, and there was free meat for everyone at Christmas, and often a brace of pheasants after a shoot. The wealth and luxurious style of living was thus to some extent justified by the way in which Sybil Monsell looked after her villagers. She talked of her welfare state in Dumbleton before the country got around to having one. She looked after the old and the ill; there was no unemployment. She built attractive homes for her estate workers. The Palaces at Dumbleton derive their name from a remark of Lady Monsell's: 'I never thought I should be building palaces for agricultural workers to live in.' There were no tumbledown cottages in the village, I was told in a letter. *Tumbledown* had been one of the very words I had initially associated with the name Dumbleton. The words might sound alike, but were opposites: Dumbleton was regarded as a Model Village.

When Josephine Staight, the daughter of one tenant, married another, she received a handsome wedding present from the Eyres-Monsells: a large hallmarked silver teapot, engraved with her initials JLS. Josie and Harry, while lacking the wealth and sophistication of their landlords, were, like them, young and handsome and happy. They farmed, first at Wormington, then, after a spell at the butcher's shop, at Cullabine. By January 1921 they had six children; that month the seventh was born, mentally handicapped. Scarcely a year later, Harry caught a chill: influenza turned to double pneumonia. It was not a lingering illness: he died almost immediately and 'his sudden death at the early age of 37,' a local obituary reported, 'has cast a gloom over the village, where he was a general favourite.'

Josie, her eighth confinement imminent, could not even attend his funeral, and only her eldest daughter was considered old enough (at 13) to go with Joe. It was April 1922, and Josie's happy carefree Cullabine life was over.

But she fared better than Ann had done. She had Joe to turn to, big-hearted Joe who was enjoying a peaceful old age with Louie and Lily (who did not marry) at the Bank Farm, where he could pursue his lifelong interest in animal husbandry. I was glad Joe turned from butchering to farming. I had found it hard to reconcile the kind man and the killer, though this is a 20th-century inhibition Ann would not have shared. In place of the large family group at the Villa in Charles Pitman Staight's day there were two Staight families, Joe's and John's, at opposite ends of the village, and a third set (Charles' children) at the butcher's shop. Joe and John were too different to be close, but they worked well together in church and village affairs. Both were churchwardens – Joe from 1901 till his death in 1927 – and witnessed dramatic changes in the church. The Victorian vogue of restoration and refurbishment came late, like most things, to Dumbleton: the church was re-opened in 1905 and not long after the Rector's 'cure of souls' was extended as neighbouring parishes, first Wormington, later Toddington, were added to his own.

When Harry died, Joe welcomed his widowed daughter and her eight* children (seven girls, one boy – almost Mr Tulliver's 'whole tribe of women') into his home, forfeiting for ever his quiet retirement. Now, in place of three people at the Bank (and his parrot!) there were twelve. Fortunately the Bank farmhouse was large enough to absorb the influx: the children slept no more than two to a room, Josie and Lily had separate rooms, and Joe (after Louie died in 1923, the year after Harry) slept downstairs. With all this tribe of chidren, Joe only once spanked one of them. The effect was hardly traumatic: today, in her seventies, she cannot remember her crime, and her reaction is one of pure astonishment that there was only *one* spanking. Although the initial impression of Joe was a forbidding one (John *looked* more benevolent) with his massive frame and stern demeanour, driving with a tall whip which to small children looked as big and threatening as the man himself, Joe's kindness and generosity extended well beyond his own grandchildren, so that even the village carter's son, William Ladbrook, would

* The Staight name-shortening habit reached its height in Josie's children. Only one of the 8 children was (is) called by the name she was christened with; even 'Mary' gets shortened: Mary Josephine (Maire), Phyllis Annie (Phyl), Lilian Evelyn (Eve), Kathleen Elsie (Kath, later Kay), Joseph Harry (Joe), Margaret Cynthia (Peg), Joan Sybil (Joan), Dorothy Winifred (Dot).

write from Canada years later about 'the very kind gentleman . . . he seemed like a Grandpa to all of us children'.

Joe's favourite hymn was 'Glorious things of thee are spoken' and how well he had hearkened to its words

> *Well supply thy sons and daughters*
> *And all fear of want remove*

He believed strongly in the old adage 'Put your money in bricks and mortar' and while Josie had just about sufficient means to leave the Bank and live elsewhere, Joe's welcome was such that there was no need to. He died in 1927, and some years later Josie left Dumbleton; her brother Pitman moved into the Bank and his cousin Ingham Staight farmed 'next door' at Cullabine.

In the years that followed, there were dramatic changes in Dumbleton. The Eyres-Monsell marriage which had looked so glamorous and golden ended sadly. Did Lord Monsell after his exciting life in the Navy, in Parliament, in High Society, find village life a trifle tame, as Sir Charles Percy, the knight of Shakespeare's day whom we met in the church, had done? The Eyres-Monsell marriage ended in divorce in 1950. The second Lord Monsell took over the Estate but declined to be the feudal landlord his mother had been, and he arranged for the village to become more self-supporting: the Estate now owns less than half the houses in the village. Nor did he live in the Hall which Edward Holland had built: the Domesday village no longer has a lord of the manor. He lives elsewhere in the village and the Hall began a new, more democratic existence as a holiday and convalescent home for Post Office employees.

In Ann's day, and in Josie's, the villagers all worked locally, within the village. As late as 1940 only two residents worked outside it. Now the whole character of the community has changed. Retired people form a large part of Dumbleton's present-day population (around 220) but of the others, few work for the Estate. Mains water came to the village, and the telephone, and electricity, but gas has never been installed. There is still no hostelry (though there is a private club for the villagers). In Ann's day, her father's smithy had gone some way, as we saw, towards meeting the deficiency by providing a meeting-place, with heat laid on, and often refreshments too! When a brewery was approached about the possibility of opening a public house in the village, it declined on the grounds of *no through trade*. In that respect the village has not changed; it is still Miss Mitford's 'confined locality'.

Did Josie, having left it behind, think sometimes of her blacksmith grandfather and uncles when she exhorted her children to action with Longfellow's words 'Something attempted, something done'?[107] As a grandmother years later – the role in which I knew her – she seldom spoke about the past (even as an old lady, a time when most old people reminisce as much as they are allowed to), and when asked about relations no longer living, would answer 'Let them rest, let them rest'. With eight fatherless children to concentrate her attention firmly on the present, we could understand her attitude and we did let them rest. Of the generation after Ann, Josie was the only niece who was old enough to remember her. She named her second daughter Annie after her (the -ie ending was detested by the recipient) but all she ever said of Ann was that she had died from Bright's Disease. She was, after all, very family-minded, quick to help needy kith and kin. Mindful of kinship, she no doubt felt no good would come from telling Ann's sad story; she made sure too that all her daughters trained for professions and acquired independence. So Josie remained silent, while earlier in another county her aunt Sarah Legge had chattered to an unheeding audience.

*   *   *   *

Sarah was the only member of the family to leave Gloucestershire and not return. Her last child, John Leslie Legge, was born at Ham Mill in March of that fateful year 1892. To reach any school from remote Ham Mill was no simple business, and John and his two sisters Nancy and Ruth rowed themselves across the river Teme to shorten the journey to Martley. Leslie and Sarah prospered at the mill, but Sarah never forgot the fact that they were only tenants. The businesswoman in her strove for betterment and at last, in 1903, they purchased their own farm, Shortwood, between Pencombe and Little Cowarne in Herefordshire. Leslie had been happy at Ham Mill and did not want to move – he wanted to be a miller not a farmer – but Sarah had her way, and they left Ham Mill. The mill itself has gone too. Just a few bricks near the weir indicate its position. The house is still there, and has kept the old name, and on a wooden sign at the gate a watermill scene is engraved alongside the words HAM MILL.

At first it was a struggle at Shortwood. The Legges had to borrow money, and Leslie had to plough with a horse and a bullock because he was unable to afford two horses. The new farm was about eighty acres, but by acquiring and clearing woodland and scrub this was increased to 120 acres. Sarah was determined to have something to leave to her son John. Just as well, as things turned out, for she had founded a dynasty. John drank rough cider at every meal including breakfast, grew to Joe-like proportions – and had 17 children! Today seven of his ten sons farm in the Bromyard area of Herefordshire, which must be some sort of a record. The quiet Leslie, who had received such a bad press from Ann, was at any rate entirely satisfactory as a grandfather. He retired more and more into his study to escape his loquacious and volatile womenfolk (Sarah, Nancy and Ruth), and worked his way through such heavy tomes as four volumes of *Echard's Roman History*. Even his death illustrates the contrasting personalities of husband and wife: when in 1926 he died quietly in bed without fuss, Sarah was hysterical, sending a small and terrified grand-daughter racing to the cowshed for John.

Sarah stayed on at Shortwood after Leslie's death, a fierce but diminutive matriarch in a long black dress, and often spoke of her sister Ann, whom neither her son John, nor his wife, nor his children knew. Sarah was a great hoarder, and in her final years relatives fought their way to her bedside through the muddles, just as at the Villa they fought their way through John's old iron to reach house or forge. Amongst Sarah's 'muddles' were Ann's diaries and photograph albums, which were beside her bed when she died. Ann's Will had left to Sarah her clothes, books and jewellery: there had been no mention of the diaries. Ann would have assumed they would be thrown away, and in any case, the flimsy form of these frail documents made their survival highly unlikely. Just as John at the Villa enjoyed Sarah's diaries in his old age, so Sarah would dip into Ann's, her eyes straining at the small cramped script of the early ones, reliving the old days when she taught Ann to do feather stitch, when she filled cushions and quilts with feathers, or won first prize for her flower arrangements at Dumbleton Show. The sisterly affection which Charlotte Brontë had praised was not ended by Ann's sudden death. Mrs Gaskell herself, who had quoted Charlotte's words about the affection of sisters in her *Life of Charlotte Brontë*, had once written to her daughter Marianne 'It is so dreary to see sisters grow old (as one sometimes does), not caring for each other, and forgetting all early home-times.'[108] Sarah had been unable to save her sister from her tragic end. She may not have been able to understand what was happening, unable to enter imaginatively into Ann's state of mind, for very positive poeple are baffled by the inertia of melancholia. Indeed, she may not have known about the Asylum until after it was all over, for it was Ann who had kept her posted with family news. But Sarah certainly did not forget the 'early home-times' as her (unheeded) reminiscences and the proximity of the diaries and albums attest.

Ann and her diaries have already been the source of some surprises – first, that a blacksmith's daughter should have written so assiduously, rooted as she was in an environment of strenuous physical labour where writing had little place; that a village girl managed to move about county and country with such mobility; that the well-regulated life documented in the diaries should have ended in such drastic disarray. And here is the final surprise, that those diaries survived the death of 'Sis'.

'Sis' had long been 'Granny Legge' and it was one of Granny Legge's grand-daughters, one of John's seventeen children, who thought some of her Gloucestershire cousins, Josie's daughters, might be interested in seeing Ann's diaries because they were set in Dumbleton, where those cousins had, like Ann, enjoyed their early years. So the diaries, which had survived removals in horse- and later motor-drawn vehicles from the Villa to Ham Mill, from the mill-house to the farmhouse at Shortwood, and from Shortwood to John Legge's second farm at Butterley, returned from Herefordshire to Gloucestershire where they had been written and where, three generations later, I first saw them.

Acknowledgements

Books of this kind depend very much on other people: the author gathers and arranges material gleaned from a wide variety of sources. This book would not even have been thought of without the generosity of Miss Mary Legge who, without (then) knowing me, lent me the diaries and albums of Ann Staight and various papers of Leslie and Sarah Legge, and who remained generous and encouraging when the loan extended from months into years. In Stow-on-the-Wold, Mrs Michael Harris was equally helpful with Staight papers and photographs in her possession. My aunts Mary and Margaret Stephens (Maire and Peg) talked and wrote to me about Dumbleton and the Staights. Peg accompanied me on many delightful research expeditions ranging from farms to mental hospitals. She was particularly good at accosting strangers and eliciting all sorts of useful information from them; and it was thanks to her that I saw Ham Mill and Robertsend, where the late Mrs Harriet Trapp without demur showed two complete strangers all over her home. In Dumbleton, Mrs Lanchbury showed us round the Villa and its beautiful gardens; the Rev Eric Giles, former Rector of Dumbleton, allowed us plenty of time to study the church records in the vestry; Mr R.C. Meadows, agent to the Dumbleton Estate, talked to us about the Monsells and the Staights and showed us over the Mill.

In Evesham, the former editor of the *Evesham Journal* generously allowed access to his archives despite their delicate state. Extracts from the *Journal* are reprinted by kind permission of the present editor.

Mr. K. Hale, formerly Deputy Sector Administrator, Gloucester Health District, supplied the vital information about Ann's final weeks and also the photograph of the Asylum. Extracts from Asylum documents are reprinted by permission of the Gloucester Health Authority. David J.T. Webster, FRCS, helped me with the medical aspects of Ann's case.

In Enfield, Mr D. Pamm, former local history officer of the Enfield Public Library, provided much useful information about the Biscoes, including the name of Mr Biscoe's public house. The photograph of the Rising Sun is reproduced by kind permission of the London Borough of Enfield Libraries.

Extracts from *The Letters of Mrs Gaskell* are reprinted by permission of the Manchester University Press; the extract from *Polly: The Story of My Wonderful Mother* is reprinted by permission of Mrs Barbara Cartland and Rupert Crew Ltd; the extract from *The Wedgwood Circle* by permission of the authors, Barbara and Hensleigh Wedgwood. Full details of all quoted material will be found in the sources.

For help with illustrations I am also grateful to Mr George Ashwin, Mr Fred Invine, Mr Peter Legge MBE, Miss Flossie Russell and Miss Dorrie Stephens.

Patricia Haigh, Karl Miller and Dan Jacobson read early drafts of the manuscript and thanks to them the book is more readable than it was. For help of various kinds I should like to thank my husband and family; members of the English and Geography Departments of University College London; and the villagers met in the course of my quest. Sadly, three of the people (including 'Dumbleton's oldest resident') whose earliest memories contributed substantially to this book, died before its publication. If by chance anyone reading this book can throw more light on any of the characters in it I hope they will write to me c/o the publishers.

Sources

First two stanzas of Dedication, The Seaside and the Fireside, *Poetical Works of Longfellow*, Oxford, 1904

'A goodly dwelling, and a rich'

1   *The Cotswold Countryside and its Characters*, Eric R. Delderfield, The Raleigh Press, Newton Abbot, 1967.
2   Grafton, *Collected Poems of John Drinkwater*, Sidgwick & Jackson.
3   See the Arden edition of *2 Henry IV*, ed. Humphreys, Methuen. V.1, note to lines 34–5
4   *2 Henry IV*, Act V. 1 & 3
5   *The Buildings of England: Glos.: The Vale and the Forest of Dean*, David Verey, Penguin Books 1970, p. 175.
6   Discussed in *Gravestones in Midland Churchyards*, by Canon J.E.H. Blake, reprinted by Oxford University Press 1928 from the transactions of the Birmingham Archaeological Society Vol LI. 1925–26.
7   *Understanding English Surnames*, Sir William Addison, Batsford, 1978.
8   Sale papers, Dumbleton Estate, Gloucester Record Office.
9   *Rural Rides*, William Cobbett, Penguin ed. pp. 387–8.
10 *Letters of Mrs Gaskell*, ed. J.A.V. Chapple and Arthur Pollard, Manchester University Press, 1966, pp. 770, 772 (letters of 31 August and 2 September 1865).
11 Holland obituary, *Evesham Journal*, Jan. 9, 1875
12 *Oxford English Dictionary*
13 The Village Blacksmith, *The Poetical Works of Henry Wadsworth Longfellow*, Nelson, Vol II, Miscellaneous Poems.
14 Told me by Mr George Ashwin, son of the Rev. Collins Ashwin, Rector of Dumbleton, 1904–1938.
15 Mrs Henry Wood, *East Lynne*, first published 1861.
16 *Life of Charlotte Brontë*, Mrs Gaskell, Penguin ed. p. 289.

Part One: The Notebook 1880, 1881

17 Marriage Certificate, Joseph Staight and Louisa Rose, General Register Office.
18 Cottage Names, *Our Village*, Mary Russell Mitford, first published 1824–32. Everyman edition p. 252.
19 *Rural Life in Victorian England*, G.E. Mingay, Heinemann, 1977.
20 A Farewell: To C.E.G., Charles Kingsley, *Collected Poems*.
21 Santa Filomena, Birds of Passage, Flight the First, verse one. Longfellow, *Collected Poems*.
22 Characteristics, *Essays*, Thomas Carlyle.
23 *Adam Bede*, George Eliot. First published 1859.

24 *Enfield Gazette*, (Occasional Notes by 'Townsman') 13.11.70
25 *The Letters of Charles and Mary Lamb*, ed. E.V. Lucas, Dent and Methuen, 1935, Vol. III, pp. 367, 239, 241.
26 *Letters*, p. 99.
27 Ebenezer Scrooge in *A Christmas Carol*.
28 Death Certificate, Ebenezer Biscoe, General Register Office.
29 *Tottenham and Edmonton Weekly Herald*, April 14, 1882.
30 See essay by Sally Mitchell in *A Widening Sphere, Changing Roles of Victorian Women*, ed. Martha Vicinus, University Paperbacks, Methuen, 1980.
31 *Victoria R.I.*, Weidenfeld and Nicholson Ltd., 1964; Pan Books, 1966.
32 Song of Solomon (Old Testament) Chapter 2, verse 5.
33 Death certificate, William Rose, General Register Office.
34 Psalm 121.
35 Verey, op. cit. p. 386.
36 *The Wedgwood Circle 1730–1897*: Four Generations of a Family and their Friends, Barbara and Hensleigh Wedgwood, Studio Vista: London, 1980, p. 198.
37 1881 Census Returns, Dumbleton, Public Record Office, London.
38 *Adam Bede*
39 *Evesham Journal*, (hereafter referred to as *EJ*) 14.9.1889.
40 *EJ* 9.9.1882.
41 *Tess of the D'Urbervilles*, Thomas Hardy, Macmillan 1891, ch. 14.
42 *Letters of Mrs Gaskell*, pp.498, 524, 744.
43 There are many more references to Thurstan (all favourable) in *The Letters of Mrs Gaskell*.
44 *Martin Chuzzlewit*, Charles Dickens, ch. 2.
45 *2 Henry IV*, 2.iv.230.
46 *The Mill on the Floss*, George Eliot, ch. 3.
47 Mr Kenneth Palmer of University College London supplied the information about Stir Up Sunday.
48 *Silas Marner*, ch. 10.
49 Tennyson, Prologue to General Hamley, pub. 1885. Concluding lines of 390, *The Poems of Tennyson*, ed. C. Ricks, Longman, 1969.
50 *The Mill on the Floss*, end of Bk 4.
51 *Aurora Leigh*, Bk 1.
52 *Pickwick Papers*, Penguin ed. p. 801.
53 *The Victorian City Images and Realities* in 2 vols. ed. H.J. Dyos and Michael Wolff. Routledge and Kegan Paul, 1973, London and Boston. Vol. I (Railways).
54 Baylis Bread. Booklet produced for Queen Elizabeth II's Silver Jubilee, Kemerton 1977; and *Victoria County History*, Worcestershire, entry on Crowle.
55 Book of Numbers (Old Testament) chapter 14, verse 9.

Part Three: The Last Diaries

56 *1200 Years of Church Life in Prestbury*, Robert Sweeney, booklet published locally. Census Returns 1881, Public Record Office.
57 *Remember and Be Glad*, Lady Cynthia Asquith, Hutchinson 1968.

58 *Middlemarch*, Penguin ed. p. 778, ch. 71. See also Verey, p. 124. Tennyson's words are quoted in *Tennyson*, by his grandson Charles Tennyson, Macmillan 1949.

59 Mingay, op. cit., p. 148.

60 *EJ* Dec, 1885.

61 The staff of the Brompton Cemetery were most helpful in locating the Legge grave for me.

62 Information from Mr R.C. Meadows, agent of the Dumbleton Estate. Census Return 1881, Public Record Office London.

63 *The Shell Book of Rural Britain*, Keith Mossman, David and Charles 1978.

64 Tennyson, *Poems*, p. 1345. No. 412, To H.R.H. Princess Beatrice, pub. 1885.

65 *John Halifax, Gentleman*, Mrs Craik, Everyman ed. Ch. 29.

66 *The Inn Album*, 2nd stanza.

67 *EJ* 6.3.1886

68 Tennyson, The Miller's Daughter, *Poems*, No. 162 (final stanza).

69 Quoted in *Portrait of Elgar*, Michael Kennedy, Oxford University Press, 1968, p. 268.

70 *Popular Fiction 100 Years Ago*. Margaret Dalziel, Cohen & West, 1957.

71 Shakespeare, *All's Well that Ends Well*, I.1.60.

72 Sarah's grandson, Peter Legge, uses the expression 'jaw pie', and I felt it appropriate to borrow it for his grandmother.

73 *Rural Rides*, William Cobbett, Penguin ed. p. 376.

74 *Under the Parish Lantern*, Fred Archer, Hodder & Stoughton 1969. Mr John Dodgson of University College London, told me about the Anglo-Saxon charter.

75 *Oxford English Dictionary*.

76 Tennyson, On the Jubilee of Queen Victoria, pub. 1887, *Poems*, No. 418 p. 1369.

77 Quoted in *Victoria R.I.*, Elizabeth Longford.

78 *EJ* 31.8.1889. Clissold Park became public property 11 January, 1889 and was opened to the public on July 24 of that year. (Information supplied by Stoke Newington Reference Library.)

79 *Adam Bede*, ch. 33.

80 Fred Archer has treated this subject in *Poacher's Pie*, Hodder & Stoughton 1976.

81 *EJ* 8.3.1890

82 *EJ* 15.3.1890

83 *Tess of the D'Urbervilles*, Thomas Hardy, Macmillan, final chapter.

84 *The Housekeeper's Guide, or Every Man his Own Doctor* (5th ed., W.W. Robinson & Sons, Leeds, 1836)

Part Four: After the Diaries

85 *EJ* 9.1.1892

86 Death certificates, Charles and Ann Staight, General Register Office.

87 Tennyson, The Death of the Duke of Clarence and Avondale, *Poems*, No. 453

88 *EJ* 16.1.1892

89 *EJ* 16.1.1892

90 *Richard II*, 3.2.65.

91 At least two Dumbleton farmers in 1881 employed private governesses for

their children (Census Returns 1881. The Returns for 1891 are not yet available.)

92 Noel Annan, review in the *New York Review of Books*, Vol. XXVI, No. 12, July 19, 1979.
93 *Testament of Friendship*, Vera Brittain, Macmillan 1940.
94 *Adam Bede*, chapter 5.
95 Asylum documents, County Record Office, Shire Hall, Gloucester.
96 Chaplain's Report 1893, County Record Office, Shire Hall, Gloucester.
97 *Highways and Byways in Glos.* Edward Hutton, Macmillan 1932.
98 Annual Reports, Shire Hall, Gloucester.
99 Death certificate, Ann Staight, General Register Office.
100 *EJ* 2.7.1892.
101 *Adam Bede*, chapter 10.

. . . And Afterwards

102 Vestry records, Dumbleton church.
103 Death certificate, Thomas Staight, General Register Office.
104 Sins of Omission. *Granger's Index of Poetry* attributes the Sin of Omission to Margaret Elizabeth Sangster (1838–1912).
105 The Sad Fortunes of the Rev. Amos Barton, in *Scenes of Clerical Life*, 1858.
106 *Polly: The Story of my Wonderful Mother*, Barbara Cartland, Herbert Jenkins, 1956.
107 The Village Blacksmith, 7th verse. See p. 15.
108 *Letters of Mrs Gaskell*, p. 435.